Non-Manipulative Selling

Selling

Second Edition

Tony Alessandra, Ph.D.,
Phil Wexler, and
Rick Barrera

Prentice Hall Press • *New York*

This book is dedicated to
Janice Alessandra,
Sue Wexler,
and
Mercedes Barrera

Published by Prentice Hall Press
A Division of Simon & Schuster, Inc.
Gulf+Western Building
One Gulf+Western Plaza
New York, NY 10023

PRENTICE HALL PRESS is a trademark of Simon & Schuster, Inc.

Library of Congress Cataloging-in-Publication Data

Alessandra, Anthony J.
  Non-manipulative selling.

  Includes index.
  1. Selling.   I. Wexler, Phillip S.
II. Barrera, Rick.   III. Title.
HF5438.25.A43   1987   658.8'5   86-43174
ISBN 0-13-623307-4 pbk.

Manufactured in the United States of America

10 9 8 7 6 5 4 3

ACKNOWLEDGMENTS

*The authors would like to thank **Garry Schaeffer** for his invaluable writing assistance, **Lynn Cablk** for her organizational contribution, **Serena Vackert** and **Trish Waynick** for their patience and tireless typing, and **Rick Roark, Lara Steinel, Steve Marx,** and **Larry Rochon** for their feedback on the manuscript.*

*A special thanks to **Ashok Deshmukh** of Tom James Clothiers, **Barry Woolf** of Walsworth Publishing Company, and **Roy Cammarano** of* International Business Times *for their insight and experiences in the form of interviews. We believe it is critical that superb managers of salespeople and programs first have been themselves superb salespeople. Each of these people was just that and their successful application of non-manipulative selling skills in the field were significant factors in their promotions to management.*

CONTENTS

PREFACE vii

1 THE PHILOSOPHY OF NON-MANIPULATIVE SELLING 1
2 RELATIONSHIP STRATEGIES 13
3 TENSION MANAGEMENT 34
4 THE FINE ART OF QUESTIONING 41
5 THE POWER OF LISTENING, OBSERVING, AND
    FEEDBACK 58
6 PLANNING 76
7 MEETING THE PROSPECT 99
8 STUDYING 125
9 PROPOSING 141
10 CONFIRMING 158
11 ASSURING CUSTOMER SATISFACTION: THE
    FOLLOW-THROUGH PROCESS 188
12 SELLING BY STYLE 204
13 THE IMAGE OF EXCELLENCE 221
14 DEVELOPING SELF-MANAGEMENT SKILLS 240
15 THREE KEYS TO SUCCESS 254
INDEX 258

PREFACE

IN 1974, Tony Alessandra was a marketing professor at Georgia State University teaching professional selling to undergraduates. Phil Wexler was the vice president of marketing and sales for a burglar-alarm company in Atlanta, Georgia. One of his major responsibilities was recruiting, selecting, training, and managing residential-security-system sales people.

We went to high school together and have been close friends since 1963. During the eleven years from 1963 to 1974, we were continually involved in business and selling projects together. In addition, no matter where we were, we continued to discuss our philosophies of selling, much to the chagrin of our wives.

One day in 1974, we were sitting in Phil's living room discussing the uneasiness we both felt over our dual lives. On the one hand, we had a philosophy of life about treating family and friends with openness, integrity, and respect. On the other hand, during business hours we had to discard those values to make our livings selling or teaching sales. Our selling techniques were fraught with tricks, innuendo, shades of gray, and psychological manipulation of our customers. We were no different from other salespeople or sales professors. On that fateful night in 1974, we decided to create another way to sell that was more consistent with our personal philosophies. From that seed, the philosophy and practice of non-manipulative selling grew.

In mid-1975, the first version of *Non-Manipulative Selling* rolled off the press in the form of a seminar workbook. We tested the concept in training programs and constantly revised the material based on the feedback we received. After three and a half years of our testing the concepts with thousands of salespeople across the United States in dozens of industries, *Non-Manipulative Selling* was first released as a book in 1979 by Courseware, then again by Reston in 1981.

When we first wrote *Non-Manipulative Selling* there were only a handful of people around the country advocating similar philosophies. In addition to us, people such as Larry Wilson with his Counselor Selling Program and Mack Hanan with his Consultative Selling Program went against the grain of the current sales thought. Today, the tide has truly turned. There are thousands of people teaching concepts similar to those in *Non-Manipulative Selling*.

Speakers and consultants have jumped on the bandwagon as well, preaching value-added selling, participative selling, and other variations of the non-manipulative theme. Upon close examination, however, both in print and in live consultation, the vast majority of "experts" prove to be inconsistent. They give lip service to the philosophy but continue to teach skills and techniques that are merely modified versions of the traditional hard sell. They are the proverbial wolves in sheep's clothing.

One reason consultants are inconsistent is that they do not like to rock their clients' boats. The non-manipulative approach may rattle the cages of traditional salespeople, who rely mostly on their sales pitches, closing techniques, and objection-handling skills to make a sale. Sales managers who teach manipulative skills also resist the philosophical changes. Therefore, many consultants water down their concepts to make them more acceptable to a larger number of clients.

Why a new edition of *Non-Manipulative Selling?* It has been more than eight years since the first edition of *Non-Manipulative Selling* was published. In that time, we have collectively presented more than 1,500 programs to more than a quarter of a million people around the world. In addition, more than 100,000 people purchased the book. Readers and seminar participants have given us many new ideas. Their collective input and specific suggestions have moved the book foward several generations. Rick Barrera's extensive contributions to

Non-Manipulative Selling in the form of specific skills and selling techniques have reenergized the concept and earned him a place as co-author. The philosophy of non-manipulative selling has not changed, only the concrete steps and activities. Jim Cathcart, our colleague and friend, provided invaluable creative input and developed the new names of the six steps of NMS: planning, meeting, studying, proposing, confirming, and assuring. Many of the concepts used in chapter 2, Relationship Strategies, originated in the audio cassette album of the same title by Jim Cathcart and Tony Alessandra (Nightingale-Co., 1985). This edition of the book has been significantly modified and expanded to include the suggestions of the salespeople "in the trenches" who took the time to tell us how non-manipulative selling worked for them and how it can work better for everyone.

Over the last twelve years, non-manipulative selling has proven to be so successful that it was put on film by Walt Disney Productions, produced as a five-part video sales training program by Coronet/MTI (Simon & Schuster Communications), and recorded as an audio cassette program by Nightingale-Conant. Many of our other successful training programs such as Relationship Strategies; Marketing as a Philosophy, Not a Department; and the Art of Managing People grew out of the basic philosophy of non-manipulative selling.

Non-manipulative selling has become the preferred sales philosophy of many *Fortune* 500 companies, including IBM, Ford, IDS/American Express, Wedkin Laboratories, Arthur Andersen & Co., Xerox, Loews Hotels, American City Business Journals, AT&T, Union Bank, Hewlett Packard, Independent Insurance Agents of America, Days Inns of America, Telecheck, Snelling & Snelling, Memorex Corporation, Tom James Clothiers, Dictograph Security Systems, and hundreds of others who have embraced our concepts in seminar, audio, video, and book form.

This new edition of *Non-Manipulative Selling* was written for people who aspire to selling with professionalism. By adopting and practicing the skills in this book, you will enter the elite 5 percent of salespeople who can virtually write their own tickets regarding earnings, choice of geographical location, industry, company, and life-style. These are the salespeople who are making more money than many corporation presidents. It is not easy to be in the top 5 percent of anything; however, the knowledge you gain from this book plus your dedication and hard work will get you there. But first you have to want it.

We are all aware that the number of women in sales has increased steadily over the years. To reflect this change and to resolve the issue of gender in language, we will alternate the use of he/she throughout the book. We hope this neither offends nor confuses anyone.

—A.J.A. and P.S.W.

1

The Philosophy of Non-Manipulative Selling

WHEN YOU HEAR the word *salesperson,* what adjectives come to mind? Typical responses to that question are "aggressive," "overbearing," "pushy." Their common denominator is always negativity, even from sales and marketing people themselves. If many professional salespeople feel negative about their colleagues, how much more likely are people outside the profession to take a negative view?

Salespeople are among the most highly paid professionals in American society, and they are very important to the economy. Why, then, do so few people respect sales as a career? Employee turnover is higher in sales than in most occupations. Ask most college students if they want to be salespeople and the answer is a resounding no!

SOURCES OF NEGATIVE SALES IMAGES

Many of the negative stereotypes people have about selling result from the way sales training is conducted. There are three problems with today's sales training: not enough training, too much product training, and inappropriate sales training.

1

Not Enough Training

Many organizations provide little, if any, training for their sales teams, despite the fact that training is the single most important function of the sales department. One reason for this negligence is that sales managers, being former salespeople, have not been "trained" to be sales trainers.

Despite the ubiquitous lack of training, most salespeople learn the ropes sooner or later. Some are naturals who excel with seemingly little effort; others learn by repeated trial, error, correction, and practice. If given the proper training and support, however, more people would become skilled communicators and problem solvers and, thus, better salespeople.

When salespeople are placed in the field without training, problems abound. They may not know what to do and therefore may rely on what they *think* salespeople should do. Their conception of the selling process could be based on role models such as Willy Loman in the Arthur Miller play *Death of a Salesman* or Herb Tarlick of the TV show "WKRP in Cincinnati"—in other words, the pushy, loud, back-slapping salesperson who offends everyone. It's no wonder there is so much tension when a salesperson meets a prospect.

Tony: My first experience in sales really reinforced this entire notion of the born salesperson. I went to a Catholic grammar school. It was a good training ground—especially for a young, budding salesperson.

One of the ways that the parochial schools generated money in those days was through selling various items to the parents, relatives, and friends of the students. Every month a school sent out its students to sell products. One month we would compete with the Girl Scouts by selling cookies. Another month we would sell those big chocolate bars with almonds in them. Every month we sold something new. I "lovingly" referred to it as the "push of the month!"

To motivate the students to sell as much as possible, there would be a prize for the top salesperson in each grade level. Fortunately, I was from a big Italian Catholic family in New York City and I always outsold my classmates.

Every month when I won the contest, people would come up to

me and say, "When you grow up, you'll be an incredible salesman because you have the gift of gab." "You're a born salesman—you can sell anything to anyone!" Year after year I kept hearing the same things: "born salesman," "the gift of gab," "great at persuading people," "able to sell anything to anyone." After a while, I started believing it. I didn't need training; I was a natural. All I had to do was keep talking!

Unfortunately, my "natural" skills were those of the traditional salesperson: talking, selling, controlling, persuading, using gimmicks, and being aggressive.

The truth is, very few people have the natural ability to be open with others and respond to their needs. Good salespeople, therefore, are made, not born. Sales skills can be learned.

Too Much Product Training

A lot of training dollars are focused on one aspect of sales training—knowledge of the product. Many organizations spend 75 to 100 percent of their training budget solely on developing such knowledge. On sales calls, new salespeople who were trained only in product knowledge usually can talk only about that subject. They exhibit "technological arrogance," that is, they talk so much about the technology that the prospect's needs are overlooked.

A classic example of overtraining someone in product knowledge is the computer store salesperson:

Phil: I had great apprehension about going into the store at all because I wasn't sure I could really work with a computer. I wasn't brought up with computers, and they seemed to be so technical and complicated beyond my scope of comprehension. I was fearful, but I wanted to go in and see what they were all about.

Computer stores definitely understand retail merchandising. In the middle of the store they had this fantastic computer setup with a color monitor and a program that was running with great color graphics and sound. I was mesmerized! Suddenly a salesman walked up behind me and said something that I'm used to hearing at a used-car lot: "It's a beauty, isn't it?"

I couldn't believe how stereotypical that sounded, but I was so awed by the computer display that I said, "Yes, it's incredible! I can't believe it. This thing is much more exciting than I expected."

The salesman responded with, "Guess what, it's 64K." I said, "My God, that expensive?" The guy roared, "No, no, no. That refers to its memory."

He then went on to explain the product in detail—how many bytes, bits, rams, roms, the storage capacity, the types of computer chips, and the add-on boards that are put in the machine. Then he took off the back of the computer and showed me the inside. That was it. I was petrified. I didn't want to know the difference between a computer chip and a potato chip! I politely excused myself and left the store, even more convinced that there was no way I could learn about computers.

If product knowledge was the most important ingredient in selling, then engineers, technicians, and research and development people would be sent out to sell products. This would not be a good idea. They would spend more time talking about how the product was conceptualized, designed, and built than about the benefits it held for the customer. Most prospects do not want to know how a product is built; they only want to know how it works and *what it will do for them,* that is, its features and benefits.

Inappropriate Sales Training

The most serious problem in training salespeople is inappropriate sales training. Twenty years ago, three topics dominated traditional sales training:

- How to give razzle-dazzle *pitches*.

- A hundred and one ways to *close* a sale.

- Power techniques for overcoming *objections*.

Interestingly enough, in traditional sales training, these remain the focus today. Too much emphasis is placed on the wrong techniques. People are being taught how to use gimmicks and shortcuts to do things *to* people. These tricks simply foster the negative image of sales. If you've been in sales for a while, you have probably had the experience of making a sale and walking out the door with a check in one hand and a contract in the other; but instead of feeling elated, you felt terribly guilty because of what you did to get the sale.

Tony: My first adult job in sales was selling cookware—pots and pans. I was taught all the commando techniques of manipulative selling. Back in 1966, when I sold cookware, I sold a ten-piece set of waterless, stainless-steel cookware for almost $300. Of the ten pieces of cookware I sold for $300, four of them were lids. There were only six pots! Talk about a tough sale! Imagine yourself returning home this evening and finding on your table a ten-piece set of cookware. You say to your spouse. "Boy that's beautiful. How much did it cost?" and your spouse says, "$300." What would your reply be?

During my first nine weeks of selling cookware, I sold $11,000 worth using traditional sales techniques. There's no question that traditional selling works—once. I can't begin to tell you how many of my customers wanted their money back. People pestered me for weeks to get a refund. In that business, however, there were no refunds. Once the contract was signed, it was also sealed and delivered. I couldn't walk down the streets of my hometown and look my customers in the eye.

What could I do? I was stuck in the middle between my company and my customers. I really felt guilty, but I thought that was the way sales were made. I thought everyone did it that way. I was selling like a traditional salesperson: tell, persuade, mesmerize, hypnotize, give a good razzle-dazzle pitch, overcome objections, and close, close, close.

I would be on some appointments for hours, long enough to wear down the prospect until she bought just to get rid of me. I was taught to grind my customers into submission. It was a win-lose situation. If I made the sale, I won and the customer lost.

I can even remember the weekly sales meetings with that slick sales manager. In retrospect, these meetings were absolutely nauseating. At the beginning of every sales meeting, regardless of how well we did the week before, he would pace back and forth like a caged tiger giving us a sideways glance, not saying a word. Finally he would yell at the top of his lungs, "I don't know what's wrong with you guys! You're not making enough sales. You're lettin' the prospects get away from you. It's a battle out there. It's a war! It's you against them. If you don't come back with the contract, you lost. If you do come back with the contract, you won and they lost."

It took me a while to realize how sick that approach was. We're not involved in a con game of one-time sales, unconcerned about the customer's satisfaction. We're all in business for the long haul, even if we sell only once to a customer. There are values, ethics, and good business sense that we must follow if we are to live with ourselves.

I'm sorry to say that in three years of selling cookware and two later years of selling life insurance, baby pictures, burglar alarms, and mausoleums, I was taught and I used all the traditional selling techniques. I made sales, but not customers, and certainly no friends.

Selling with gimmicks and shortcuts, acting sincere when you are not, and acting defeated when you are not—these are neither the way to sell nor the ethical way to do business.

TRADITIONAL SELLING VS. NON-MANIPULATIVE SELLING

Every sales call has similarities to others, but the techniques employed differentiate the non-manipulative salesperson from the traditional salesperson.

In figure 1.1, you can see that non-manipulative selling emphasizes the early steps of the sale whereas traditional selling stresses the close. You can also see there are differences in the terms each uses. In non-manipulative selling, the salesperson's words have no connotation of manipulation or superficiality. They express concern, preparedness, cooperation, and the intent to continue the relationship after the sale.

In figure 1.1, you will also notice that the emphasis placed on each phase of the sale is represented by the width of the shaded area surrounding it. The traditional salesperson spends an inordinate amount of time trying to convince the customer to buy. The non-manipulative salesperson, however, takes more time in the beginning to plan, meet, and study in order to be of service to the client. In the following series of steps you can compare the two selling processes.

	TRADITIONAL SELLING	NON-MANIPULATIVE SELLING
INFORMATION GATHERING	PROSPECTING SMALL TALK FACT FINDING	PLANNING MEETING STUDYING
PRESENTATION	PITCHING	PROPOSING
COMMITMENT	CLOSING/ OVERCOMING OBJECTIONS	CONFIRMING
FOLLOW-THROUGH	RESELLING	ASSURING

FIGURE 1.1 **The Sales Process**
A COMPARISON OF THE TIME SPENT
IN EACH PHASE OF THE SALES PROCESS

Step 1: Planning vs. Prospecting

One of the major differences between the two selling processes is the amount of time spent in the beginning phases of the sale. Non-manipulative salespeople devote a lot of time to planning their territory and managing their time and accounts. Traditional salespeople take a shotgun approach to prospecting, which, unfortunately, is very inefficient in the long run. Contacting the *right* prospects is more productive than contacting a large number of them. The best combination is to contact a large number of the right prospects.

Step 2: Meeting vs. Small Talk

The purpose of meeting your prospect, initially, is to begin building a business relationship. Professional salespeople know that a solid business relationship goes beyond the immediate product or service being offered. The relationship and, therefore, the sale, require the establishment of trust and the building of credibility. When the prospect knows the salesperson sincerely has the prospect's best interest at heart, the rest of the sales process can continue. Today's buyers are appreciative of salespeople who show an interest in them and their business or family.

Step 3: Studying vs. Fact-Finding

Traditional salespeople spend a minimum amount of time studying the prospect's situation. They operate under the assumption that a need exists based on the target market in which the prospect falls.

Non-manipulative salespeople spend a great deal of time studying their prospects' businesses. They look not only for needs but for opportunities. Looking for needs implies that customers only have problems that need to be solved. Looking for or creating opportunities puts the salesperson in the position of a consultant who can take the status quo and improve it.

Non-manipulative selling is analogous to the holistic medical movement. When studying a patient's symptoms, a holistic doctor looks at virtually every facet of the person's life. The prescription includes ways for the patient to take an active role in getting well. A traditional doctor treats symptoms without giving much thought to the big picture. You can see how this approach is similar to that of traditional sales.

In non-manipulative selling, you encourage the prospect to become involved in the selling process. By asking well-structured questions, offering thought-provoking possibilities, and studying the many facets of the prospect's operation, you engender cooperation.

Step 4: The Proposal vs. the Pitch

After meeting with the prospect and studying his or her problem, the next step for the non-manipulative salesperson is to propose a solution to the problem. Both traditional and non-manipulative selling allocate approximately the same amount of time to the presentation. Beyond the time factor, however, the similarities disappear.

Traditional salespeople give an identical presentation to all prospects and customers, regardless of their needs. In fact, they may use a "canned" presentation that ignores the prospect's individuality.

The non-manipulative sales approach, by contrast, is one in which the presentation is custom-tailored to the prospect's needs. Benefits are discussed as they apply to specific problems. This is made possible by the comprehensive discussions the salesperson has had with the prospect.

Step 5: Confirming the Sale vs. Closing

To non-manipulative salespeople, the confirmation of the sale is a logical conclusion to the continual communication and agreement that has been taking place with the prospect. Since they have worked together on a common goal since the beginning, there are few reasons why the prospect would voice objections at this point. There may be details to work out, but they don't get in the way of the sale.

Traditional salespeople spend most of their time and training on the close. In fact, the ability to overcome objections becomes a point of pride with some salespeople, many of whom flaunt their ability the way Sumo wrestlers flaunt their weight. Certainly this is an exaggeration; the point is that objections are a source of information that the salesperson should have uncovered earlier. If she had done so, there would be no objections, only a confirmation of the sale.

When Phil Wexler was a fledgling burglar-alarm salesman, his company provided him with a small flip chart. On each page was a possible objection and the salesperson's response. This was designed to give the salespeople all the ammunition they needed to overcome the customer's objections.

Phil: One day as I was sitting in a customer's house, I realized the absurdity of using such a tool. I was playing a game with the customer. When the customer raised an objection, I remembered the page, flipped to it, and gave the answer. When the customer raised a second objection, I looked at the customer and said, "Mr. Jones, I have this book that my company gave me. It's designed to give me the answers to all these objections you've come up with. How about if I just give you the book, you flip from page to page, read the answers to all the objections, and let's see if we can come to the reason why you're resisting buying this burglar alarm. If it's something you ought to have, let's go ahead and buy it. If it's something you shouldn't have, just tell me so and I'll leave you alone. I'll leave the book with you and go sit in the other room for a while. You decide if the burglar alarm is what you ought to have."

Salespeople have to recognize that the resistance many customers show is not resistance to the product but resistance to the salesperson. Prospects often create objections to cover up for the lack of a sales relationship. Traditional selling is an anachronism that used to thrive (in the short term) on the cat-and-mouse game, "Can you come up with more objections than I can handle?"

In non-manipulative selling, the confirmation becomes a question of "when," not "if." If resistance occurs, it simply indicates there is a need for gathering more information or clarifying some details. Gaps in communication are not a problem in professional sales because the salesperson is willing to spend the time with the prospect until everything is understood.

Step 6: Assuring vs. Reselling

The problem with traditional sales is that the prospect has usually been rushed into buying. Several undesirable consequences can ensue. After a while, the customer may experience buyer's remorse. This requires going back to do a reselling job so the sale does not fall through. Needless to say, this is a waste of time and, especially when unsuccessful, creates a lot of ill will.

Traditional sales methods often cause another problem. If the sale was closed and the buyer was left feeling resentful, when the salesperson goes to recontact the buyer, the salesperson has to start from scratch reestablishing the relationship. If another salesperson is given the account, he has to overcome the grudge the customer still holds. Non-manipulative selling avoids these problems by making sure the customer is happy after the sale.

Non-manipulative salespeople thrive on satisfied customers and see them for what they are—assets! The salespeople begin assuring customer satisfaction after the sale by changing hats from salespeople to quality-control people. They make sure the customer received the proper order on the right delivery date and help the customer track the results and analyze the effectiveness of the product or service for the specific problem(s) addressed. In general, such salespeople stay in touch and become the type of person the customer can also consider an asset.

By assuring the satisfaction of each customer, non-manipulative salespeople build a clientele that will guarantee future sales and become annuities.

In literature, every great story has a premise. In business, every great philosophy has its guiding principles. Non-manipulative selling is no exception. The six guiding principles of NMS that reflect its level of professionalism and integrity are:

1. A professional is known not by the business he or she is in but by the way he or she is in business. In sales, your expertise in an industry is lost when you change industries. Your professionalism, however, goes with you no matter who you work for.

2. If two people want to do business together, the details will not stand in the way. On the other hand, if two people do not get along well and do not want to do business together, no detail will pull it together and make it happen.

3. The sales process must be built on a foundation of trust and mutual agreement. Relationships that are open, honest and free of tension create long-lasting business associations that pay off in many ways for many years.

4. In selling, as in medicine, prescription before diagnosis is malpractice. A non-manipulative salesperson does not offer solutions before he completely understands his customer's business.

5. People buy because they feel understood and appreciated by the salesperson, not because the client was made to understand the salesperson's product or service.

6. People like to make their own decisions, regardless of how wise or unwise those decisions are. If you impose solutions upon clients, they will resent both you and your solution. A salesperson can help a customer solve a problem, but should do so in a way that makes the customer a partner in the solution.

These guidelines, along with the philosophy and six steps of NMS, have worked wonders for people's careers. Roy Cammarano is an excellent example of what non-manipulative selling can do for a career. A former client and now a friend of the authors', in 1983 Roy started out making $18,000 a year selling memberships to a health club. He attended a non-manipulative sales (NMS) seminar and read the first edition of this book; three years later he was the executive vice president of California Business Times, a subsidiary of American City Business Journals. In 1986, Roy was making more than $100,000 a year plus stock options, perks, and expenses. He attributes most of his success to non-manipulative selling and shares some of his experiences throughout this book.

Roy: After I adopted non-manipulative selling, I went from being a "hammer" to being helpful. Before NMS, I would pound people by leading them with very manipulative questions, ones that had only one or two possible responses. Whatever answer they gave, I would just continue with my planned questions. My perception was that since they were talking to me, they must want to do business.

I find now with NMS that my customers and I make decisions together. They feel much better about their decisions, so my follow-up procedures have become much more enjoyable. In the past I was constantly reconfirming the sale because my customers felt they had been hustled. As a result, they were not as open and honest with me in subsequent business transactions. They thought I was going to take more from them. Now my clients feel I give them more than they ask for. The relationships are more open and honest. I'm no longer a taker, I'm a giver. I realize if it's in everyone's best interest, we'll do business. I've gained the reputation of being someone who is able to give more to people, and that has moved me higher in my career.

I think the most important part of non-manipulative selling is the information-gathering phase. During that phase, you give to people more than anyone else ever has, especially other salespeople. You give them insights into their business that hadn't occurred to them. You get them thinking about how they could be more successful in their business. For that, you are remembered in a much better light. And you do all this in a way they are comfortable with. Relationship strategies are so important. It's a matter of asking your questions in a tone that they are comfortable responding to.

After I started using NMS, I got so involved in information gathering and considering people's personality styles that I found I was given much more information. That gave me the ability to find opportunities to help them more and people responded differently to me. They wanted to help me as well. My career took off. I was able to penetrate accounts more and get more referrals and repeat business.

Part of my success can be attributed to my commitment to myself. A commitment to being a better, all-around person has made everything more fun because I do it better. When work and play are fun, you like to do it more and you become more successful.

2

Relationship Strategies

IN YOUR DEALINGS with other people, have you, on the one hand, ever experienced a personality conflict? Most of us have. Have you, on the other hand, ever met someone for the first time and after fifteen minutes or so, felt as though you have known that person for many years?

Your ability as a non-manipulative salesperson to develop such a positive chemistry with all of your prospects and customers is crucial to your success in sales. In sales, the *first* thing you have to sell before anything else is *yourself*; and you can do it every time.

Most salespeople try to create positive chemistry in their sales relationships by practicing the Golden Rule: "Do unto others as you would have them do unto you." It is the contention here, however, that practicing this rule verbatim increases your chances of creating more conflict than harmony with your prospects and customers. Taken literally, the Golden Rule says a person should treat others from his own perspective, not theirs; the person should speak to people the way he likes to be spoken to, manage them the way he would like to be managed and, most importantly, *sell* others the way he would like to be sold. The authors disagree. Let's take Tony's mother as an example.

Tony: My mother is so outgoing she makes the television aerobics instructor Richard Simmons look like an introvert! She's the type of person who walks into a restaurant and, on the way to her table, stops to introduce herself to total strangers. It's unbelievable. She'll approach people and say, "Hi, I'm Margie Alessandra. What's your name? Betty? Nice to meet you. Are you Italian? No? Oh, too bad. What are you eating? Would you recommend it?"

She means well, but not everyone appreciates having their meal interrupted by someone that person has never seen before. Other people, however, look at her and think she is the greatest. They actually wish their mothers were like her. Whether they appreciate her or not, my mother doesn't care. She inflicts her way of doing things on other people. She doesn't do it maliciously or selfishly; she actually believes people like to be treated the same way she does.

The authors suggest you learn to practice the *intent* or spirit of the Golden Rule: "Treat people the way they want to be treated." For the purposes of this book, "Sell people the way they like to be sold." This may be called the Platinum Rule.

BEHAVIORAL STYLES

To practice the Platinum Rule effectively, you need to be able to read people. To communicate with someone on her wavelength, you must first know what frequency she is tuned into.

Throughout history, people have categorized one another in different ways in an attempt to understand human behavior. For example, ancient astrologists turned to nature for their explanations of personality. They devised a system of twelve signs in four groups characterized by water, fire, air, and earth.

Over the course of hundreds of years philosophers and scientists, from Hippocrates to Jung, developed personality theories. It is interesting to note that these theories had one thing in common: as in astrology, they divided people into four distinct styles. Most modern theories follow suit.

It is important to keep in mind that no style is more or less

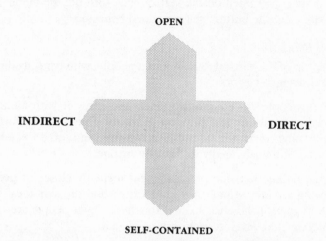

FIGURE 2.1 *The Two Dimensions of Behavior*

desirable than another. They all have positive and negative aspects. What annoys one person may be appealing to someone else.

Relationship strategies, based on the authors' research and observations, is an updated system that gives you a practical way to recognize people's preferred styles of communicating. The four styles are based on two dimensions of behavior: openness and directness. These are depicted graphically in figure 2.1. The concepts are readily understood if taken one axis at a time.

OPEN VS. SELF-CONTAINED BEHAVIORS

Openness is the ease with which a person shows emotions and responds to other people. A very open person is willing to share thoughts and feelings and jump into new relationships where a self-contained person would remain aloof. Self-contained people do not mind being alone and frequently prefer it. Open people are more people oriented; self-contained people are task oriented.

In figure 2.1, the range of behaviors between open and self-contained are represented on the vertical axis with the top being open behaviors and the bottom self-contained behaviors.

Open Behaviors

At the top of the vertical axis are open people, who typically display the following behaviors:

- Open people are emotionally open and show it with animated facial expressions and physical gestures. They are comfortable expressing their joy, sadness, confusion, and other emotions quickly and unabashedly to virtually anyone.

- Open people become physically and mentally closer to people. During a conversation, they practically stand on your toes. They are huggers, hand shakers, and touchers. Open people are more outgoing and develop relationships quickly.

- Open people are informal and enjoy quickly breaking down the walls of formality. They like to swap first names as soon as possible. They prefer relaxed, warm relationships.

- Open people love loose, amusing conversations. They would rather digress and hear about your brother-in-law's surgery than discuss the business at hand. Interaction in a conversation is more important than content.

- Open people do not like to structure their time and don't become upset when other people waste their time. In fact, they balk at imposed schedules and agendas and prefer to go with the flow.

- Open people are feeling-oriented decision makers. They value their hunches and the feelings of others. They come to their decisions by realization rather than cogitation.

Self-Contained Behaviors

The other end of the vertical axis represents self-contained people, who typically exhibit the following behaviors:

- Self-contained people do not readily show their emotions. They could be called poker faces. Physically, they are more rigid and less expressive than open people. Self-contained people are guarded and well behaved. They are never boisterous or rowdy. If you were a stand-up comedian, you wouldn't want an audience full of self-contained people; their laughter is more inward than outward.

- Self-contained people keep their distance, physically and psychologically. They are less easy to get to know than open people, but once you know them, they are like everyone else. At first they tend to remain aloof and value their privacy. Their offices are arranged more formally and assure a comfortable distance from the people whom they meet. With strangers, they prefer to keep everything on a business level.

- Self-contained people are task oriented. A conversation with a self-contained person will rarely stray from the business that initiated the contact. They dislike digressions from their agendas.

- Self-contained people are fact-oriented decision makers. They want to see statistics and other hard evidence. In the workplace, they prefer to work alone and put little value on opinions and feelings. On the surface, they appear to operate in an intellectual mode, not an emotional mode.

- Self-contained people are champions of time management. They are the efficiency experts of the world, who create and follow rigid plans and schedules. They implore other people to respect their time and not waste it.

DIRECT VS. INDIRECT BEHAVIORS

Directness refers to the amount of control a person attempts to exert over people and situations. The amount of effort a person uses to try to gain control also reflects her attitudes towards risk taking and change. Directness is measured on the horizontal axis in figure 2.1.

Direct Behaviors

Direct people occupy the right end of the directness scale and typically exhibit the following behaviors:

- Direct people, to borrow a Wall Street metaphor, are bulls. They are forceful, Type A personalities, who confront conflict, change, risk, and decision making head on.

- Direct people are outspoken communicators and often dominate business meetings. They will tell you their opinions even if you don't want to hear them, and if they want your opinion, they'll give it to you.

- Direct people are competitive, impatient, and confrontative. They bulldoze their way through life. They argue for the sake of arguing. They hold eye contact longer than average and possess an air of confidence. Their handshakes are firm.

- Direct people thrive on accomplishment and are not overly concerned with rules and policies. They are more likely to look for expedients to attain their ends than to accept obstacles. Ambiguity does not deter them; it encourages them. Their attitude is, "It is easier to beg forgiveness than to seek permission."

Indirect Behaviors

At the left side of the horizontal axis are indirect people, who display the following behaviors:

- Indirect people are bears, to use the Wall Street metaphor again. They approach risk, decision making, and change cautiously. They are the meek who shall inherit the earth. They are Type B personalities, who are slow paced and low key.

- Indirect people are tentative, reserved communicators, who are not contributors in meetings. When their thoughts are solicited, they often preface their statements with qualifications such as "I'm not sure if . . ." or "According to my sources . . . ."

- Indirect people avoid conflict whenever possible. They are diplomatic, patient, and cooperative. On unimportant issues, they will conform rather than argue. When they have strong convictions about an issue, however, they will stand their ground. When they are less convinced, they carefully weigh an issue's importance against the discomfort of confrontation.

- In a stressful situation, there are two basic responses: fight or flight. Indirect people choose flight. This does not mean they are cowards; one can avoid conflict with smooth talk, diplomacy, and finesse.

- Indirect people are low profile, reserved, and gentle. For example, their handshakes are sometimes soft, and they speak at a slower pace and lower volume than direct people. They don't take the initiative at social gatherings but wait for others to approach them.

DETERMINE YOUR OPENNESS AND DIRECTNESS

As you read the above descriptions of openness and directness, you undoubtedly did what everyone does: you compared yourself to the characteristics being described. That's good. At this point, you will find it helpful to go back over the descriptions to determine where you stand on the two axes.

Now think of a "difficult" person with whom you would like to have a better relationship. Determine that person's position on the two axes and mark on those places. More often than not, you will find that people with whom you have conflicts have opposite personal styles from yours.

In determining your personal style or that of someone else, look for overall patterns. How do you act most of the time? Which descriptions of yourself did you identify with first before you started thinking, "Yes, but . . ."?

People are not simple; they are infinitely complex. Even though everyone has one dominant personal style, they also possess characteristics from all the styles. You may do some things in an indirect way and others in a direct way; in some situations you are very open and in others self-contained. The more comfortable you feel, however, the more you are acting in accordance with your dominant style.

FOUR BEHAVIORAL STYLES

The four behavioral styles, when combined graphically as in figure 2.1, form four quadrants. These quadrants and their unique com-

FIGURE 2.2 *The Four Styles of Behavior*

binations of behaviors identify four styles of relating to the world. Figure 2.2 shows the placement of the *socializer, director, thinker,* and *relater.*

The Socializer

Socializers have a behavioral style that is high in both directness and openness, readily exhibiting characteristics such as animation and intuitiveness. They can also, however, be viewed as manipulative, impetuous, and excitable when displaying behavior inappropriate to the situation.

Socializers are fast-paced people whose actions and decisions are spontaneous. They are seldom concerned with facts and details and try to avoid them as much as possible. The authors' favorite socializer, Phil Wexler, has a motto: "Don't burden me with the details." This disregard for details sometimes prompts socializers to exaggerate and generalize facts and figures. It also gives them a built-in excuse when they are wrong on something. "I didn't have all the facts!" They are more comfortable with "best guesstimates" than with exact, empirically backed data. They are the type of people who rush into a bank, hail an officer, show a bounced check, and exclaim, "I can't be overdrawn, I still have checks left!"

Socializers are idea people. They are very creative and have a dynamic ability to think quickly on their feet. They always seem to be chasing dreams, and they have the ability to get others caught up in their dreams because of their strong persuasive skills. Their emphasis is on influencing others and shaping the environment by bringing others together to accomplish results. They seem always to be seeking approval and recognition for their accomplishments and achievements.

Socializers are true entertainers. They love an audience and thrive on involvement with people. They tend to work quickly and enthusiastically with others. If they had a motto that would aptly describe their behavior, it might be, "When you're as good as I am, it's hard to be humble."

Socializers are stimulating, talkative, and gregarious. They tend to operate on intuition and take risks. They are enthusiastic and optimistic as well as emotional and friendly. They like involvement, and their greatest irritations are doing boring tasks, being alone, and not having access to a telephone.

The primary strengths of socializers are their enthusiasm, persuasiveness, and delightful sociability. Their primary weaknesses are getting involved in too many things, being impatient, and having a short attention span, which causes them to become bored easily. Many socializers have occupations such as public relations specialists, talk show hosts, trial attorneys, social directors on cruise ships, hotel personnel, and other glamorous, high-profile careers.

In the business environment, they like other people to be risk takers and to act quickly and decisively. In a social environment they like others to be uninhibited, spontaneous, and entertaining. Some famous people who epitomize socializers are the show business figures Carol Burnett, Lucille Ball, Burt Reynolds, Dom Deluise, and Tom Selleck; the prizefighter Mohammad Ali; and U.S. President Ronald Reagan.

If socializers had theme songs that reflected their personalities, they could be, "Celebration!," "Let the Good Times Roll," "All Night Long," or "Don't Rain on My Parade."

Certain environmental and proxemic clues indicate the presence of socializers. (Proxemics is the study of personal space and the movement of people in it.) Socializers design and use their space in a disorganized and cluttered manner; however, they know if something is missing. Their office walls may contain awards, stimulating posters or notes, and motivational, personal slogans. Their office decor is open, airy, and friendly, and the seating arrangement indicates warmth, openness, and a willingness to make contact with others. Socializers like contact and often move to an alternative seating arrangement when talking with visitors. Socializers are touchers and don't mind a slap on the back or a warm handshake. They don't mind people getting close to them, so there is very little danger of alienating a socializer by standing too close or playing with something on their desk.

To increase their flexibility and achieve more balance, socializers need to control their time and emotions; develop more of an objective mindset; spend more time checking, verifying, specifying, and organizing; concentrate on the task; and take a more logical approach to projects and issues.

The Director

Directors are self-contained and in control. They are firm in their relationships with others, are oriented toward productivity and goals, and are concerned with bottom-line results. Closely allied to these positive traits are the negative ones of stubbornness, impatience, and toughness. Directors tend to take control of other people and situations and are decisive in their actions and forthright in their decisions. Always in a hurry, they like to move at a fast pace and are impatient with delays. It is not unusual for a director to call you and, without saying hello, launch right into the conversation, "You've got to be kidding; the shipping from Hong Kong will kill us . . . by the way, this is Jack." When other people cannot keep up with their speed, they view them as incompetent. The director's motto might be: "I want it done right and I want it done now" or "I want it done yesterday!"

Directors are high achievers who exhibit very good administrative skills. They get things done and make things happen. They are like jugglers in that they like to manipulate many projects at the same time. They start juggling three things at once, and when they feel comfortable with those three things, they pick up a fourth. They keep adding more until the pressure builds to the point where they turn their backs and let everything drop. They call that "reevaluating their priorities." After reducing their stress, they immediately start the whole process over again. The theme of a director seems to be, "Notice my accomplishments."

Directors are motivated toward high achievement and have a tendency toward workaholism. Therefore, doctors would say that directors are in the high-risk category for heart attacks. Impatient, Type A personalities are also prime victims of ulcers. Directors, however, don't just get ulcers; they give ulcers to other people!

Directors specialize in being in control. They tend to be independent, strong-willed, precise, goal oriented, cool, and competitive, especially in a business environment. They accept challenges, take authority, and go head first into solving problems. They tend to exhibit great administrative and operational skills and work quickly and impressively by themselves. Directors try to shape their environment to overcome obstacles to their plans. They demand maximum freedom to manage themselves and others. Directors can have a low tolerance for the feelings, attitudes, and inadequacies of their co-workers and subordinates. They use their leadership skills to become winners.

The primary strengths of directors are their ability to get things done, their leadership, and their decision-making ability. Their weaknesses tend to be their inflexibility, their impatience, their poor listening habits, and their neglect of taking time to "smell the flowers." In fact, they are so competitive that when they do finally go out to "smell the flowers," they return and say to others, "I smelled twelve today. How many did you smell?"

In a business environment, directors like others to be decisive, efficient, receptive, and intelligent, and in a social environment they want others to be congenial, assertive, and witty. A director's ideal occupation might be a hard-driving newspaper reporter, stockbroker, independent consultant, corporate CEO, or drill sergeant.

Famous people who are directors in their behavioral style are the actors Telly Savalas as Kojak, William Shatner as Captain Kirk on the television program "Star Trek," Bea Arthur as Dorothy in the TV show "Golden Girls," Ed Asner as Lou Grant, and Clint Eastwood; the television anchor Barbara Walters; and British Prime Minister Margaret Thatcher.

The theme song of a director would be "My Way."

Directors' desks will appear busy with lots of paperwork, projects, and material separated into piles. Their offices are decorated to suggest power, for example, by having a hatchet buried in the wall. There are often large planning calendars. Directors are formal and keep their distance physically and psychologically. Their offices are arranged so that seating is formal; that is, a big desk symbolizing power separates directors from their visitors. They don't like people talking three inches from their noses, and becoming your friend is not a prerequisite to doing business with you.

To achieve more balance, directors need to practice active listening; project a more relaxed image; and develop patience, humility, and sensitivity. They need to show a concern for others, use more caution, verbalize the reasons for their conclusions, identify more as a team player, and be aware of existing rules or conventions.

The Thinker

Thinkers are both indirect and self-contained. They seem to be very much concerned with analytical processes and are persistent, systematic problem solvers. They can also be seen as aloof, picky, and critical. Thinkers are very security-conscious and have a high need to be right, leading them to an overreliance on the collection of data. In their quest for information they tend to ask many questions about specifics, and their actions and decisions tend to be extremely cautious. Although they are great problem solvers, thinkers could be better decision makers. They are slow to reach a decision, but given a deadline, they will rarely miss it.

Thinkers tend to be serious and orderly and are likely to be perfectionists. They tend to focus on the details and the process of work and become irritated by surprises and "glitches." Their theme is, "Notice my efficiency," and their emphasis is on compliance and working with existing guidelines to promote quality in products or service.

Thinkers like organization and structure and dislike too much involvement with other people. They work slowly and precisely by themselves and prefer objective, task-oriented, intellectual work environments. They are precise, detail oriented, disciplined about time, and often critical of their own performance. They tend to be skeptical and like to see things in writing. They like problem-solving activities and work best under controlled circumstances.

The primary strengths of thinkers are their accuracy, dependability, independence, follow-through, and organization. Their primary weaknesses are their procrastinating and conservative nature, which promotes their tendency to be picky and overcautious. They tend to gravitate toward such occupations as accounting, engineering, computer programming, the hard sciences (chemistry, physics, math), systems analysis, and architecture.

The greatest irritations for thinkers are disorganized, illogical people. In business environments, they want others to be credible, professional, sincere, and courteous. In social environments, they like others to be pleasant and sincere.

Famous people who are outstanding examples of thinkers are the television actors Leonard Nimoy as Spock in "Star Trek," and Jack Webb as Sargeant Friday on "Dragnet," and the fictional British detective Sherlock Holmes.

Thinkers generally have offices with highly organized or clear desk tops and charts, graphs, exhibits, or pictures pertaining to the job on the walls. They are noncontact people who are not fond of huggers and touchers and who prefer a cool handshake or a brief telephone call. This preference is reflected in the functional but uninviting arrangement of their desks and chairs.

The thinkers' theme song could be "Step by Step," and their type of music is classical, the more complex the better.

To increase flexibility, thinkers need openly to show concern and appreciation of others, occasionally to try shortcuts and time savers, and to try to adjust more readily to change and disorganization. They should also work to improve timely decision making and the initiation of new projects, to compromise with the opposition, to state unpopular decisions, and to use policies more as guidelines than as rigid decrees.

The Relater

Relaters are open and indirect, relatively unassertive, warm, supportive, and reliable. They are sometimes seen by others, however, as compliant, soft-hearted, and acquiescent.

Relaters seek security and, like thinkers, are slow at taking action and making decisions. This pace stems from their desire to avoid risky and unknown situations. Before they take action or make a decision, they have to know how other people feel about the situation.

Relaters are the most people oriented of all of the four styles. Having close, friendly, personal, first-name relationships with others is one of their most important objectives. They dislike interpersonal conflicts so much that they sometimes say what they think other people want to hear. They have tremendous counseling skills and are extremely supportive. People feel good just being with relaters. Relaters are excellent listeners and generally develop relationships with people who are also good listeners. As a result, relaters have strong networks of people who are willing to be mutually supportive.

The focus of relaters is on getting acquainted and building trust. They are irritated by pushy, aggressive behavior. Their theme is, "Notice how well liked I am." They ask about any proposal, "How will it affect my personal circumstances and the comraderie of the group?" They are cooperative, steady workers and excellent team players.

The primary strengths of relaters are relating to, caring for, and loving others. Their primary weaknesses are that they are somewhat unassertive, overly sensitive, and easily bullied. Their ideal occupations cluster around the helping professions such as counseling, teaching, social work, the ministry, psychology, nursing, and human-resource development. They are good at being parents.

In the business environment, relaters like others to be courteous and friendly and to share responsibilities. In a social environment, they like others to be genuine and friendly.

Famous people who are relaters are the television personages Mary Tyler Moore, Jean Stapleton as Edith on "All in the Family," David Hartman on "Good Morning, America," Jane Pauley on the "Today Show," and Mr. Rogers from the children's show, "Mr. Rogers' Neighborhood."

The songs that best reflect the personality of relaters might be "Feelings," "People," "Getting to Know You," "You've Got a Friend," and "We Are the World."

As for environmental clues, relaters' desks contain family pictures and other personal items. Their office walls have personal slogans, family or group pictures, serene pictures, or mementos. Relaters are high-touch in a high-tech world. They give their offices a friendly, warm ambiance and arrange seating in a side-by-side, cooperative way.

To increase flexibility, relaters need to say no occasionally, to attend to the completion of tasks without over-sensitivity to the feelings of others, to be willing to reach beyond their comfort zone to set goals that require some stretch and risk, and to delegate to others.

Here is a joke that will help you to get a handle on the four behavioral styles: Four eighteenth-century French nobles, each of a different behavioral style, were convicted of a crime and sentenced to death by decapitation. On the day of the execution, they mounted the stairs of the scaffolding together and were placed in a special four-person guillotine. The executioner pulled the rope, and the blade came down but stopped inches from their necks. This was interpreted as a sign that they were innocent and they were set free. The men stood up with joy. The director immediately turned to the others and yelled, "You see, I told you I was innocent!" The socializer let out a scream, "Let's PARTY!" The relater went to the hangman, hugged him, and said, "I just want you to know I didn't take this personally. You're a nice person at heart. Why don't you come over for dinner sometime?" The thinker paused, looked up at the mechanism, scratched his chin, and said, "Hmmm, I think I see the problem."

BEHAVIORAL STYLES AND INTERPERSONAL PROBLEMS

An awareness of behavioral styles becomes important when people of different styles meet. If each person behaves according to his or her style, negative tension can result and slow down or short-circuit the sales relationship.

Besides differences in openness and directness, the styles differ in pace and priority. Directors and socializers are faster paced; thinkers and relaters are slower paced. Directors and thinkers are more task oriented; relaters and socializers are more people oriented.

To avoid unproductive relationships when meeting with others, you must meet their needs, especially their behavioral-style needs. In short, you must treat them in the way that they want to be treated—sell them in the way that they want to be sold. If they move fast, you move fast. If they like to take their time and get to know you, allow more time for the appointment. When you meet another person's behavioral-style needs, a climate of mutual trust begins to form. As trust develops, the other person will begin to tell you what he or she really needs. Instead of a contest, there will be a productive relationship and, hopefully, an eventual sale and long-term customer.

Rick: I had a luncheon meeting with a major client so she could meet me to determine if she would like me to speak at her firm's annual meeting. I went to the lunch with two friends who worked for the company's regional office, and the three of us met the woman from the head office who was in charge of hiring me.

I was introduced to the woman and immediately felt that I was in the twilight zone. Everything she did was in slow motion. It seemed as if she took an hour to extend her hand; she gave my hand about a half a pump and said, "How do you do?" I immediately determined that she was self-contained, task oriented, and judging by her speed, she was indirect. That made her a thinker.

Throughout the rest of the meal I consciously slowed my pace and kept the subject on business unless she chose to digress. After we ordered I said, "We're here today to discuss these five points. There is some information I need, then I can give you the data you need and you can tell me what you think." We proceeded to do that, and at the end of the meal she hired me. She made it a point to tell me, "You know, I've never hired a speaker before on the first meeting. I usually meet with people several times before I'm comfortable awarding a contract."

The two friends who accompanied me to the meeting and who know me quite well thought I was ill or had had a stroke and didn't know it because I was moving and talking so slowly. I also wasn't being as overly friendly as I usually am. It worked. I now have a strong, ongoing relationship with that company.

HOW TO RECOGNIZE BEHAVIORAL STYLES

You now have some knowledge of the four personality patterns and how important it is to interact appropriately with a person's behavioral style. But how do you identify which of the styles your prospect represents? And, how do you do it quickly? To identify your prospect's style, you must observe what that prospect does; you must be sensitive to both verbal and nonverbal actions. Two procedures help you quickly, accurately, and simply to identify a prospect's behavioral style: Note the prospect's environment, and observe the prospect's actions.

The Prospect's Environment
First, notice the environment in which your prospect works. How is the office decorated and arranged? What is on the desk, walls, and bookshelves? What is the seating arrangement between you and your prospect? If you see family pictures on the desk and walls, nature posters, a round desk, and a separate seating area with a sofa and two side chairs, what is your first impression of the prospect's behavioral style? By comparing these environmental clues with those discussed earlier, you'll see that you are probably dealing with a relater, either that or an interior decorator who is a relator.

Environmental indicators, however, are only one kind of clue to behavioral style. Do not use them as the sole determinant. Your client may have had little control over her environment or may have changed the environment in order to meet other needs, such as an intense work load, a headstrong boss or spouse, or budgetary constraints.

The Prospect's Actions
The second method of identifying behavioral style is to observe it in action. This is the most crucial and accurate method. There is one catch, however; in order to observe someone's behavioral style, you need to observe a range of verbal and nonverbal behaviors. This

requires you to stimulate more behaviors by asking questions and "actively" listening.

Observable *open* behaviors include animated facial expressions, considerable hand and body movement, flexible time perspective, storytelling and anecdotes, little emphasis on facts and details, sharing of personal feelings, contact orientation, and immediate nonverbal feedback.

Observable *self-contained* behaviors include little facial expression, controlled and limited hand and body movement, disciplined sense of time, conversation focused on issues and tasks at hand, required facts and details, little sharing of personal feelings, non-contact orientation, and slowness of nonverbal feedback, if any at all.

Observable *indirect* behaviors would be soft handshake; intermittent eye contact; low quantity of verbal communication; questions for clarification, support, and information; tentative statements; limited gestures to support conversation; low voice volume; slow voice speed; little variation in vocal intonation; hesitant communication; slowness in moving.

Observable *direct* behaviors are firm handshake; steady eye contact; high quantity of verbal communication; more rhetorical questions asked to emphasize points or challenge information; emphatic statements; points emphasized with gestures and challenging tone; high voice volume; fast voice speed; and speed in moving.

To identify behavioral styles using the openness-directness axes, first mentally locate the prospect's position on the openness axis, then determine the degree of directness demonstrated. The result is a placement of the prospect into one of the four quadrants of behavioral style through a simple process of elimination. For instance, if you determine that your prospect is exhibiting open behaviors, you are automatically eliminating the styles with self-contained behaviors, those of director and thinker. Likewise, if you determine that your prospect is also high in directness, you automatically eliminate the indirect styles, those of relater and thinker. Therefore, by the process of elimination, you are left with the socializer style for your prospect.

The following three scenarios illustrate different personal styles. See if you can identify which ones they are:

- The seminar was to begin at 8:30 A.M. following an 8:00 coffee-and-doughnut session. When I arrived at 7:45 A.M., a participant was already in the room with a pad and pencils neatly laid out in front of him. He said nothing until I approached, and we politely shook hands. He was totally noncommittal. I asked a few questions for which I received polite, to-the-point answers.

- Around 8:15, with several other people in the room, a woman stopped hesitantly at the door and softly asked, "Excuse me, am I at the training seminar for salespeople?" On being told yes, she breathed a sigh, walked in, and took a cup of coffee while stating how interesting the seminar would be for both business and home. She asked a few questions, listening intently to my remarks, and expressed some concern about role playing in front of a group.

- At this moment, another participant strode in, loudly asking, "Hey, is this the sales seminar?" On hearing, yes, this person dramatized a faked sense of relief and started asking where the coffee was, explaining that he couldn't function without his "black poison." He had overheard our role-playing comments and leaped in on the conversation to say how he liked doing those things. He followed this with a tale of how he overwhelmed everyone in the last role-play situation in which participated.

What would you call the style of the first person described? The second? The third?

The first participant is clearly self-contained, which indicates that he is either a thinker or a director. His low quantity of conversation and restrained gestures place him as indirect, therefore, a thinker.

The second participant volunteered information about personal feelings and gave rapid feedback in the form of a sigh and by her comments. These are characteristics of openness, suggesting a relater or socializer. The soft voice, questioning for clarification, and hesitance all suggest indirectness, thus this person demonstrates a relater style.

The third participant, telling stories and responding quickly, is high in openness. His directness is also on the high side—speed in responding, fast movements, high quantity of conversation—which are the traits of a socializer.

By checking the prospect's environment and observing and labeling the behavioral style, you can identify his or her style. You cannot expect the prospect to adapt to you. You, therefore, must adapt your selling style to your prospect's buying style. This requires behavioral flexibility.

BEHAVIORAL FLEXIBILITY

Behavioral flexibility should apply to your own actions, not those of others. It occurs when you step out of your comfort zone and style preference to meet another's needs. It occurs each time you slow your pace somewhat for a relater or a thinker, or when you quicken your pace for a director or socializer. It occurs when a director or thinker takes time to listen to a human-interest or family story from a relater or socializer.

Behavioral flexibility is independent of behavioral style, and it varies greatly within styles. No style is "naturally" more flexible than another. You can choose to be flexible with some people and inflexible with others. You can choose to be flexible with one person today and inflexible with that same person tomorrow. It is an individual decision to manage your own style in order to meet a prospect's style needs and reduce the possibility of that prospect experiencing negative tension.

Practicing behavioral flexibility means modifying your own style preferences when they differ from those of your prospect. This does not mean being phony or manipulative for the sake of a sale. The idea is not to change colors as a chameleon does. Rather, flexibility is part of learning to communicate with people in their language. What would you do if you wanted to do business with someone who spoke only Spanish? Would you continue to speak English or would you speak their language? Naturally you would speak Spanish or hire an interpreter. There is nothing phony or manipulative about this.

When you deal with directors and thinkers, speaking the same language means getting down to business quickly. With socializers and relaters, it means spending time to get to know them.

Rick: I flew to a city in the Midwest to talk to the executive vice president of a company that was considering hiring me for a big consulting project. He picked me up at the airport at 9:00 A.M., wined me and dined me, gave me a comprehensive tour of the city, and returned me to the airport in time for my 5:00 flight. Fifteen minutes before my flight, after not mentioning a word about business all day, he said, "About that proposal of yours, I'm going to recommend it."

It's clear that some people want first to feel comfortable with the people they do business with. Had I forced the issue and talked about business all day, I would not have gotten the consulting project.

Selling, by its very nature, is a people business. In addition to your product knowledge, you must also have knowledge of people. Treating people the way they want to be treated is one of the master skills of non-manipulative selling. You will find it to be an indispensible asset for building any type of relationship, especially business relationships that can become lifelong assets.

Individual products and services can be relatively short-lived. Over the course of your career, the companies you represent will, most likely, change from time to time. Your ability to make and maintain solid business relationships, however, will be the keystone to your success, no matter whom you are working for. Investing in the understanding of others is the first step to becoming a professional, non-manipulative salesperson. The other master skill of non-manipulative selling, tension management, will be discussed next.

3

Tension Management

IS TENSION BAD? Most people would emphatically answer yes! You may be surprised to learn that, contrary to the Anacin commercials, tension, in and of itself, is not bad. What determines the effect of tension is how much there is. We all have a level at which we function best. Below that level we are under-stimulated; above that comfortable level we are over-stimulated. The optimal level is our "comfort zone."

There are many sources of tension. Once they are distilled to their essence they break down into three groups: personal tension, relationship tension, and need tension.

PERSONAL TENSION AND TRADITIONAL SALES

Personal tension is an internal nervousness caused by negative thoughts, expectations, fears, anticipation and so on. Traditional salespeople and the nature of their sales techniques cause unnecessary tension in selling situations for a number of reasons.

Being unprepared. Walking into a prospect's business without having done your homework is good cause for tension.

Pressuring clients. Salespeople do have consciences, so when they pressure a customer into buying, they sometimes feel guilty about it.

Lack of confidence in one's skills. Traditional sales is a skill-intensive business. A newcomer who is unsure of his or her ability to make a presentation or answer questions or objections will have more tension than the old pro.

Pressure to make the sale on the first visit. Traditional sales managers either implicitly or explicitly convey a tension-producing message to their salespeople: make the sale or fail; produce or perish.

Phil: One of my client companies had the "one call close" so deeply ingrained in their sales system that they changed their language rather than changing their philosophy. Their analysis revealed that the majority of their sales were made on the second call. So they gave the first call a new name—the "pre-call." The second call then became the "first call." This change in language allowed them to continue in their old ways. Unfortunately, this corporate attitude created a great deal of tension in the salespeople.

Cold calls. Cold calls, that is, a call in which you walk in not knowing a thing about the prospect and have to give a canned pitch to a possibly inhospitable skeptic, are the most dreaded part of sales for traditional sales people, understandably so.

Personal Tension and Non-Manipulative Selling

The good news is that non-manipulative selling reduces the causes of personal tension inherent in the traditional-selling approach.

- Non-manipulative salespeople do not pressure their customers. The customer is an equal partner in the selling process and is agreeing with every step along the way. When it is time to write up the order, it is a foregone conclusion, not a tactical close.

- Non-manipulative salespeople are not unsure of their skills because they are prepared, practiced professionals. Their communication skills and the nature of their relationships with prospects make it easy for them to say, "Listen, I sense a misunderstanding; let me clarify this."

- Cold calls are not the norm for non-manipulative salespeople. There are times, however, when a cold call can be used, especially for a product that has a short sales cycle. Non-manipulative salespeople make a cold call differently. They would only call on a prospect in their target market; they are more sensitive to the needs of the prospect; they enter with a different attitude and convey it immediately by saying, in effect, "Some people I can help, some people I can't help; do you mind if I ask you some questions so we can both determine if I may be of service to you?" Non-manipulative salespeople are also sensitive to the fact that they do not have an appointment and may be there at a bad time.

In general, the nature of non-manipulative selling will eliminate most personal tension in both you and your prospects. It is important for professional salespeople to reduce their own tension so they can concentrate on managing the tension of the customer. This will make for a more productive working relationship.

RELATIONSHIP TENSION

Relationship tension is the normal tension that exists between two interacting people. The tension can be either constructive or destructive, but it is always present. The tension is caused by the differences in the way people handle themselves and others, preferences of closeness and self-disclosure, and other fascinating nuances of personal style.

One technique for managing relationship tension in a constructive, professional manner was discussed in the previous chapter on relationship strategies.

Tension and Productivity

The relationship between personal tension and productivity has been the focus of many theories, the most notable being that of Yerkes and Dodson. They found that people function best within a range of tension that has become known as the "comfort zone."

Figure 3.1 graphically depicts the relationship between tension and productivity.

As the figure shows, if there is no tension, there is no productivity. As tension increases, so does performance, to a point. Beyond that point, if tension continues to increase, productivity decreases. In other words, either a lack of stimulation or too much stimulation are bad for performance. Between the two extremes is one's "comfort zone," or area of optimal productivity, which is different for everyone.

Tension Management and Relationships

Everything you do to help your customer be in his comfort zone enhances the relationship. Everything you do to take him out of that comfort zone worsens the relationship. Non-manipulative salespeople are constantly measuring the tension level between themselves and the people around them. Learn to observe your customers and be sensitive to their tension level. Let's look at an hypothetical example.

Imagine the following scenario: A customer of yours starts out for work one morning, and everything goes wrong. His car won't start, his second car has a flat, he calls a cab and it arrives an hour

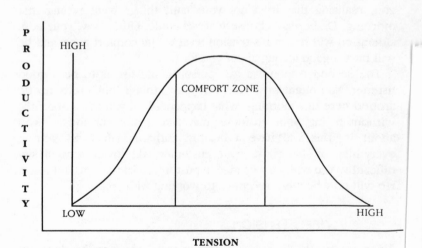

FIGURE 3.1 *Tension Level and Productivity*

later. Everything that could possibly go wrong between his home and the office does exactly that, goes wrong. He finally gets to work and he's livid. You walk in the door for your scheduled meeting with him and find him tense and in no mood to see you.

The first thing you may do is interpret the customer's mood as being a reflection of you. You take it personally. This is a mistake, however, because it is not you he doesn't like; it's the way his day started. You haven't changed or done anything to change the relationship; he's changed. What should you do?

There are two ways to handle this situation. One is politely to say, "Gee, Mr. Jones, it appears that things are pretty hectic here this morning. Would another day be more convenient for you?" This shows sensitivity, which your customer will appreciate.

Notice the words that were used in the handling of the situation above. The salesperson did not say, "Gee, you look as if you're in a bad mood." Instead, it was, "Things look hectic around here." There is a good reason for this. You *never* want to accuse someone of being in a bad mood. Doing so will often make him defensive and more tense. Put the blame on the environment, not on the person.

As soon as the customer is given the opportunity to reschedule, he will relax a bit. The customer may relax enough to meet with you, realizing that it is not your fault things went wrong that morning. Or he may choose to reschedule. Either way, your consideration will return his tension level to the comfort zone, and he will have a good feeling about you for it.

The second response a salesperson could use is to be a good listener. You might say, "Gee, Mr. Jones, things look pretty hectic around here this morning. What happened?" If you ask innocently, without prying, your customer may take a moment and tell you about it. This will have a healthy, cathartic effect. By getting everything off his chest, your customer will lower tension significantly. You will see a change in posture, facial tension, and voice. He will now be more receptive to working with you.

NEED TENSION

Need tension is the stress a person feels when reality does not match the desired situation. This discrepancy between the real and the ideal creates what is called a need gap.

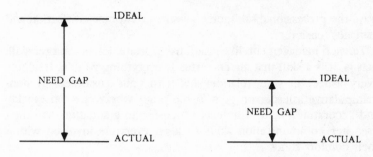

FIGURE 3.2

As figure 3.2 shows, the larger the discrepancy between what you want and what you have, the greater your need gap. The more closely aligned the ideal and actual, the smaller the need gap. This source of tension is based on expectations, wishes, and attitude vs. current circumstances. In figure 3.2, which person do you think will buy?

As a non-manipulative salesperson, part of your job is to find out what your prospect's need gap is. Most prospects know they have a need gap, although they would not call it that. Other customers may require extensive questioning and discussion to make them aware of their existing need gap. Prospects often do not see the forest for the trees. A prospect who does not perceive a need gap will not be motivated to consult with you. That is why it is important to ask questions such as, "What is your company's five-year goal?" or "What is your mission?" and then ask the prospect to compare the present situation with the plan or goal. You can also ask, "What would you like to see happen to achieve that goal?"

When a need gap is recognized by you and your prospect, you can then propose a solution that will close the gap and eliminate that source of need tension for your client.

Assuring customer satisfaction involves periodic follow-ups to see if the need gap is still closed. The ideal solution to a customer's problem will keep the gap closed for good; however, there are times when it will reopen in your absence. In this situation, it is your job to propose a solution, which may be something as simple as providing additional training. Chapter 11 discusses the many ways the professional salesperson assures customer satisfaction and manages tension.

Tension management, like relationship strategies, is a master skill; that is, it is a skill that affects virtually everything you do. It affects every aspect of your relationships with your customers. A non-manipulative salesperson gets to the point where she can quickly and accurately size up the level of tension in a situation. She then uses her communication skills to keep everyone involved within their comfort zones.

The following section on information gathering and communicating skills will take you the next step, from knowing what you *need*, to knowing what to *do* to meet that need.

4

The Fine Art of Questioning

THE FINE ART OF QUESTIONING is the keystone of information gathering; in turn, information gathering during the study phase is one of the hallmarks of a non-manipulative salesperson. So the ability to ask the right questions in the right way is paramount to a successful career. An example is a salesman Rick knew in Buffalo, New York. His story illustrates how a sales situation can suddenly take a turn for the better after the posing of one astute question.

Rick: I recall a Yellow Pages salesman, Mike Rucker, who called on me early in my career. He asked several questions and seemed to be getting nowhere until he asked, "Who is your competition?"

"I don't have any," I replied.

"No competition?" he asked gently.

"No one in town does exactly what I do," I said, "and most people don't understand what I do."

"That sounds like a nice competitive advantage," he remarked, "but it doesn't help you if people don't know what you do."

"That's the real problem," I told him.

"Let me ask you this," he said thoughtfully. "Whom do your customers or potential customers view as your competitors?"

"That's a big problem too," I admitted. "They think I'm just like Dale Carnegie." Then it hit me. Hey, I could place an ad next to Carnegie's in the Yellow Pages and people would call me to compare programs and prices!"

This is called a lay-down. The rest of the sale was a piece of cake for him.

Questioning is such an important communication skill that it not only simplifies your job but makes your job possible. After all, without the information provided by your prospect, you cannot function as a non-manipulative salesperson. Well-phrased questions help prospects reveal their thoughts and feelings. The proper questioning will give you tremendous insight into your customers' needs, motivations, business climate, and fears. All this information will do two things: It will help you serve your clients as well as you can, and it will increase your sales.

The conversation stimulated by your questions will smooth the way for the building of a business relationship and will help you accomplish four important goals:

- Manage tension.

- Build trust.

- Uncover prospect's needs and opportunities.

- Identify behavioral style.

It is obvious that questioning does more than gather the nuts-and-bolts information you need to match your product or service to the prospect's needs. As a brief aside, it is worth mentioning the difference between needs and opportunities. Needs are the gaps between what a client wants and what he has. Needs cannot be created, they exist. Opportunities, on the other hand, can be created. They are potential sources of new markets, avenues of distribution, promotional vehicles, and the like that can be developed by the astute business person.

OPEN AND CLOSED QUESTIONS

Asking questions is similar to painting a picture. If you were to set up a canvas to paint a breathtaking vista, what would you paint first? You would probably use a large brush and paint the background first. After the background, you would use a smaller brush to paint small details, and as time went by you would keep reducing the size of your brush to paint smaller and smaller details.

Questioning begins the same way. You start with a broad brush, that is, an open-ended question. An open-ended question is one that requires a narrative for an answer. The question gets the prospect involved in the conversation immediately. A closed-ended question requires only a yes, no, or brief, factual answer such as a number.

Open Questions

Open-ended questions have the following characteristics and uses:

- They cannot be answered with a simple yes or no.

- They begin with what, why, where, how, who, or when.

- They do not lead the person in a specific direction.

- They increase dialogue by drawing out the prospect.

- They help the prospect discover things for herself or himself.

- They can be used to encourage the prospect to think about your product or service.

- They create a situation in which the prospect will reveal her or his behavioral style.

Open-ended questions should be phrased thoughtfully. Do not just ask, "How's business?" or "How are you doing today?" People have pat answers for those questions. Ask open questions that require some thought and a sincere answer. Some examples of open questions to begin with are the following:

1. What are some of the ways you would like your office to be more efficient?
2. Tell me about your present billing system.
3. At present are there any plans to computerize any aspects of your operation?
4. How, if at all, do you see a computer fitting into *your* office?
5. What functions do you plan to computerize?

When you have finished painting the background, that is, gathering information with a broad, open question or two, it is time to be more specific. Ask more focused open or closed questions at this point.

Closed Questions

Closed-ended questions allow your customer to answer quickly and to the point. They have many uses:

- They extract simple and specific facts.

- They are useful for giving feedback during a conversation.

- They are used to gain commitments and gather specific information.

- They can be used to direct the conversation in specific directions.

Some examples of closed questions are as follows:

1. Have you had any experience with small-business computers?
2. Does your office produce a lot of paperwork?
3. Is anyone in your office computer-literate?
4. Would you prefer delivery on the weekend or during the week?

THE MANY USES OF QUESTIONS

In addition to knowing the two basic forms questions can take, you should be familiar with their uses. Questions can be used effectively to draw out information you seek from prospects. The use of the following types of questions will help you diagnose a prospect's situation.

Clarifying Questions

Clarifying questions restate the prospect's remarks or refer directly to them. They are a form of feedback that is accompanied by a rising voice inflection that implies a question, even if one is not directly asked. "So, you'll be here on Tuesday," is a statement, but with a rising inflection it implies the additional, "Isn't that so?" Examples of these questions are as follows:

1. If I hear you correctly, you're saying that you need at least one copy for each secretary.
2. Are you speaking about peripherals or just the central processing unit?

Clarifying questions may be successfully used as follows:

• They express in different words what the prospect just said.

• They invite the prospect to expand or clarify an idea previously expressed.

• They help clarify ambiguities and broad generalizations.

• They uncover what is on the prospect's mind.

Developmental Questions

Developmental questions ask the prospect for further details on specific subjects. In the case of a vague word or broad generalization, the developmental question will ask the prospect for more definition in the picture she is trying to paint. For example: "There are many software programs available. When you look up clients on the computer, will you want to find them by name, address, or account number?"

Developmental questions help you ask for additional information and encourage the prospect to expand and elaborate.

Directional Questions

As the word implies, directional questions steer the conversation in other directions. As a consultant, you navigate your way through the prospect's situation to a destination that will reveal his needs and opportunities.

Directional questions are appropriate when you want to move from one topic area to another. Consider these examples:

1. Do you send a lot of form letters?
2. Do you often have to look up client files quickly, for example, when clients are on the phone?

Well-used directional questions help in the following ways:

• They direct the conversation through logical steps.

• They provide a means of supplying necessary information to the prospect, such as delivery dates, financial information, and so on.

• They give the prospect an additional way to participate in the information exchange. For example, "Many people in your industry have found that using a computer has saved them money. Which uses do you feel will save you the most money?"

It should be noted, however, that directional questions, if not used carefully, can be perceived by prospects and customers as leading them to respond in a manner that they do not intend. Such a practice can then be perceived as manipulative. Be sure, then, that your use of directional questions follows the guidelines given above.

Testing Questions

Testing questions allow you to determine where the prospect stands on an issue or if she is keeping up with you in the discussion. At the end of a sales call, testing questions give the prospect an opportunity to express any additional thoughts that may arise. Some examples of testing questions are as follows:

1. How do you think that might help you?
2. Does that sound reasonable?
3. What's our next step?

Third-Party Questions

Third-party-opinion questions combine a statement and a question. They question indirectly by telling the prospect how others feel or react to a particular subject. They then ask the prospect to give his opinions and reactions concerning the same subject. Research indicates there is a greater acceptance of a statement if a well-known and respected person or corporation endorses the statement, so long as mention of the name is not perceived as name dropping. Third-party-opinion questions, therefore, are used as follows:

• They increase prospect confidence in the way problems or needs can be met by suggesting that others have solved a similar need in a similar way. For example, "*Consumer's Union* has rated this product as the best available for its price range. Is this the price range you're interested in?"

• They increase prospect pride in a decision or perception. "That's a good selection. Mr. Jay at Beech Manufacturing, the president of the national manufacturers' group, has used this product successfully to cut his downtime by 30 percent. Do you have similar downtime considerations?"

FACT-FINDING VS. INFORMATION GATHERING

There is a subtle but important difference between fact-finding and information gathering. Fact-finding is what traditional salespeople do most of the time. They ask for specific information to determine the prospect's need for their product or service. Information gathering is a tool of non-manipulative salespeople. She asks questions that give her the big picture of the prospect's business. In this way, non-manipulative salespeople act as consultants rather than as pushers of products or services. Asking information-gathering questions uncovers opportunities as well as needs.

Information-gathering questions are both open and closed, but they should begin open. Some examples are as follows:

1. What is the overall mission of your company?
2. How do you view the option of investing in a new computer system versus upgrading your old system?
3. Do you currently have a plan for improving white-collar productivity?
4. Is security a problem?

Fact-finding questions are useful after you've grasped the big picture. They are closed questions such as these:

1. How many work stations do you want the computer to service?
2. How many accounts do you want this data base to be able to handle?

The Importance of Flexibility

One of the biggest mistakes made by salespeople is that they lack flexibility in questioning. They start at the beginning of their list and ask the questions one by one, in order, regardless of the answers they receive. It is almost as if they are not listening to the answers.

The proper way to question a prospect is to conduct an interview as if you were a journalist. Ask a question, see where the answer takes you, and respond with a relevant question that will help the prospect elaborate on the information he just gave you. When you have exhausted that subject, look at your list and ask another question. It is much more effective to ebb and flow with the conversation in this manner.

It is important to be creative in your choice of words. Avoid repeating, "Tell me about this," "Tell me about that." Phrase your questions as you would if you were getting information from a friend.

Another key to remaining flexible during the questioning is to come prepared with a *customized* list of questions. Most salespeople use the same questions for every prospect, regardless of the business they are in. You, however, are aspiring to be a minority, that is, one of the 5 percenters talked about in the preface of the book.

Before you meet with your prospect, prepare a list of questions based on the homework you've done on her industry, market, and individual business. The list does not have to be twenty questions long; it can be a simple list of general areas to cover. The list should be tied in to the objective of the call. If it is an information-gathering meeting, use broad, open questions. If you are fact-finding, use specific questions.

Flexibility will not only result in more information and a better grasp on how you can help your client, it will also build the relationship by showing how sensitive you are.

How to Compose Questions

To help you compose your questions for information gathering and fact-finding, keep these guidelines in mind:

Ask permission to ask questions. Show respect and you will not intimidate or alienate people. Help your prospects relax by explaining why you want to ask some questions. A simple question will work: "Would you mind if I ask you a few questions so that I can better understand your situation and serve your needs?"

Start with broad topics and narrow the focus with later questions. "Could you tell me a little about your business?" is an example of a broad, open question. Keep in mind that your opening question will be very important in creating a good impression with your prospect. For this reason, you need to size him up as quickly as possible so that the first question matches his style. The book will talk more about questioning by style later.

There are major benefits to asking such a broad question as, "Could you tell me a little about your business?" A question like that gives your prospect complete freedom to answer in any way he chooses. This has a relaxing effect. It also reveals to you his behavioral style, the knowledge of which will help you shape your subsequent questions. Last, the answer to this question may reveal needs and opportunities. If it does not, they will become apparent as you build subsequent questions around this answer.

Build on previous responses. The easiest and most effective way to build a conversation around someone's responses is to take the operative word in the sentence or sentences and create a question based on it. A simple example will clarify this. Imagine two people meeting on an airplane:

"Hello, my name is Ellen, what do you do for a living?"
"I'm a *writer*."
"A writer," Ellen continues. "What kind of writing do you do?"
"Mostly *humor*. Occasionally I write something serious or philosophical, but people laugh at that too."
"That's very interesting," Ellen says. "I don't know a thing about writing, especially humor. Tell me about it."
"Well, you take one part sarcasm, add two parts irreverence and one part creativity, shake violently, and hope it doesn't blow up in your face."

In a business context, using the operative word or words would look something like this:

"Could you tell me a little about your business?"

"I'm a distributor of *sporting equipment* to *colleges* and *universities.*"

"That's interesting. What kind of sporting equipment?"

"Everything found inside a *gymnasium.* We don't get into the larger things like bleachers, goal posts, and football fields."

"What colleges and universities do you sell to?" (This plays off the second operative word in the original answer.)

"We sell to every school *west of the Mississippi* with *more than 5,000 students.*"

"Is there a reason you confine your business to schools west of the Mississippi?"

"Yes, they're easier to reach for service."

. . . And so on. You get the idea. This technique quickly and effectively works in both social and business situations. There is a built-in, logical order to this method of questioning, and it shows the prospect that you are listening and following along.

Keep questions free of jargon, buzz words, or technical vernacular that may be confusing. Every field has its own jargon, and you may be an expert in yours; however, your prospect may not be as well versed as you. Avoid questions that will confuse your prospect or worse, make him feel inferior. Instead of asking, "Was the baud rate of your present system satisfactory?" ask in a way that he can relate to, such as, "Were your telephone transmissions of data fast enough?"

Keep the questions simple. Ask about one topic at a time so that your prospect can concentrate on an answer that will be useful to you. If you ask about two things in one question, one will be answered and the other may be forgotten completely. An example of a question containing too many thoughts is the following: "Would you mind telling me a little bit about your personal and professional objectives, as well as some of the things you find that have been helping or hindering you in the accomplishment of those goals?" If you overwhelm your prospect with a question like this, he may say, "Yes, I do mind." You would be better off breaking this down into four questions and tackling them separately.

Keep questions in a logical sequence. If you ask a lot of unrelated questions, your prospect may become uncomfortable for fear that you are trying to manipulate him. When your line of questions follows the operative words in his answers, the prospect will see your logic and know where your questions are headed. This will reduce his tension and increase cooperation.

Pose nonthreatening questions. At the beginning of a sales relationship, NEVER ask a prospect, "How much money do you want to spend?" This is guaranteed to raise tension with 99 percent of the prospects you will meet. Talk about other things and avoid the sensitive issues of finances, business stability, personal health, age, and politics. There will be time later to discuss the details.

If you have to ask a sensitive question, explain why you are asking. There are times when you have to ask about a prospect's ability to meet financial obligations. When necessary, just be straightforward, but explain why you need the information. Prospects will respect you for your candor and give you the information. If a prospect is not willing to give you a reasonable amount of sensible information, you may be wasting your time. Don't jump to this conclusion; simply reduce your prospect's tension level and come back to the question later.

Phrase sensitive questions as diplomatically as possible. Don't ask, "How much money do you make a year?" Create a context and ask how it relates to their situation. For example, you might say, "We require our applicants to earn $50,000 a year or have a $5,000 down payment. Is that a problem?"

A loan officer at a bank was told that the bank was having trouble collecting loans from underage borrowers; therefore, future applications required the person's age before processing. When faced with a middle-aged customer, the loan officer would say, "Mrs. Jones, the bank loan committee requires a statement of a customer's age so that we know the person is of legal age to make a loan. Some of my customers prefer to say, 'twenty-one plus.' Is that all right with you?" He received a lot of laughs and smoothed over a potentially awkward moment with finesse.

Ask what general benefits are desired. Many prospects will not know all the benefits of your product or service. Therefore, do not ask them what benefits they are looking for; tell them what benefits will be theirs. When you ask them what they want, have them generalize about the improvements they would like to see. If you were to ask a prospect, "How do you expect a computer to streamline your office?" you may make her feel ignorant. She has never owned a computer, so she probably has no idea of all its uses. It would be better to ask what general improvements she would like to see, as in the question, "What are some of the duties in the office that you find tedious and time consuming?" This will free her of needing computer knowledge to answer the question. She'll answer: "The payroll, accounts receivable, accounts payable," and so on. You will then have the information you need to recommend the hardware and software.

Give prospects flexible questions. Traditional salespeople ask, "Would you prefer to meet at 8:00 or 10:00?" This is manipulative and a bit of an insult to the customer. A better way to ask is to give the client all the flexibility, as in, "How do your mornings look for an appointment next week?"

Maintain a consultative atmosphere. Remember, you are a liaison between your company and your customers; you are a consultant. As such, you want to question your prospect in a way that will yield the maximum amount of information with the least effort. To do so, take the pressure off the questions. Ask them in a relaxed tone of voice. Give time for the answers, even if it means sitting quietly and waiting. Don't be in a hurry to get to your next appointment. The investment you make in time now will pay off handsomely when the prospect evolves into an annuity.

Phrase questions so prospects answer positively. Research has shown that people prefer to agree to something rather than voice an objection. You can make things easier for your prospect by the way you ask questions. If you sense that a prospect has a preference for something, ask in a way that lets her say yes. For example, you could say to a prospect, "This computer has the capability to handle the accounting function, inventory control, and mailing lists. I sense from your comments that you'd prefer to discuss the accounting functions today. Is that so?"

Questioning in this way saves time, acts as feedback for the customer and as feedback for you so you know the two of you are on the same wavelength.

All of these tips will take you a long way toward constructing questions and conducting interviews as a consultant. The greatest tip, however, is the ability to gear your questions to the person's behavioral style.

QUESTIONING BY BEHAVIORAL STYLE

The way you phrase your questions should be determined by the behavioral style of your prospects. Doing so will assure they "hear" you and their responses will be more valuable to you.

Directors

You have to be careful with directors. They hold competence above everything else and will not tolerate ignorance on your part. You have to show that you've done your homework; otherwise you will find your meeting suddenly cut short. When you begin questioning a director, make a statement that shows you are knowledgeable and then ask a question. Questions can pertain to industry trends, the growth of the company, and the director's role in it, future directions the company might take, and so on. For example, "Mr. Williams, competition is fierce in the fast-food business, and yet you've remained an industry leader. What would you consider your competitive edge?" Directors love to talk about themselves and their accomplishments in business. Keep in mind that they are also very competitive and goal oriented.

More specific questions should ask about their bottom-line goals. "What type of bottom-line benefits would you expect to gain from our product?" "As a result of purchasing our product, do you expect to reduce your office staff?"

Thinkers

Thinkers expect you to be very well organized and precise in your questioning. If you have six questions to ask, tell them so. If you say, "I'd like to ask you a couple of questions," and then ask six, you may make them angry. They like accuracy. You could say, "I have a number of questions to ask; it will take no more than twenty-two minutes." This gives them an idea of your expectations and leaves you with some leeway.

The questions you ask should focus on facts and details. Phrase your questions carefully. For example, you could say, "How many checks a month are in your payroll?" "What is the budget you are working with for your new computer system?" "What are the parameters you have established for the purchase of the computer?"

Relaters

Relaters like to become friends before doing business. Plan on spending time with them. Questions such as "Tell me how you got into this business," or "Tell me about your business," will be well received. This question focuses on building the relationship and serves to gather information.

Relaters are often only one of many decision makers. It would pay for you to ask, "I was wondering what other people might be involved in this decision and what their roles might be?"

Socializers

Socializers, like relaters, enjoy building a relationship first. Asking them, "This is a fascinating business. How did you get into it?" will work well. Socializers also like to talk about concepts and dreams. Questions such as, "Where do you see yourself/your business in five years?" will stimulate socializers. In fact, if you can uncover a dream or mission and help a socializer achieve it with your product or service, you will be a star.

Answers and Insights

The way people answer questions will give you insight into their style. Relaters and socializers tend to give longer, broader answers. Thinkers and directors give terse, focused answers. If you cannot determine the person's behavioral style before you ask your first question, look around and pick up cues from the office, the way you are greeted, and the seating arrangement.

Questioning, and its close relative, listening, are two of the most difficult communication skills for Americans to learn. This may sound like an extreme statement, but it is true. Americans are primarily output oriented; we love to talk about ourselves.

Rick: I was on a flight to Chicago, and sitting next to me in first class was a Japanese businessman. After we took off, he turned to me and politely asked, "What do you do for a living?" I told him I'm a professional speaker. He then said, "Oh, that's very interesting. I do not know anything about professional speaking, tell me about it." For the next hour and a half I spilled my guts to this man. I told him everything I know, all my trade secrets, my marketing strategy, secrets that I planned to put in a book someday, you name it.

At the end of my lecture, after I slumped exhausted into my seat, he turned to the man on the other side of him and asked "What do you do?" The man said, "I'm an electrical engineer." The Japanese man said, "Oh, that's very interesting. I do not know anything about electrical engineering. Tell me about it." For the rest of the flight, another hour and a half, the engineer told our mutual friend about a new invention of his, the design details, marketing and promotional plans, expenses and so on.

When we landed, the three of us were standing together waiting to deplane. I realized I hadn't asked the Japanese man what he does, so I asked. His response was a shock: "I am an electronics engineer." I asked him what he was doing in Chicago. He replied, "There is a consumer electronics show here this week. I am going to be lecturing about new-product development and marketing."

The engineer and I felt we had been somewhat used. The engineer had just given away the invention of a lifetime, and I had just exhausted myself telling this man things he already knew. It brought home a powerful message. Unlike the Japanese, who are more receptive and input oriented, we Americans are too output oriented. We need to learn to receive more, not in a way that makes someone feel used but in a way that's useful for everyone.

The skills of questioning and listening are absolutely indispensible in establishing business relationships, gathering information, and fact-finding. The best consultants do not go into a company and immediately tell them what to do. They ask questions, listen, diagnose, and make recommendations. At least half of the consultant's job is to ask the right questions and listen carefully to the answers.

Questioning skills will not only bring valuable information to the surface, they will also show your prospects that you are truly interested in their business or buying needs. Listening skills give you the ability to absorb what is said. The best questioning combines what you have learned in this chapter with what you learned in chapter 2 on relationship strategies. When you have neither, you make the mistake illustrated in the next story.

Ash Deshmukh is a sales manager with the Tom James Company. The firm manufactures and sells expensive, custom-made men's clothing, which it markets directly to clients. All of their services are provided in the client's office. For the last four years, Ash has been supervising fifteen sales people. Before he discovered Non-Manipulative Sales, he was the traditional salesperson with a pitch.

Ash: I thought I was doing a great job of selling, but a pattern was emerging. The suits and shirts would fit great, but I had trouble getting another appointment with my customers. The answer didn't dawn on me until I ran into one of my clients in a social situation. After exchanging greetings, I said, "I just want to ask you if you're mad at me." He said no. I asked, "I thought the suit and shirts fit you great. Why couldn't I sell you again?" He replied, "Well, it's true, the suit fits great. In fact, it's the best-fitting suit I have, but the way you sold me, after you left, I felt as if you had taken everything out of me. I was exhausted!"

He went on to say, "The only way I could answer the questions you asked was in your favor. I felt that I had been manipulated. I figured if I had to go through that every time you came in, I'd rather wear a product that wasn't as good. At least I wouldn't have to be put through the wringer every time I bought a suit."

I decided to develop a non-manipulative approach in which the customer could tell me how I could best be of service to him. Selling became a lot easier. By answering my questions, the customer was effectively telling me how he could be sold because he told me what was important to him. I could then tailor the presentation to his needs. Now, after I introduce myself and my company, I ask, "If you would consider doing business with me today, what are some of the things you would want me to do for you that would make you happy with my performance?" Customers tell me specifically what I need to do to make the sale. They enjoy being sold that way.

After I started using non-manipulative sales techniques, not only did my sales increase but I was able to retain customers whom I may have lost after one sale using traditional sales techniques. I'm not a wizard; I just read the book and applied it.

5

The Power of
Listening, Observing,
and Feedback

TRY TO IMAGINE that you have just finished your information gathering and are about to begin your presentation to your prospect. You're about to tell her your recommendation for the needs the two of you have just discussed. Just as you begin your presentation, your Fairy Godmother walks in. She waves her magic wand and instantly everyone in the room is frozen in time. She taps you on the shoulder and asks you to write down on one side of a piece of paper everything you know about that prospect. As soon as you've finished, with a wave of her magic wand, miraculously on the other side of the page appears, for every piece of information you had about the customer, a new piece of information of equal importance. When she's finished, you know twice as much about your prospect, in both quality and quantity, as you knew before.

Do you think having twice as much information would help you make the sale? No one would doubt that the chances of making the sale would increase dramatically. The more you know about your prospect, the better your chances of selling that prospect.

Unfortunately, you have no Fairy Godmother to wave her magic wand. So how can you accomplish this great feat without her? Improve your listening skills!

58

Selling requires an information exchange and that exchange cannot be one-way. Listening is, by definition, part of the process. Prospects and customers provide information about problems and opportunities in exchange for information from you about potential solutions. If you were a poor listener, there would be at least two detrimental effects: your solutions would be faulty or inappropriate, and your prospects might turn the tables and not listen to you. Active listening, by contrast, encourages cooperation and understanding. In fact, active listening is the key to tension management.

Roy: The most important thing is to take your ego out of everything. That's the biggest problem. You can't be a know-it-all. You have to let other people tell you what they think. Even if you know what they're going to say, you have to bite your tongue and let them tell you. If you stop them and say, "Oh, what you mean is . . ." and continue talking, they won't hear what you're saying because they're stuck on wanting to tell you what's on their mind. So you've lost them. Non-Manipulative Sales makes you a sounding board. You learn to control your impulse to interrupt, which is good, because interrupting is rude.

Unfortunately, listening skills are often ignored or just forgotten in sales training. While businesses are willing to spend money to send executives to sales courses, they rarely direct personnel to courses designed to improve listening habits, even though effective salespeople spend the majority of their time listening. This is due to the misconception that listening is the same as hearing. This is not so.

Ralph Nichols and Leonard Stevens, in their book *Are You Listening?* (McGraw Hill, 1957), point out that most people listen with approximately 50 percent efficiency. Furthermore, information is lost as the message is passed from one person to another. In other words, people hear entire messages and still lose or distort their meanings when conveying them to someone else. It is much like the childhood game of "Telephone," in which everyone whispered a sentence from person to person around a circle. The fun came when the last person to receive the message said it aloud and compared it with the original message. The two were not even close. At early ages we learned that communication is an inexact skill. The same process takes place in the business world. Imagine a message going from the customer to the salesperson to the sales manager to the production department and then to the delivery and installation people. It takes good listening to keep the message the same all the way down the line.

A distinction must be drawn between listening and remembering. Listening is the process of receiving the message the way the speaker intended to send it. Memory is simply recall over time. Listening and time have profound effects on memory. An untrained listener is likely to understand and retain only about 50 percent of a conversation. After forty-eight hours, this relatively poor retention rate drops 25 percent. Think of the implications. Memory of a conversation that took place more than two days ago will be incomplete and inaccurate. No wonder people can seldom agree about what has been discussed and therefore put contracts in writing.

Active listening takes effort. It involves concentration and causes noticeable physical changes. During active listening, your heart rate increases, body temperature rises slightly, and circulation is stepped up.

THE THREE LEVELS OF LISTENING

Whenever people listen, they are at one of the three basic levels of listening. These levels require various degrees of concentration on the part of the listener. As you move from the first to the third level, the potential for understanding and clear communication increases dramatically.

Marginal Listening

Marginal listening, the first and lowest level, involves the least concentration, and typically the listener is easily distracted by her own thoughts. During periods of marginal listening, a listener will exhibit blank stares, nervous mannerisms, and gestures that tend to annoy the prospect and cause communication barriers. The salesperson hears the message, but it doesn't sink in. There is enormous room for misunderstanding when a salesperson is not concentrating on what is being said. Moreover, the prospect cannot help but feel the lack of attention, which insults him and diminishes trust. It may be funny in comedy when family members continually patronize each other with, "Yes, dear," regardless of what is said. In real life, however, it is *not* funny.

Prospect: What I need, really, is a way to reduce the time lost due to equipment breakdowns.

Salesperson: Yeah, OK. Let's see, uh, the third feature of our product is the convenient sizes you can get.

Salespeople of all experience levels can be guilty of marginal listening. Beginners who lack confidence and experience may concentrate so intensely on what they are supposed to say next that they stop listening. Old pros, by contrast, have heard it all before. They have their presentations memorized and want the prospect to hurry up and finish so the "important" business can continue. These traditional salespeople forget that the truly important information lies in what the prospect is saying.

Evaluative Listening

Evaluative listening, the second level of listening, requires more concentration and attention to the speaker's words. At this level, the listener is actively trying to hear what the prospect is saying but isn't making an effort to understand the intent. Instead of accepting and trying to understand a prospect's message, the evaluative listener categorizes the statement and concentrates on preparing a response.

The evaluative listening phenomenon is a result of the tremendous speed at which a human can listen and think. While a person speaks at an average rate of 120 to 160 words a minute, the mind is capable of thinking six to eight times that speed. It is no surprise that evaluative listening is the level of listening at which we listen most of the time. Unfortunately, it is a very difficult habit to break, but it can be done in practice.

Prospect: What I need, really, is a way to reduce the time lost due to equipment breakdowns.

Salesperson: (defensively) We have tested our machines in the field, and they don't break down often.

In this example, the salesperson reacted to *one* aspect of the prospect's statement. Had the salesperson withheld judgment until the end of the statement, she could have responded more objectively and informatively.

In evaluative listening, it is easy to be distracted by emotion-laden words. At that point, you aren't listening to the prospect. Instead you are obsessed with the offensive word and wondering what to do about it. This is a waste of time for both you and the prospect. It increases personal and relationship tension and throws your communication off course. To avoid the problems of marginal and evaluative listening, practice active listening.

Active Listening

Active listening is the third and most effective level of listening. The active listener refrains from evaluating the message and tries to see the other person's point of view. Attention is not only on the words spoken but on the thoughts and feelings they convey. Listening in this way means the listener puts herself into someone else's shoes. It requires the listener to give the other person verbal and nonverbal feedback, which will be discussed later in this chapter.

> **Prospect:** What I need is a way to reduce the time lost due to equipment breakdowns.

> **Salesperson:** Could you tell me what kind of breakdowns you have experienced?

In the example above, the salesperson spoke directly to the prospect's concerns, not around them. Her desire to make a presentation was deferred so she could accomplish a more important task: effectively communicate with the prospect.

Active listening is a skill that, in the beginning, takes practice but after a while becomes second nature. The logic behind active listening is based on courtesy and concentration, as you will see in the following guidelines.

Listen to Words and Thoughts

This may seem obvious, but when someone speaks to you, she is expressing thoughts and feelings. Despite the logic of this statement, most of us listen only to the words being said. Spoken language can be an inexact form of communication, but it is the best we have in this stage of our evolution. If you come back 2,000 years from now, you can, perhaps, communicate with your prospects via mental telepathy. For now, given the limitations of our words, you have to look beyond them to hear the entire story.

Listen *behind* the words for the emotional content of the message. These are conveyed in the nuances of voice and body language. Some people, such as directors and thinkers, on the one hand, will give you very little emotional information. That's all right because you will deal with them in a very factual, business-only style. Relaters and socializers, on the other hand, will reveal their emotions and in turn, will appreciate your acknowledgment of their feelings. It will be appropriate to discuss their feelings and treat them more as friends than strictly business associates.

There are several ways to hear the emotions behind the words. First, look for changes in eye contact. After you have established a comfortable and natural level of eye contact, any sudden deviations from the norm will tip you off to emotional content in the message. People tend to look away from you when they talk about something embarrassing. When this happens, make a quick mental note of what it pertained to and treat that subject delicately. You should also give them the courtesy of looking away momentarily yourself, as if you are saying, "I respect your privacy." The dynamics of interpreting voice quality will be discussed later in this chapter under the section "Feedback."

Listen *between* the words for what is not said. Oddly enough, people reveal more in what they don't say than in what they choose to say. Part of this is due to the emotional content of the message and part is due to the information they are giving you. A story will illustrate this point.

Rick: I was talking to the president of a large paper mill. I simply asked him what kind of training he had for his sales people. He went into a two-and-a-half-hour discourse on all the seminars, training films, video tapes, and cassettes they had from the parent company, suppliers, industry associations, and in-house programs. I sat, listened, and took notes. At the end of his speech I said to him, "I noticed you didn't mention anything about time management for sales people." He raised his voice and emphatically said, "You know, just this morning I was talking to a guy and I told him we have to have some time-management training for our sales people."

The lesson here is to get the prospect talking and listen actively. Take notes, look for clues to emotions, and don't interrupt or start thinking about your next question. Concentrate.

Reduce Noise

Noise is anything in the environment that causes a distraction during your conversation. If you were talking to a prospect in the middle of his factory, you would have a lot of noise around, both literally and figuratively. Noise can occur in a quiet environment as well. If you were nervously to tap your pencil on the table, you would distract your customer.

Internal noise is something that distracts you but cannot be sensed by the other person. For example, a headache would be noise that only you would know about. Your thoughts about the prospect or questions to ask are another source of internal noise. The best way to stop this interference is to look right at your prospect and listen intently.

It is essential to reduce or eliminate as much noise as possible when you meet with a client. If the prospect's environment is too distracting, see if you can find a better place to talk. One possibility is another office. You can also go across the street to a coffee shop, if one is available. Coffee shops are good places to meet; however, you should avoid rush hours, and, be sure to ask the waiter to bring your coffee and leave the two of you alone. You don't want to substitute one form of noise for another.

Meetings are never 100 percent noise-free. There will always be some distractions to cope with, so make every effort to remain on track. Providing the best possible environment for the meeting will help both you and your prospect accomplish your missions.

Organize What You Hear

Taking notes will improve your memory because notebooks don't forget. Ask permission to take notes and do it as unobtrusively as possible. Most people take notes as if they were recording the meeting for someone who wasn't there. You don't have to do that. You can take cryptic notes and, later, when you have the time, go back and fill in the details. Don't bury your face in your notebook, looking up only to breathe. Just jot down key words and phrases and maintain your eye contact as much as possible.

Your ear for operative words, developed in the chapter on questioning, will come in handy again. Listen for and write down operative words. Listen for the main ideas your prospect is talking about. Use testing questions to get feedback so you know you are understanding what is being said.

IRRITATING LISTENING HABITS TO CHANGE

No one is perfect. We all have some bad listening habits that we get away with when we talk to our family and friends. In a business context, however, you must leave these bad habits behind and practice active listening. To give you some insight into your listening habits, an extensive list of common irritating listening habits is provided here. Read through the list and be honest with yourself. Mark those that you are guilty of and use this awareness to begin eliminating them from your listening habits.

1. You do all the talking.
2. You interrupt when people talk.
3. You never look at the person talking or indicate you are listening.
4. You continually toy with a pencil, paper, or some other item while talking.
5. Your poker face keeps people guessing whether you understand them.
6. Because you never smile you come off as too serious.
7. You change what others say by putting words in their mouths.
8. You put people on the defensive when you ask a question.
9. Occasionally you ask a question about what has just been said, showing you weren't listening.
10. You start to argue before the other person has a chance to finish the case.
11. Everything that is said reminds you of an experience you've had, and you feel obligated to digress with a story.

12. You finish sentences for people if they pause too long.

13. When you are talking, you become angry when someone finishes a sentence for you.

14. You wait impatiently for people to finish so you can interject something of your own.

15. You work too hard at maintaining eye contact and make people uncomfortable.

16. You look as if you are appraising a woman talking to you, looking her up and down as if considering her for a job as a model.

17. You constantly measure people's words as being "believable" or "unbelievable."

18. You overdo the feedback you give—too many nods of your head or uh-huh's.

19. You sit too close to or too far from people.

20. You act as if you know it all, frequently relating incidents in which you were knowledgeable, shrewd, or the hero.

21. You make judgments about people while they speak.

22. You feel obligated to listen rather than being sincerely interested in or empathic toward people.

23. You become distracted by words that are, for you, emotionally laden, and you miss part of the message.

The National Society of Sales Training Executives conducted a survey among purchasing agents in the United States. They asked, "What are the major shortcomings of salespeople today?" The answer was a resounding, unanimous POOR LISTENING SKILLS!

Good business relationships depend on active listening. As an active listener, you will be able to develop intelligent, relevant questions and prove what an indispensible consultant you are.

FEEDBACK

The flip side of listening is feedback. The three forms of feedback you give and receive are verbal messages, voice inflections, and nonverbal behavior, or body language. These forms of feedback are bi-directional. To acknowledge the speaker's message you *give* feedback. The inverse occurs when, as the receiver, you *observe* or *hear* the feedback *you* are being given. You can think of these forms of feedback as three coins, all of which have two sides—giving and receiving or observing.

Giving Verbal Feedback

Giving verbal feedback requires that you ask questions, make statements, and give descriptions and other comments. You are asking for clarification of thoughts or feelings. You may also repeat your key points to make sure your customer is understanding what you intended.

Verbal feedback is especially useful for checking the pace and priorities established in the meeting. For example, you could say, "My manager tells me I sometimes get carried away with my enthusiasm and move along too quickly. Would it be more helpful if I slowed down a bit?" This not only shows a sensitivity to the customer's needs but lets the customer understand you better and encourages him to ask you to slow down or speed up the presentation.

Another question you could ask is, "Would you like me to get right into the details of the proposal, or do you have some other questions?" This lets the customer know his preferences are most important. The answers will clue you in to the way he likes to do things. Always look for or solicit some form of feedback so you can adjust your pace and priority.

Verbal feedback lets you convey how you are interpreting the customer's verbal, vocal, and visual messages. For example, based on your prospect's comments, you could ask, "Shall we explore that issue some more?" or "How do you think that will work?" If you see your customer squint or frown, you should say something like, "I get the impression I'm not coming across clearly. Is there something I can explain for you?"

Feedback should become a natural part of communicating with anyone. During a sales call, give and receive verbal feedback. If it is not offered, ask for it. Some of the ways to accomplish this follow:

- During your presentation, describe to your customer the impressions you have to make sure you're both on the same wavelength.

For example, you might say, "You mentioned earlier you have several production problems. Let me show you exactly how this product will solve these problems."

- Ask thought-provoking questions to solicit feedback. Questions can be phrased creatively, such as, "What do you think of when I say a computer is user-friendly?"

- Restate the customer's message in your own words instead of repeating what she said verbatim. For example, if you were selling a computer software program to a customer who wants a continuous training and upgrading program, you could say, "Let me make sure I understand you correctly. You would like to be kept informed of any changes in the program and periodically trained in its new features?"

- Give verbal feedback statements that begin with such statements as these:
  "Let me be sure I understand your major concerns."
  "Let me briefly summarize the key points we've discussed."
  "I hear you saying . . ."
  "As I understand it, you're saying . . ."
  "Did I understand you correctly?"
  "Was I on target with what you meant?"
  "Were those your major concerns?"
  "Does that about sum it up?"

Observing Verbal Feedback

Receiving or observing verbal feedback is simply being an active listener. The subtleties of active listening, noticing vocal qualities, and observing body language will be covered subsequently.

Giving Feedback with Voice Inflections

As mentioned earlier, there is more to the spoken word than its dictionary meaning. The emotions behind words carry most of the weight of the message. When you give feedback, you should use your voice to your advantage. Controlling your vocal intonation will improve the quality of your feedback and communication in general. Just as you listen for the hidden meanings behind your customer's words, so too, she will receive impressions from the emotions behind yours. Given this awareness, you can prevent doubt, fear, boredom, or fatigue from undermining your message.

Vocally you should strive to convey the qualities people expect from a professional: enthusiasm, confidence, and sincere interest. These can be achieved by varying your volume, inflection, and rate of speaking. For example, confidence is conveyed by projecting with a strong, full voice. Speaking clearly and distinctly is a sign of intelligence. Sincerity is shown by lowering your voice and being relaxed; and you know how to convey enthusiasm.

The ability to relax and give vocal feedback will lower tension and build trust in your relationships. Your use of vocal variation will add impact to your words and increase your prospect's understanding and retention of what you say.

Observing Voice Inflections

The flip side of using voice inflections is noticing and interpreting them. One word can have myriad meanings depending on the inflection used with it. A good example of this phenomenon is the word *Oh*. The dictionary meaning is an interjection. An interjection is a part of speech and, in reality, "Oh" has no meaning without the voice inflection that accompanies it. Think about it. Depending on how you say it, "Oh" can convey surprise, understanding, cynicism, doubt, fear, or anticipation. The only thing that gives us a clue to the speaker's meaning is the voice tone and occasionally the body language that accompanies it. And yet the interpretation of that voice inflection has become second nature to us; we don't have to stop and analyze it.

Your perception of all your prospect's voice inflections is second nature, but you may not be concentrating enough to let them sink in. As a non-manipulative salesperson who practices active listening and feedback, you should *hone* your powers of concentration and let what you perceive register in your mind.

The first step in perceiving someone's vocal inflection is to note what is normal. The normal speed and volume of speech will also give you clues as to the person's behavioral style, if you don't already know. Directors and socializers speak quickly and relatively loudly. Relaters and thinkers are more soft-spoken and slower paced. In addition to speed and volume, become used to your customer's inflection. Is he normally expressive or does he speak in a monotone?

After you have a good idea of what is normal for someone, you are in the position to observe and interpret changes in that person's vocal expression. Regardless of the direction or degree, there is always significance in the change. When you perceive it, acknowledge it somehow. Ask a clarifying question or in some other way solicit feedback. This is especially important if the change was for the worse. Any lapse in communication or deterioration of trust should be corrected as soon as possible, if not immediately.

Changes in vocal inflection rarely occur without accompanying changes in eye contact. This makes your job easier because two clues will jump out at you at once. For example, an angry customer will speak loudly and use irregular inflection and high speed. At the same time he will look away from you and look for something to throw or hit. These subtle clues are your cue to run for cover. Seriously, the clusters of vocal inflections and eye contact are familiar to everyone; what is unfamiliar is the concerted perception and use of that data to maximize communication.

With all the things you have to keep in mind while talking to a prospect, it is not unreasonable to expect that you might forget one thing or another. When listening, the observation you are most accustomed to making is the person's eye contact. So when you see a change in someone's eyes, use it as a reminder to listen for vocal clues as well.

Giving Nonverbal Feedback

It's amazing how much can be expressed without uttering a word. The subtleties of body language are fascinating to contemplate. The art of giving nonverbal feedback is an important one for non-manipulative salespeople; after all, no one likes to be interrupted.

Using body language keeps the conversation flowing and gives you a silent way of indicating you are following what is being said. Keep these tips in mind when giving nonverbal feedback:

• Nod your head when you understand or agree, but do it *in moderation*. You don't want to look like one of those toy dogs with the bobbing heads that people put in the rear window of their cars.

- Face your prospect and maintain good eye contact. This will show you are interested and have the confidence to look her in the eyes.

- Lean forward in your chair and you will convey that you are sincerely interested.

- Keep your arms open and at your sides. Crossed arms imply that you are not open to what is going on. A hand on your chin or face makes you look bored.

- When you speak, you can wave your eyeglasses or pen for emphasis, but don't wave it at the person; otherwise you'll look like a school teacher. When you're not speaking, don't play with it.

- As an active listener, withhold judgment while listening. If you slip into evaluative listening, be sure at least to suppress facial expressions that would reveal what you are thinking. When you realize you've slipped, return to active listening by increasing your concentration.

- If you are working with a relater or socializer, a gentle pat on the back when saying hello or goodbye can convey warmth and be appreciated. Smiles work with everyone.

There are innumerable gestures and clusters of nonverbal behaviors that you could give. The important thing to be aware of is the effect of your body language. Sitting or standing in a relaxed, open position will invite more interaction, cooperation, and trust than holding yourself in a tight, nervous manner.

Observing Nonverbal Feedback

Non-manipulative salespeople are always cognizant of the tension in a relationship. One of the most salient clues they have to tension is the other person's body language. Those subtle yet revealing postures, gestures, and movements often tell more than the giver or receiver is aware of. Some gestures, in fact, are more expressive than words. Imagine a man slapping his forehead and groaning. Without asking, you immediately know he has just remembered something important. Now imagine that person slapping his forehead, then his arm, then his leg; what do you conclude? Mosquitos! All this without words.

The observation and interpretation of body language is very rapid. Research has shown that people can interpret a situation or gesture in the time it takes for one frame of a film to be exposed—1/24th of a second. The trick, as with voice inflection, is to have the observation register in your mind so you can use it. To do this, you have to practice being observant.

Body language, being a direct reflection of the unconscious mind, is often more reliable than the words people say. In fact, it often contradicts the verbal message. If you are a practiced observer, you can read a person's current level of sincerity, trust, and interest through body language. This will enable you to sense your progress in a relationship and, if necessary, make an adjustment for the better.

Many books and articles describe ways of interpreting individual movements of the hands, eyes, mouth, and so on. The easiest way to understand body language, however, is to observe clusters of gestures and postures. Within a context and combined with observations of voice inflection and verbal feedback, you should have no problem inferring a person's attitude from the following guidelines:

Openness. In this situation, your customer signals sincerity and cooperation as he wants to work toward an agreeable solution with you. Openness is characterized by open hands, uncrossed legs, arms gently and loosely crossing lower body, unbuttoned coat, taking coat off, moving closer together, leaning forward, smiling, and good eye contact.

Enthusiasm. Enthusiasm is characterized by an inward smile, erect body stance, hands open and arms extended, eyes wide and alert and lively, voice lively and well modulated.

Readiness. This positive state is characterized by leaning forward in a chair to an open position, hand possibly placed mid-thigh, relaxed but alive facial expression, standing with hands on hips with feet slightly spread, nodding in agreement, good eye contact, close proximity.

Acceptance. A customer shows acceptance by displaying honesty and sincerity. These are indicated by hands to chest, open arms and hands, good eye contact, moving closer to the other person, touching the other person.

Confidence and Authority. These easily recognized gestures include steepling of hands (fingers together, pointed up; the higher the hands held, the greater the confidence), stretching out legs, leaning back with hands laced in back of head, continuous eye contact, proud and erect body stance with shoulders squared, thumbs in coat pockets, hands on lapels, reduced hand-to-face gestures, smiling inwardly, tipping back in chair.

Evaluation. When your customer is listening intently to your words in order to judge their merit, he will show evaluative gestures including sitting in the front portion of the chair with the upper torso projected forward; slightly tilted head; hand-to-cheek gesture, where head is often supported by the hand; stroking the chin or pulling the beard.

Boredom or Indifference. These states are shown by relaxed posture, slouching, doodling, drooping eyelids, little eye contact, yawning, slack lips, legs crossed and foot kicking, tapping of fingers on desk, expressionless stares, little visual feedback, staring at hands or fingers, supporting head with hand, posture aimed toward the exit.

Reassurance. In order to reassure themselves, customers may pinch the fleshy part of their hands; gently rub or caress some personal object such as a ring, watch, or necklace; bite fingernails; or examine cuticles.

Self-control. Self-control gestures are manifested when your customer is holding something back. They include wrists gripped behind the back, crossed and locked ankles, fists clenched, pupils contracted, and lips closed or pursed.

Defensiveness. When your customer feels psychologically defensive, his behavior will be characterized by rigid body, tightly crossed legs and/or arms in protective gestures, pursed lips, clenched fists, fingers clenching the crossed arms, head down with chin depressed toward the chest, little head movement or a stiff neck, and minimal eye contact with occasional sideways or darting glances.

Suspiciousness and Secrecy. These attitudes can be recognized by such gestures as failing to make eye contact or resisting glances from you, glancing sideways at you by slightly turning the body away, rubbing or touching the nose, and squinting or peering over glasses. The first sign of suspicion and secrecy may be a conflict between what your customer says and what her body projects.

Nervousness. Common indicators of nervousness are clearing the throat, hand-to-mouth movements, covering the mouth when speaking, tugging an ear, twitching lips or face, playing with objects and fidgeting, shifting weight while standing, and tapping fingers on a desk. Other indicators are waving foot in circular motion, plucking at collar or ringing neck with finger inside shirt collar, incongruently laughing, pacing, sighing deeply, whistling, cigarette smoking, biting or picking nails, poor eye contact, preoccupation with clothing, and jingling money in pockets.

Frustration. Customers exhibit frustration through the following gestures: tightly clenched hands, hand wringing, rubbing back of neck, controlled and shallow breathing, staring into space, running hands through hair, tightly closed lips, stamping a foot, and pacing.

Remember, body language will imply *what* the person is feeling, not *why* it is being felt. You must, therefore, ask questions to determine the reason for the change in emotion.

Giving and observing verbal and nonverbal feedback comes naturally for most people, but like listening, you may not do it well. Like everything else, it gets easier with practice. Remember to use feedback in the following situations:

To define words. There will be times when your prospect uses a word or phrase you don't understand. Ask her to define it for you. By the same token, if you use a twenty-five-cent word and your customer looks confused, restate your thought using five- and ten-cent words. After all, a word is only as valuable as its effectiveness in accurately conveying ideas. A twenty-five-cent word that is misunderstood is worth less than a clearly received five-cent word.

In lieu of assumptions. Like gunpowder, assumptions are not safe to make; when handled improperly, they could blow up in your face. Before acting on your assumptions, test them. Ask your prospect what he means by a statement. Imagine a situation in which a prospect smiled a lot and answered your questions. If you didn't check to see what he was thinking, you would be proceeding blindly. After all, the prospect may be uninterested but smiling to be polite. If you don't ask, you won't know. So ask questions, questions, and, if necessary, more questions.

Create transitions between phases of the sales process. A convenient and professional way to move from one phase to another is to sum up what has been covered so far and ask the prospect if all is clear and if she is in agreement. For example, you might say, "We've talked about a lot of things here. Let me briefly summarize them." After your summary you would ask, "As I see it, X, Y, and Z seem to be most important to you. Am I on target?"

It's the Changes That Count

A key point in this discussion is this—be on the lookout for *changes* in behavior. Just as every scientific experiment starts with the observation of the norm, so too, your inferences from the feedback you receive will be based on changes in the individual's normal mode of expression. In the beginning, if you learn nothing else, learn to recognize when you have lost a customer's interest. Heed the warning sign: a lowered level of response, both verbally and nonverbally. When you sense this happening, use questioning, change your pace, and/or change the topic of conversation. If your prospect prefers, adjourn for the day and come back another time to begin fresh. Don't wear down your prospect. You are there to create a mutually satisfying interaction.

The concept of natural selection or survival of the fittest applies to the business world as well as the animal kingdom. In the animal kingdom, members of a species who are weak simply do not survive. In the business world, the strength of your listening, observing, and feedback skills will dictate whether or not you survive. If poor listening habits are the number one shortcoming of salespeople in America, then those with great skills should not only survive but *thrive* and join the ranks of the elite 5 percent.

6

Planning

MOST SALESPEOPLE do not analyze their accounts because it requires more time, thought, and paperwork than they want to devote. The authors implore you to be the exception to this rule. Remember, you are trying to climb the ladder to the top 5 percent. The only way to do it is to climb one rung at a time and the rung of account analysis is a very important one.

It costs money to make money, and your expenses should be carefully planned, not recklessly spent. The most effective way to minimize your sales expenses and maximize the profits from your territory is professionally to plan and manage your territory.

The plan you devise will, to a large extent, determine your success in penetrating your market. Effective territory management takes into consideration market analysis, account analysis, prospecting, and call preparation.

Remember: As a non-manipulative salesperson, you are in business for yourself. You are your immediate boss and favorite employee. Therefore, you must take an active role in planning every facet of your business, from targeting markets to promoting yourself. Planning your success is the only way you will achieve that success.

COMPANY AND PRODUCT KNOWLEDGE

As a professional salesperson, you represent your company. In reality it goes further than that. You are your company. When you make a good impression, your company benefits from the good will. It is absolutely necessary, therefore, for you to have the most thorough knowledge possible of your company. There will be times when you will have to sell your company as well as your product or service. Buyers want to buy from reputable firms, and your knowledge and assurance will often come in handy. This is especially true with thinkers and directors. They are more likely to ask, "Who is your company?" "How long has it been around?" and "What is its track record?"

In addition to learning the history and development of your company, you should also know its mission statement. Every company is in business for a reason other than to make money. Find out what prompted the founding of your company.

In addition to knowing your company, you must, of course know your product. Product knowledge is so important that salespeople who work for companies like IBM and Xerox are expected to know every facet of their products and their competitors' products. They are trained and tested extensively in programs that take anywhere from many months to years. In some cases, salespeople are not allowed to talk to prospects until they have completed these rigorous training programs. These companies are industry leaders and their salespeople are perfect reflections of their companies.

Many industries require their salespeople to have educational backgrounds in specific areas. For example, the pharmaceutical and medical technology industries often require backgrounds in biology or premedical subjects. Some companies are even willing to send their salespeople to school as part of their training. Their reasoning is sound; if sales reps are going to consult with doctors and hospital administrators, they had better have a thorough understanding of their product and its operation and be able to speak and understand their customer's language.

It is essential that you know everything about your product and those of your competition. When talking to a prospect, you should be able effortlessly to compare the features and benefits of your product with those of all your competitors. You must be an expert in your field. In fact, you should know so much that you could go to work for a competitor without much training.

TERRITORY MANAGEMENT

The logical procedure for managing a territory is first to analyze what the trends, problems, and opportunities in the market are. The next step is to analyze individual accounts to determine profitability and the allocation of your time.

The plan you formulate will be similar to the plan your company uses to penetrate potential markets. Naturally, your plan will have a narrower scope, but the overall strategy should parallel your company's marketing plan. Find the answers to these questions and you will begin to get a firm grip on your own marketing plan.

1. What industries, and within those industries, what specific businesses will be your target market?

2. What is the most cost-effective way of reaching these prospects?

3. Who are likely to be the best accounts and what sources should be used to research them? If you work for a large company that has a marketing department, ask them if they have market data that you can use.

4. When is the best time to reach these prospects? If you are in a seasonal business, you may have to plan, study, and meet with prospects during a particular time of year.

5. What business trends and market conditions will affect your prospects? Given the rapid changes that take place in the business world, you should continually think about ways to avoid problems and anticipate opportunities for yourself and your prospects.

MARKET SEGMENTS

The two most common ways to manage a territory are geographically and by categories or market segments. The former is an obvious way of dividing up prospects. The latter means this: within your territory there will be different types of businesses that will use your product or service. For example, if you sell water-purification systems, you can sell them to restaurants, hospitals, office buildings, and private homes, to name a few. Each of these is a different market segment.

If you are given a choice, you should choose a limited number of market segments on which to concentrate. This will give you two major advantages. First, it will allow you to become known in the industry.

Second, and most important, you will become industry-wise, such as an expert in that industry. By reading trade journals and attending association meetings, you will learn all the details necessary to make you an effective consultant.

If you are not given a choice and your prospects cover many market segments, divide them into categories. This will help you be better organized and point the way toward trade journals that you should read for background information.

MARKET ANALYSIS

How do you divide your territory into market segments? It's simple; just list all the possible uses of your product or service and brainstorm all the appropriate industries. Next, determine the number of companies in each category, their sizes, and where they are located.

The advantage of selling to a small number of market segments is that you can take the time to determine the sales potential in each. There are numerous sources for data on sales, sales trends, and projected sales by geographical location, industry, and so on. Some of the many sources for this information are as follows:

- Industry and trade journals

- Local business newspapers

- The *Wall Street Journal*

- Annual Report on Business published every January in *Forbes*

- *Standard & Poor's Industry Surveys*

- *Moody's Industrial Manual*
- *Encyclopedia of Business Information* sources
- Your company's marketing department
- Noncompeting salespeople
- Support groups such as TIP and Winner's Circle
- Your own creativity

The information you uncover will help you determine which market segments are most promising. It makes sense to spend more time on those markets that have been most profitable in the past. This is also true of individual accounts within each market segment.

Competition Analysis

You must be aware of your competitors—what they are doing right, what they are doing wrong, and what share of the market they hold. Knowing your competition will give you a more objective perspective on your company, product, or service's strengths and weaknesses.

To analyze the competition, determine how they compare in terms of sales volume, reputation, pricing, quality, customer service, market share, growth, and financial stability. Often there is no cut-and-dried answer to the question of which company is better. Your competitors may be stronger in some market segments and weaker in others owing to the unique nature of customer needs in those industries. Different market segments value different features and benefits; yours appeals to some, your competitors' appeal to others. Your product's strengths and weaknesses in different market segments should be part of a competition analysis.

After you have compiled all this information, analyze why your competitors are either better or worse than your company for each market you serve. Ultimately, the question is, How can you capture more of a market share, capitalize on your strengths, and minimize your weaknesses?

Account Analysis

The way to get the most out of your territory is to spend more time on those accounts with the biggest payoff. To set your priorities, it is necessary to analyze your accounts with an objective system that leaves no doubt as to which side of your bread is buttered.

You have probably heard the expression that 80 percent of your business comes from 20 percent of your accounts. This being true, you need to establish a list of "preferred" customers. They will be the ones who give you the maximum return on your investment of time and money.

There are four steps for determining which accounts are your most profitable. These analyses can be done for both present customers and prospects.

Estimate Your Potential Sales. For each of your accounts, do the following:

• Look at last year's gross sales. Let's say, for example, that Acme Agar gave you $10,000 in business last year.

• Take an educated guess as to how much business they will give you this year. Let's look on the bright side and project next year's sales to be an additional $2,000, for a total of $12,000.

• Multiply the projected sales figure, in this case, the additional $2,000 by a probability factor. The probability factor is a percentage that is based on how optimistic you are that your sales projection will actually be met. It's handy to work with three levels of confidence: high = 80 percent, medium = 50 percent, and low = 20 percent. Hypothetically, if you had a medium amount of optimism, you would multiply $2,000 by 0.50 and get 1,000; this figure added to the original $10,000 = $11,000. This would be the number you would use as your potential sales quotient.

• For prospects, the same procedure applies. The only difference is in your sales projection. To estimate a prospect's sales, compare their business to similar businesses that are already accounts. You can also use industry trends and statistics for your forecast. Make an educated guess and go with it. Calculate the potential sales quotient based on your estimate.

Calculate How Much Your Time Is Worth. It is useful for your edification and for the next calculation to determine how much you earned last year on an hourly basis. This is a rough estimate that will be used to help compare one account to another. Whether it is 100 percent accurate is unimportant as long as you use the same value for all the comparisons.

Take the amount of money you grossed last year and divided it by the number of hours you worked. Did you work a 40-hour week? Did you put in a lot of time at home, making your week a 50- or 60-hour week? A 40-hour week works out to be 2,000 hours a year, a 50-hour week is 2,500 hours a year, and a 60-hour week is 3,000 hours a year. Whatever you worked, enter it into the equation:

Hourly Rate (last year) ($/hr) = Gross Income/# hrs. worked

Determine How Profitable Your Accounts Are. Objectively to determine an account's profitability, you need to calculate your return on time invested (ROTI). This is simply the relationship between the effort you expended and the result. Sales results will be your gross commissions from one account; sales effort will be the amount of time spent on that account multiplied by your hourly rate. Mathematically stated,

$$\text{ROTI} = \frac{\text{Sales Results}}{\text{Sales Effort}} = \frac{\text{Gross Commissions}}{\$/\text{hr.} \times \text{hrs. worked}}$$

An example will help clarify this. Your total commissions from the Bermuda Prism Company were $15,000. The amount of time required to plan, meet, study, propose, and assure their satisfaction was approximately 300 hours at $20 per hour. Your ROTI for that account is 2.5. A ROTI of 1.0 means you are making the same hourly rate on that account as last year. A ROTI of less than 1.0 shows you are making less money than last year. Any account with a ROTI of less than 1.0 should be handled in one of four ways: (1) *Your first preference should be to try to increase their sales*. If that is not possible, then (2) cut back the amount of time invested in the account; (3) hand them over to your company's telemarketing department, if there is one; or (4) service the account by mail or telephone.

As you repeat this process for every account, you will find their ROTIs to be quite different. The higher the value, the more profitable the account.

Classify Your Accounts. Once you have a ROTI for each account you will be able to classify the accounts into three levels of profitability. The highest 20 percent will be designated as A accounts. Obviously these are your most profitable accounts. The next 30 percent will be called B accounts. The next 40 percent will be C accounts. These percentages add up to 90, not 100. By design, the bottom 10 percent of your accounts should be dropped to allow time for upgrading the top 90 percent and researching and prospecting for new accounts that have the potential to be A accounts. By dropping 10 percent, it simply means you are going to spend next to no time servicing them. Hand them off to telemarketing, sell them by mail, or literally drop them.

One way to find new A accounts is to look at your present A and B accounts to see if there are any patterns that stand out. These industry patterns will suggest who your new As will be. You then know where to direct your prospecting efforts.

After classifying your accounts into As, Bs, and Cs, you can determine the appropriate allocation of your time for each account. As will require the most time but will give you the highest return on the time invested. Bs and Cs have to be nurtured and brought up to A status.

Using the formulas given above, you can determine what would be necessary to turn each account into an A account. By reducing the amount of time invested in the account or increasing the account's sales, you upgrade its classification. Please note: *It is essential to maintain the quality of the service you give an account. To cut back on the amount of time you invest, you have to work smarter.* Cut back gradually and realize that it may take a year or more to bring it up to an A. An example will show you how this works mathematically. Here is a hypothetical A account:

$$\text{ROTI} = \frac{\$15,000}{300 \text{ hrs} \times \$20/\text{hr}} = \frac{\$15,000}{\$6,000} = 2.5$$

A 'B' account might have the following values:

$$\text{ROTI} = \frac{\$5,000}{250 \text{ hrs} \times \$20/\text{hr}} = \frac{\$5,000}{\$5,000} = 1.0$$

A 'C' account would look like this:

$$\text{ROTI} = \frac{\$3,000}{160 \text{ hrs} \times \$20/\text{hr}} = \frac{\$3,000}{\$3,200} = 0.9$$

In order to change the B account into an A account or the C to a B, you have either to increase their sales or decrease the amount of time spent. Assuming sales will stay the same, plan to cut back your time, but by how much? To find out, rearrange the ROTI formula to determine sales effort.

Sales Effort = Sales Results
               ROTI

Using the values from the B account,

Sales Effort = $5,000/2.5 (target ROTI) = $2,000 (target sales effort)

To get Sales Effort, you have to divide $2,000 by $20/hr
               Sales Effort = 100 hours

This tells you that your goal is to spend a total of 100 hours per year on this account to turn it into an A account. The same calculation will determine how many yearly hours to spend on a C account to bring it up to a B account.

Through the manipulation of the numbers, you can see how and where to spend your time and, in turn, begin to control the return on the time you invest. Knowing where you are going to invest your time will allow you to set territory objectives.

TERRITORY OBJECTIVES

The opportunities you uncover will lead to objectives or goals that you will set for yourself. These objectives, like the classification of accounts, serve as priorities that motivate you and focus your efforts where they will have the greatest payoff.

Some examples of territory objectives are as follows:

1. Upgrade a certain percentage of C accounts to B accounts and B accounts to A accounts.
2. Increase your entire gross sales for the year.
3. Increase the percentage of high-profit products or services.

4. Reduce your expenses for the entire territory.
5. Increase your prospecting efforts on a monthly basis.
6. Break into new market segments or expand some you are in already.

Your territory objectives will depend on your customers, territory, products or services, and company. Strive for them the same way you strive for your personal goals.

So far the majority of the discussion on planning has centered around established customers. Every salesperson knows, however, that career advancement and increased income depend on new customers.

PROSPECTING

As a non-manipulative salesperson who thinks like a consultant, you know that the only way new business will come your way is if you go after it. Of course as you gain contacts and establish long-term relationships, referals will come your way, but you can't sit back and wait for them. Part of your monthly routine must include prospecting.

The vast majority of salespeople experience sales slumps. The reason dry spells occur can be understood with the aid of figure 6.1.

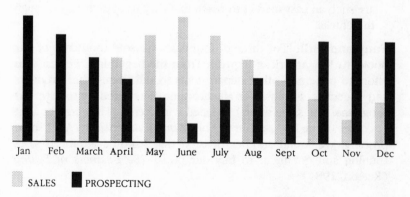

SALES   PROSPECTING

FIGURE 6.1

Let's say you start a job in January and spend a lot of time prospecting. In fact, it takes up 90 percent of your time. Naturally, there is lag time between your initial contact with a prospect and the confirmation of a sale. This is called the sales cycle, and, generally, the higher the price of the product, the longer the sales cycle. As time goes by, sales increase; your prospecting activities begin to pay off. You become more and more impressed with yourself. You're making customers happy, your sales manager is thrilled, and your bank statement looks better all the time. As sales increase, you keep decreasing your prospecting activities because you think, "I don't need to prospect; I'm making sales!" Months later you enter a dry spell but can't figure out why. The answer is simple; you stopped prospecting. The prospecting groundwork you laid in the beginning of the year has already paid off, and your well of new business is starting to run dry.

Sales slumps can be avoided by continually prospecting. There are numerous ways to gain exposure, uncover new markets, and establish new business contacts. There is no "best" strategy. They all work, so find the ones that work best for you and your product, company, and industry. Some of the many sources of prospects are the following:

Satisfied customers. People with whom you have business relationships should be systematically approached to see if additional needs exist. This takes place during the assuring phase of the sale and will be discussed in chapter 12. Satisfied customers are such an easy market to reach that they frequently slip through the cracks.

Tony and Phil: "For three or four years we sold thousands of our books to IDS/American Express. From the beginning, we made an effort to penetrate other departments to sell them other products and speeches. Finally after all that time they hired us to give our programs. The same thing happened with Xerox. They bought a lot of copies of the first edition of *Non-Manipulative Selling*. After some probing, we found another division that handled advanced sales training and got them to buy our book, *The Business of Selling* (Reston, 1984).

Keep in mind different departments, divisions, parent companies, and other spin-offs of your present customers. In addition, when your company introduces new products or services, your entire customer list becomes a prospect list. At least once a year you should go through your customer list and a list of your products and services to see if new opportunities exist.

New prospects. In traditional sales, if you don't make the sale, you automatically ask the prospect if she can refer you to someone else. Often the prospect will not; after all, what kind of friend would give your name to a pushy saleman? In non-manipulative selling, however, the first priority is the relationship; the second is the sale. Therefore, when you ask for a referral, the prospect doesn't feel as if he is doing a friend a disservice by giving out the friend's name.

Company leads. Often your company will provide leads from ads, direct-mail responses, telephone campaigns, and other valuable sources. These leads are generally of high quality because the prospect has already expressed an interest in your company. In this situation, don't procrastinate; approach the prospect quickly.

Friends and social contacts. As a non-manipulative salesperson who is a consultant and not a vampire, you will have friends who will not be afraid to refer you to their friends.

Civic and professional groups. Get involved. Join trade associations and business groups, especially those in your target industries. The chamber of commerce is another good group to join and be active in. The higher the level of your involvement, the more exposure you will have and the more business you will do. Put in the time to work on committees and climb the ladder to the board of directors or other official positions. Visibility will give you credibility and build trust. When you show that you care about your community, people will believe you also care about your clients.

Centers of influence. Centers of influence are prominent people in your community who can direct you toward new prospects. A center of influence may not become a customer, but can be an excellent resource nonetheless. Your priest, rabbi, minister, or congressperson or influential business people can all be called upon for help.

Orphan accounts. These are former customers who, for some reason, have stopped buying. Often the reason is simply that they have fallen through the cracks and have not been called on in a while. These accounts represent a gold mine right under your nose.

Phil: Dictaphone Security Systems found they were losing a lot of good salespeople because the sales cycle was relatively long. Salespeople who were on 100 percent commission would get frustrated and quit within eight or ten weeks, even though they had been told the average sale is made approximately twelve weeks into the job. Dictaphone began a pilot study that later became known as the Hohokus Project, named after the town in New Jersey where they first tried it. Here's what they did: They dug into their huge files of orphan accounts and gave each new salesperson fifteen or twenty of them. The salesperson was instructed not to sell the accounts anything but to call simply to make an appointment to bring them some updated information. The information was a revised handbook on crime and fire protection. The salesperson would also say that he would check their security system and would promise not to try to sell them anything. "I won't even bring my briefcase in. I just want to make sure your system is working effectively." When the salesperson made the call, after checking out the system, he would ask the customer if the customer had any friends who might need security systems. It was strictly a means of obtaining leads. The project reduced the length of time between being hired and making a sale by 60 percent, which in turn decreased the turnover rate dramatically."

Conventions and trade shows. As a consultant who will immerse yourself in your industry, you will undoubtedly attend trade shows and conventions. These are full of opportunities. There may be times when your company chooses not to participate in a trade show. If the booth fee is manageable, get involved in the show yourself. Create an exciting theme for your booth and everything in it. Decorations, brochures, and prizes can all be thematically related. Give away products, services, or a trip to Hawaii so you have a way to collect business cards. In addition, it is essential that you be the primary salesperson in the booth to make the contacts; and be sure to follow up after the show.

Directories, indexes and Yellow Pages. There are innumerable directories to the businesses in your industry and geographical location. The local library and chamber of commerce are invaluable resources. If you are not familiar with their directories and indexes, ask for help.

Support groups. Support groups such as Winner's Circle and the Tip Club are excellent sources for further education and contacts. They often have professional speakers present programs on sales and marketing. You will also have the opportunity to meet noncompeting salespeople who will help you brainstorm ways to penetrate markets and reach specific prospects. If there are no support groups in your area, start one!

Direct mail. This is a relatively inexpensive way to reach a large number of people. An attractive, professionally written, one-page flyer can be very effective. Every salesperson's dream is to have people calling him or her.

To most people, a direct-mail campaign is a major project. To a non-manipulative salesperson, it should be an on-going process. The three authors of this book practice what they preach. They use Tony's brother, Gary Alessandra's business, Professional Speaker's Marketing Group of La Jolla, California, to send monthly direct-mail pieces to their large customer base. The response has been enormous, and, if nothing else, decision makers across the country are seeing their names on a regular basis.

Consider starting a newsletter to keep your customers abreast of the latest developments in your company and the industry in general. If you do not have the expertise or the time to write the newsletter, work with other people in your company or industry or hire a professional writer. It will be worth the time and expense.

Public speaking and seminars. If you can get in front of an audience to educate and entertain them, you will discover an endless source of prospects. It is not even important to be paid for your speaking engagements. Your payoff will come when business increases dramatically. This is a common practice that pays off for financial planners, insurance salespeople, lawyers, and so on. This method will make you an expert in the eyes of the public, and you will be the first person they think of when they have a question.

Fly first class. This may seem like an unusual suggestion, but the authors' experience bears out its truth. In general, who flies in first class? People who can afford it, which means they are successful in some form of business. These are exactly the people you want to meet. Many airlines offer memberships in frequent-flyer clubs merely for signing up. These members are allowed to upgrade their fares from coach to first class for next to nothing. You can also ask to be upgraded to first class even if you are not a frequent flyer. At the gate, tell the ticket person you would like to upgrade to first class if it isn't full. If there is room, they will let you move up, sometimes for free and often for a small additional fee. It pays to take advantage of all these ways to get into first class to make contacts. One contact can change your whole life.

Prospects are everywhere. Be observant. Keep your eyes, ears, and mind open to the people and situations around you. You never know when your expertise will be needed.

Identify Top-Quality Prospects

Top-quality prospects are those that have the decision-making authority and the money to purchase your product or service if they need it. Some research and an account analysis will give you a lot of insight and allow you to rate a company as a potential A, B, or C account.

It is important to create the criteria that your prospect will have to meet before you invest a lot of time in them. Make a checklist that includes the prospect's apparent needs, credit, accessibility of the decision maker, and so on.

Timing is very important in prospecting and varies depending on the industry. Decision making takes time, so you need to allow for that. For example, products sold during Christmas are often purchased during the summer. Your prospect may require a month to make a decision and two to three weeks for the study phase of the sale. Taking all this into account you need to meet this prospect in April or May.

Create a System for Prospecting

The more organized you are, the less likely you are to lose names and numbers, forget about prospecting, or make other costly mistakes. The first step is to start a file and, if necessary, get help in setting it up. Keep track of everything about the prospect including dates of contact, who referred you, possible needs or opportunities, and so on.

Your system should indicate steps to take for each prospect. A minimal amount of research will be required to identify those who will be most promising. You also need a system for direct-mail contact and follow-ups. To organize your client and prospect files, consider this system:

Use a hanging file system with 8½-×-11-inch file folders. Label twenty-six of the files A-Z. These will be your master files for your client list. You can either have a separate master prospect file or, if there is room, combine them with present clients.

Give each client his or her own page and record all the permanent information you have on the company, the decision maker, your contacts, addresses, telephone numbers, birthdays, spouse's names, everyone's hobbies, the dog's name, and so on. Attached to this master sheet will be a contact report. Every time you talk to this client, make a note of the reason and outcome and the date of your next contact.

To remember when to approach customers, set up a tickler file. You probably have one already, but consider improving it with some of these ideas. You can use either a notebook, several notebooks, or a small card file. Whatever system you use, it should be divided into twelve months. There should also be a section for the current month, and it should be divided into four or five weeks. For each client or prospect there will be an index card on which you will write the client's name and contact date. As you plan contacts and follow-ups, simply put the cards in the appropriate week. At the end of each week, spend some time reviewing the up-coming week's calls and put those cards in your daily reminder notebook or daily tickler file.

After you talk to a customer, enter your notes on the contact report and put the tickler file card in the week of the next contact. There is a good reason to keep your master files and tickler files separate. Imagine you are in your office and a client calls. You quickly have to dig up your information on the account. If that information is in alphabetical order in the master file, you know exactly where to look. If it were attached to the tickler card and filed under a date somewhere in the future, you would not know where to find it unless you happened to remember when you were going to talk to that person again.

Setting up a system like this may seem like a headache; however, it is worth the effort. There are also some alternatives. You could solicit the help of a well-organized friend. You could use one of the many computer programs that will organize you. You could also work with a secretary who would take the paperwork off your desk and put it in files rather than piles. Your secretary would also update your files and keep you from interfering with the system. If you choose the latter idea, an efficient and time-saving tactic is to dictate the information and have it transcribed and filed.

No matter what system you use, it is absolutely essential to follow through with your prospects. Always keep the ball in your court. Don't expect them to call you back. If you spend the time to follow through, you will find your appointment book filling up with new names and numbers.

Customers were mentioned earlier as annuities. Prospecting can be compared to acquiring a new life insurance policy each time you develop a long-term business relationship. In the long run you will build a business base that will pay you the annuities you deserve.

PRECALL PLANNING

Throughout this book the authors are continually stressing that non-manipulative salespeople do their homework. They plan and research their territories and individual accounts even before approaching a prospect for the first time. An important part of professionalism is being prepared. Therefore, precall planning will take place before the meeting, studying, proposing, confirming, and assuring phases of the sale.

There are many benefits to precall planning, some of which are the following:

- It saves time. Customers appreciate it when you take up as little of their time as possible.

- It makes you look professional. Being organized allows you to be informed and to communicate quickly and effectively. Never contact a client, even on the telephone, without first reviewing the account file.

- It reduces tension. Beginning salespeople who are well prepared have less to worry about.

- It allows flexibility. There is no substitute for knowledge and preparation. Precall planning will give you both.

- It increases your sales. The more prepared you are, the more effective you will be in everything you do.

Uncovering Decision Makers

The research you conduct before the initial contact should uncover the name of the decision maker you will have to deal with. This information can be obtained by calling a receptionist and asking, "Who is the person responsible for ...?" or "Who is in charge of ...?" You can also ask noncompetitive salespeople who are familiar with the company. Other sources are industry journals, annual reports, and local business newspapers.

If you are in an industry in which you sell only to very large accounts, you know that there are often times when you have to use a multilevel, team-sell approach. The more complex and technical your product, the more salespeople will be involved in selling and the more buyers will be involved in the decision making. There may be three decision makers in different departments and levels of the corporation. One may be in accounting, another in engineering, and the third may be the president of the firm. Each will have to be consulted by a salesperson on your team who has the required expertise. Someone who sells well to technical people will meet with the engineer. Someone who works well with accountants will call that person and so on. Knowing this in advance will allow you to plan your penetration into the company with your sales manager and other members of the sales team.

Setting Call Objectives

Every type of contact with a prospect or customer has a purpose. Your call objectives will vary depending on the phase of the sale and your relationship with your client. It is important to establish your call objectives prior to contact. Whether you are contacting your client by letter, telephone, or in person, you have to have a clear idea of what you will say and why you are taking up your customer's time.

Figure 6.2 is an example of a precall grid that can be used for organization. It lays out in front of you all the steps to take in the sales process. As you complete each step, check it off and go on to the next. Another advantage of this grid is that it lets your sales manager quickly see the status of your accounts at any given time. When he asks, simply take out the grid and show where you are along the scale.

Some of the many reasons to contact a customer are to introduce yourself and your company, products, or services; to make as many appointments as necessary to build the relationship and gather information; to propose a solution to the prospect's problem; to confirm the sale; and to follow up to assure customer satisfaction. All of these take preparation.

Telephone Contact

It is essential to gear your pre-call planning to the needs inherent in telephone contact. Telephone calls in any phase of the sale should be short and to the point, which means you must be organized. Some of the many reasons to call are to break the ice and become known to the prospect, to set up appointments, to follow up on a proposal, to introduce new products, to collect money, or to confirm information gathered previously.

A Telephone Planning Sheet (see figure 6.3) will help you quickly focus on the purpose of each call. Fill out this form in advance for each call to be made and your calls will sound better, take less time, and accomplish your objectives.

The items on the Telephone Planning Sheet are for you to use verbatim or to adjust to your needs. The organization of the sheet will prevent you from digressing too far, forgetting your train of thought, or hanging up and realizing you forgot to mention something. This is especially useful when calling long distance.

1.0 — **Mail Contact**
1.1 — Introductory Letter—Self
1.2 — Introductory Letter—Product
1.3 — Special Sale Letter

2.0 — **Phone Contact**
2.1 — Busy
2.2 — Not In
2.3 — Spoke—Neg. Response
2.4 — Spoke—Pos. Response—Call Back
2.5 — Spoke—Made Appointment

3.0 — **In-Person Contact**
3.1 — Established Relationship
3.2 — Determined Behavioral Style

4.0 — **Studying**
4.1 — Decision Making Process
4.2 — Needs Summary
4.3 — Success Criteria
4.4 — Made Appointment for Presentation

5.0 — **Proposing**
5.1 — Proposal Document
5.2 — Individual/Group Presentation
5.3 — Demonstration
5.4 — CSU Summary

6.0 — **Confirming**
6.1 — Ask for Commitment
6.2 — Yes, Go to 6.4
6.3 — No, Reason Why?
6.4 — Commitment Letter

7.0 — **Assuring**
7.1 — Thank You Letter
7.2 — Delivery Dates
7.3 — Training Schedules
7.4 — Follow-Up Schedules

8.0 — **Additional Business Within Company**
8.1 — Reorders
8.2 — Contact Other People/Departments
8.3 — Additions
8.4 — Contact Parent Co. or Subsidiary

9.0 — **Referals**
9.1 — Ask?
9.2 — Testimonial Letters
9.3 — Check Style, Possible Needs of Referal
9.4 — Contact Referal (go back to 1.0)

10.0 — **New Product Sales to Same Company**
10.1 — Begin With 1.0 If New Person
10.2 — Begin With 2.0 If Same Customer

FIGURE 6.2 **The Precall Grid**

Company: _____

Contact: _____

Telephone #: _____ Secretary's name: _____

Best time to call: _____ Date of last contact: _____

Market segment: _____

Background

Information: _____

_____

Call objective (primary): _____

   (secondary): _____

Initial-benefit statement: _____

_____

Key points to cover: _____

_____

What I will ask client to do: _____

_____

Potential concerns/questions #2: _____

_____

Answer: _____

_____

Potential concerns/questions #2: _____

_____

Answer: _____

FIGURE 6.3 *Telephone Planning Sheet*

The two items "Potential concerns/questions" and "Answers" will be very useful for telephone calls and in-person meetings. An important part of being prepared is having the ability to anticipate the prospect's concerns and have answers and information ready. This will draw on your product knowledge, understanding of the industry, and the insight you gain from researching the individual account.

In-Person Contact

Seven steps should be undertaken before any meeting with a client. These steps will focus your attention and creative energy and increase your success significantly.

1. Do all the research possible.
2. Write out the questions you intend to ask as well as the general topics you plan to cover in the meeting.
3. Anticipate the prospect's answers and brainstorm possible problems and opportunities that may arise.
4. Visualize your success. Whatever your call objectives may be, spend time sitting quietly with your eyes closed and imagine yourself with the prospect successfully achieving your objectives. This is a powerful tool that really works!
5. Role play with a fellow salesperson. Many salespeople avoid this exercise, but those who use it swear by it. Role playing will sharpen your ability to anticipate questions and issues. Your role-playing partner should stretch your imagination without harassing you for the fun of it. It is also helpful to record your role-playing session on audio or video tape. The insight you will gain from listening or watching the session will be quite valuable.
6. Go over your call objectives, ideas, questions, and overall plan of action with your sales manager. Get feedback and input as to how to improve your approach.
7. Sleep on it. You will be amazed what you will think of when you let all the information percolate in your mind. You will think of additional questions, issues, and creative ideas. Give yourself as much time as possible before the meeting to let your unconscious do its job. You may come

up with a great idea that needs some lead time such as a video demonstration or a special brochure.

This seven-step program of pre-call planning will serve you well if you use it routinely. Of course, for a brief meeting with your customers you need do only some of the steps. For example, if you are going to stop by to drop off information, you don't have to go through most of the steps, but you do have to refamiliarize yourself with the details of the account.

This generic, pre-call, seven-step process will vary only in the type of research and preparation you do for the different types of calls. The needs of each phase of the sale—meeting, studying, proposing, confirming, and assuring—are discussed in their respective chapters.

A word on common sense. It is essential to have everything ready and at your disposal when meeting with a prospect. Plan ahead. Take enough business cards, literature, brochures, and other documents you may need. If you will be riding in your car with the prospect, make sure it is clean. If you will be giving a presentation, make sure your equipment is in top working order. Take extra slide projector bulbs. Video tapes should be cued to their starting points. Photocopied documents should be stapled and carried in something that will protect them. Give as much forethought to your presentation as you do to your studying phase. Visualize both and you will avoid embarrassing surprises.

Simply stated, planning is everything you do before contacting the prospect. You begin by taking a bird's-eye view of your territory, individual accounts, and prospects. You analyze where your time will be most profitably spent, and then you research and plan everything up to the moment of contact. In a nutshell, this is the phase in which you can exert direct control over your career.

7

Meeting the Prospect

THE INTRODUCTORY MEETING is the point at which everything comes together. Your understanding of behavioral styles, body language, and image, and your listening and questioning skills and product knowledge all have an impact on the impression you make in the first few minutes of a meeting. In that short, precious time you often make or break the sale. In that time your prospect sizes you up and determines if you are the type of person with whom he would like to do business.

There are three ways you can meet a prospect: in person, over the telephone, or by letter. Each makes a different impression and has its advantages and disadvantages. Table 7.1 shows how the three methods compare in terms of quality and quantity (a score of three is the best).

The quality of a contact is its effectiveness based on two criteria: your ability to receive feedback from the client and your ability to reach some degree of resolution. The resolution may not be "the big close" but a commitment to the next step in the sales process. Personal contacts provide the best opportunity for feedback, both verbal and nonverbal. The telephone is a less effective means of

Table 7.1

Comparison of Methods of Contact

Type of contact	Number of possible contacts	Quality of contact	Total value
In person	1	3	4
By telephone	2	2	4
By mail	3	1	4

contact, and direct mail is the least effective, as the scores in table 7.1 indicate.

The number of contacts possible using a given method is inversely related to the degree of personal contact involved. Obviously, more people can be reached in a given day by direct mail than by telephone; and the telephone allows more contact than in-person calls.

What is the best method? Looking at the third column of table 7.1, you can see they all add up to the same value. The answer, therefore, is to use all three methods. They all serve different purposes and are appropriate for different impressions. There is no *best* way. The most effective approach is to use all three in an organized, on-going effort in which you continually send letters, follow up with telephone calls, and make appointments to meet prospects in person.

It is important to understand the difference between a sales effort and a marketing effort. Many of the techniques are the same. For example, they both employ direct mail, telephone calls, and in-person contacts. The primary difference, however, is the number of prospects reached. A marketing campaign is often aimed at an enormous number of people. The Publishers' Clearinghouse Sweepstakes is a case in point. It is sent to millions of Americans.

A sales effort, by contrast, is aimed only at the number of people on whom you can realistically follow up. A few days after your letters go out, you must telephone your prospects. If you bite off more than you can chew, some of your prospects will fall through the cracks and never be called. That would be inefficient and wasteful of good prospects.

There is no doubting the importance of quality, but without someone to talk to, quality is worthless. If given the choice between a salesperson with impeccable sales communication skills who sees only a few prospects versus a less-skilled salesperson who is an excellent prospector, the authors would take the prospector. There is no question that quantity is a major factor in the formula of success. Although this book is about the quality of your sales ability, you should not forget about quantity. By learning all the elements of non-manipulative selling, you will increase the number of sales you make for a given number of prospects, but this does not reduce the importance of contacting as many prospects as you reasonably can.

MAINTAINING A CONSTANT SUPPLY OF CONTACTS

Think of the sales process as a funnel, as depicted in figure 7.2. The most important step of the sales process is the beginning—the

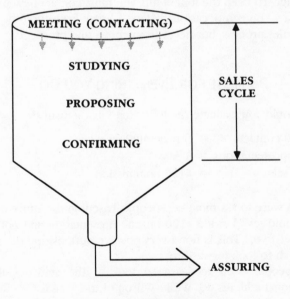

FIGURE 7.2 *The Sales Funnel*

meeting phase. Without a fresh source of prospects, the rest of the sales process is impossible.

The time from the initial contact to the confirmation of the sale is called the sales cycle. When sales are down, it is not because of today's activities but because of a lack of activity in the beginning of the cycle.

Phil: A friend of mine who is also a professional speaker was feeling down because she wasn't getting the number of bookings she had grown accustomed to. I asked her a few pointed questions and discovered she had been very, very busy for the last 90 to 100 days and had not contacted anyone new during that time. I told her that no matter how busy she became, she had to continue to contact a minimum number of new prospects each day or week in order to avoid a sales slump.

A sure-fire way to prevent yourself from running out of leads is to keep filling the sales-cycle funnel. You *must continually* put new contacts in the top in order to produce sales from the bottom. It's like manufacturing; without the raw material, you cannot fabricate a product. To keep the funnel full, you must contact new prospects every day. You can occasionally take a break from the other phases of the sales process, but never from contacting prospects.

PAYMENT FOR EVERYTHING YOU DO

How would you evaluate the following sales statistics?

10 contacts	= 3 presentations
3 presentations	= 1 sale
1 sale	= $120 commission

If you were to ask most salespeople, based on the above numbers, they would say "I made $120 on one presentation and nothing on the other two." This is not a very positive outlook and doesn't give you much to look forward to.

Salespeople need to learn to look at the statistics the way professional athletes do. Willie Wilson of the Kansas City Royals hit .333 in 1982 and was the major-league batting champion. A .333

hitter who is a decent fielder is worth about $1 million a year. Yet, evaluated the way a salesperson would evaluate himself, he failed to get a hit two out of three times. If a baseball player looked at it that way, how motivated do you think he would be? Not very motivated. Instead, the professional baseball player thinks to himself, "I got one third of a hit every time I stepped up to the plate." Now he's motivated.

The reality of the sales statistics above is this: the salesperson did not get a $120 commission for one presentation and nothing for the others; he got $40 for each presentation. Taking it a step further and using the baseball analogy, the salesperson received $12 for *each contact* rather than $120 for one and nothing for the other nine.

If someone were to offer you $12 for every contact you made, that is, every time you wrote a letter, made a telephone call, or met someone in person, what would you do? Would you work hard to make as many contacts as you could or would you take an extra half hour for lunch or slack off on your prospecting? You would work hard.

Most salespeople feel they are paid to make sales. Not true. You are paid to make contacts. Without contacts you cannot make sales. In fact, you are paid for every step of the sales process. Improving the quality or increasing the quantity of your contacts will increase your productivity.

The example of a 3:1 presentation/sale ratio is hypothetical. You can plug in your own numbers for number of contacts, presentations, sales, commissions, salary, and so on. Calculating your contact yield will show you exactly how you are paid for everything you do.

THE INITIAL-BENEFIT STATEMENT

Why should a prospect meet with you? She doesn't know who you are and may not be familiar with your company. Therefore, there has to be a way for you quickly to convey to her who you are and how you might be able to help. This has to be expressed in a way that shows you are not a traditional salesperson but a non-manipulative salesperson, who serves your clients as a consultant.

A telephone contact will be used as an example because it is so common. The first thing to do is tell your prospect who you are and what company you are with. This is obvious. What is not obvious is your next step. Traditional salespeople would launch into a canned pitch to tell the prospect how they can be of service. The traditional salesperson projects this kind of image: "Howdy, Mr. Prospect. If you'll just sit down and keep your mouth shut, I'll tell you what your problems are and how to solve them. If you'll sign this contract and write me a check, I'll implement the solution as well. I can do it all."

How do you feel about this salesperson? Have you ever been that type of salesperson? Most of us have.

The non-manipulative salesperson presents the possibility of help and gives some background as to why he is in a position to give it. He projects a better image to the prospect: "Quite frankly, Mrs. Brooks, there are some people I can help and some I can't help. The only way we're going to know which category you fit into is to spend a few minutes together. We'll talk about what you do and what I do and see if there is a common ground on which we can do business. At the end, if I think I can help you in any way, I'll tell you and ask for a little more time to learn even more about your situation. On the other hand, if there doesn't seem to be a need for my services, I'll tell you so and be on my way."

An initial-benefit statement would sound like this: "Mrs. Brooks, I've worked with many banks in the area and have shown them how to increase their bottom-line profits by decreasing their accounts-payable expenses. I'd like to spend a few minutes learning about your operation to see if you are one of those people I can help."

The purpose of the initial-benefit statement is immediately to show a prospect what the benefits would be. This will give them a reason to talk to you. It makes sense to tell your prospects up front rather than wait until you're halfway through the sales process. Most customers, regardless of their behavioral style, are benefit oriented. They may be concerned with cost and interested in features, but the bottom line is always benefits.

LETTERS

It is essential for a prospect to have seen or heard your name before you talk to her. This will prevent the prospect from saying, "Who?"

Instead, it will be, "Oh, yes, I received your letter recently." For this reason, letters are often a logical precursor to telephone calls and personal visits.

Letters serve well as introductions and can be even more effective if they include a third-party referral. Don't be afraid to be an honest name dropper; names are better than keys at opening doors. Letters can also be used to do the following:

Secure appointments. Long-distance appointments can be confirmed well in advance by letter.

Answer questions. Providing information or asking further questions of a customer costs less by mail.

Reach busy people. Doctors, company presidents, and other inaccessible people prefer letters. They often find it impossible to answer all their telephone calls.

Follow up on a sales call. It is helpful to summarize with a letter the key points agreed upon during your sales meeting. This will provide you and your customers with a written record of what transpired and show them you do business in a professional way. Thank-you letters also show professionalism.

Provide updates. A brief letter with enclosures will keep your customers informed of new developments in your field or company.

Stimulate business. Direct-mail pieces of promotional specials and introductory offers will increase sales.

Regardless of the purpose of the letter, it will strengthen trust, maintain interest, and keep the lines of communication open between you and your clients.

Personal Letters

Nine times out of ten, personal letters are the only way to go. They show you care enough to take the time to write, and it is this kind of personal attention that builds solid business relationships. If you cannot take the time to write a letter, dictate one and have it transcribed by a secretary. Another alternative is simply to jot down what you want to say and have a secretary write it for you.

Never follow up a sales call with a form letter. If you do, you might as well kiss the account good-bye. Form letters are only appropriate for promotional direct-mail pieces.

The art of concise letter writing is one that requires practice. To make the best impression possible, be sure to do the following:

Use good stationery. Your letter is an extension of you and your professional image. Use paper that looks and feels good.

Personalize your letters. Use your company's letterhead for all your letters and be sure to enclose your business card.

Type your letters. Unless they are very brief notes, handwritten letters look amateurish. If you don't have a typewriter, beg, borrow or steal one. If you can't type, then beg, borrow, or steal a secretary. Most cities have professional typing services. Use one if necessary. The small fee will be well worth it. Find one that has a computer so it can save the originals of all your personal letters and direct-mail pieces. In the future it will cost less to modify letters that are on the computer.

Break up the text. Write in short, well-focused paragraphs. Avoid long sentences and keep your ideas separate. Use one paragraph for each idea and get to the point quickly. Resist the temptation to socialize when writing to directors and thinkers. With relaters and socializers, however, it's all right to open the letters by asking them about their trip to Mallorca.

Use a strong introductory sentence. The reader should know the purpose of your letter after reading the first sentence. Give an initial-benefit statement. The rest should be supporting details.

When you write to prospects whom you have not met, the best letters are personal letters. Even though you do not know the prospect, your research should uncover enough information to form the basis of a letter. Include the following elements:

1. Use your prospect's name in the salutation and be sure you spell it correctly.
2. Identify yourself and your company.
3. Mention who referred you, if appropriate.

4. Make an initial-benefit statement that will capture your prospect's attention. For example: "Our new software program can increase billing speed on your computer by 20 to 30 percent."

5. Identify an area of probable interest that you discovered in your pre-call preparation.

6. Write in the language of your customer's industry. Use the vernacular your prospect uses daily. This will show you are knowledgeable in his field.

7. State one or two reasons for the customer to see you. Make the reasons relevant to the person's business. These reasons should be tied in to the benefit statement.

8. Include a brochure to increase interest.

9. Indicate when you will follow up with a telephone call.

10. Be brief. Your letter should be a maximum of one page.

Once you have composed your letter, give it to friends and family to read. Be open to their comments and prepared to rewrite it until you have achieved perfection.

Computers make correspondence infinitely easier than typewriters. If you do not own one and cannot have access to your company's computer, ask a professional word-processing firm about all their services. They will explain how their computers can combine mailing lists with your letters to produce sales letters that look personal.

Roy: In my company, we have the benefit of a complete computer system, so we have designed and stored direct-mail letters that are geared toward different personal styles. For example, in our business, we have found most media directors to be thinkers. The opening paragraph of that letter would appeal to a thinker. We do this even before we have met the person.

We also go a step further. We have four different colors of account-record sheets, each corresponding to a behavioral style, and our accounts are computerized and cross referenced by industry *and* behavioral style. This is really helpful for direct-mail campaigns.

After we've met the person and know her style, we use the color of the account-record sheet that is appropriate. When you're talking to that person on the telephone, you can look at her record sheet and immediately know how to ask questions that are in line with her style.

Inspired by Roy's clever ideas, the authors composed some sales letters to give you an idea of the way an opening paragraph can appeal to different personal styles.

Sample Letter to a Director

Dear Mrs. Johnson:

> **"Prescription without diagnosis is malpractice."**
> **—Dr. Tony Alessandra**

In business, as in medicine, we believe this is true. That is why I'd like to meet with you to learn about your business and help you find some creative ways to meet your goals.

I'll call you in a couple of days to set up an appointment for us to get together.

Sincerely,

Rick Barrera

P.S. I've enclosed a copy of our latest issue and thought the article on page 10 would be of interest to you.

Sample Letter to a Thinker

Dear Mr. Cognito:

> **Recent Research Shows:**
> **Four-Color Ads Increase Readership 45% More**
> **Than Black-and-White Ads**

We are the only four-color, business-to-business publication in the greater Newark area.

If you would like to learn more about how we can help increase your readership, enhance your image, and impact your bottom line, call me at 123-4567.

Sincerely,

Phillip S. Wexler

P.S. Surveys have also indicated that two-page spreads increased readership by 38 percent.*

*Source: *Analyzing Communication Trends,* a series of reports by Technical Publishing, a Dun & Bradstreet company.

Sample Letter to a Socializer

Dear Ms. Gregarious:

What do Xerox, IBM, and Mercedes Benz have in common?

They all use *Business Times of San Bernadino* to enhance their image and increase overall sales.

They've told us our targeted business-to-business publication is the most effective use of their advertising dollar.

If you would like to discuss how you can get these important benefits, please call me at 123-4567.

Sincerely,

Tony Alessandra

P.S. Our up-coming real estate issue may be of interest to you. It will be out the first week of December.

Sample Letter to a Relater

Dear Mr. Caresalot:

We started *Business Times* because we wanted to provide an efficient way for local businesses to communicate with one another. In addition, we want to make business better for everyone in Lower San Diego County.

Due to our extensive circulation and high pass-along readership, you will find our publication to be an excellent medium for advertising your products and services to the local business community. We will open doors for you every month with customers whom your sales team has not had time to see yet.

Each month your message can reach 8,000 business decision makers for a fraction of what you are currently paying your salespeople. Don't, however, get rid of your salespeople! You will need them to follow up on the leads your ad will generate.

I will be calling you in the next couple of days to see if you would like to discuss how you can get these and other benefits from working with us to make Lower San Diego County a better business community.

Sincerely,

Rick Barrera

P.S. Your salespeople will find doors open more easily when prospects have read your ad and are familiar with your business.

Tips for Better Letter Writing

When writing your letter, it's best to talk in terms of your prospect's interest rather than your own. One way to do this is with an "I" count. Read your letter and count the number of times you use the words *I, me, my,* or *mine.* You will be surprised at how often they show up. Rewrite the letter and focus on your prospect and his needs by using "you" and "your." Instead of saying, "I have a product that . . ." say, "You'll be interested in knowing that . . ."

It is important to avoid hype in your letters. Your sense of professionalism should tell you that enthusiasm, when carried to extremes, will come off as overzealous. Convey your enthusiasm in a low-key, meaningful way.

When critiquing your letter, ask yourself if it accomplished what you had planned. Is the purpose of the letter clear? Does it describe the product or service without giving too much information? It is important to pique your prospect's interest without giving enough details to allow him to jump to a conclusion.

Always keep a copy of your correspondence. This will help you document your progress with prospects. In addition, you can use the best letters for other contacts.

If you analyze the sample letters, you will discover how to write your letters:

1. In your salutation, use Mr., Mrs., or Ms. Take the time to find out whom you are writing to and the proper spelling of the person's names. Never write "Dear Sirs" or "To Whom It May Concern."

2. If there was a referral, the first paragraph reminds the prospect in a brief, simple style.

3. The second paragraph shows you did your homework and then gets to the point of the letter.

4. The third paragraph says something about the prospect's company and makes a brief, low-key benefit statement.

5. A meeting is suggested and a follow-up telephone call is mentioned.

6. Always include a brochure and promise to have more information when you meet.

Dictation

Many people find dictation to be a valuable time saver. Buy a pocket tape recorder and utilize your travel or waiting time. For example, after a sales call, you can dictate a thank-you letter for your secretary to type.

Dictation takes practice because you have to think in an organized way. Many people find it difficult to organize their thoughts and speak simultaneously. For this reason, you should write an outline first. The outline will incorporate all the key ideas in the exact order to be covered. Make notes on examples, prices, data, times, dates, and other details to be included. After you have outlined your letter completely, follow the outline and dictate slowly.

After your dictation, be sure to listen to what you have recorded. When the letter is transcribed, be prepared to edit and polish it. Letters must be written in proper English rather than the loose style most of us use when speaking.

Form Letters

The advantage of form letters is that they reach the maximum number of people in a minumum amount of time. The disadvantage is that they are impersonal and, therefore, not always appropriate. Form letters should be used only for large, direct-mail promotions. The following tips will help you write effective form letters:

1. The lead sentence must immediately draw the reader's attention.

2. The lead paragraph should be no more than two or three sentences.

3. The opening paragraphs should promise a benefit to the reader.

4. Fire your biggest gun first.

5. There should be a strong motivating benefit behind your proposition.

6. Arrange your thoughts in logical order.

7. Write in a believable style, avoid hyperboles.

8. Make it easy for the prospect to respond, that is, to order, call, or write for more information.

9. Include an order form and tie the text of the letter to it.

10. Write about your prospect, not about yourself or your company. Go through the letter and count "I s."

11. Give the letter a light, conversational tone.

12. Write simply, avoiding twenty-five-cent words and unfamiliar jargon.

13. Avoid beginning sentences with "a," "an," or "the."

14. Use active rather than passive verbs. For example, say "It rotates 360 degrees" instead of "It can be rotated 360 degrees.

15. Eliminate unnecessary "thats".

16. Keep paragraphs down to six lines.

17. Do not use underscoring, exclamation points, and capitalization for emphasis. Enthusiasm should be conveyed with words.

18. Get feedback from people who know good advertising copy. If this seems like a lot of work, be assured it will pay off handsomely. Anyone familiar with direct mail will tell you a well-written sales letter is worth a mint.

Computer Letters

Computers make correspondence today infinitely easier than in the old days of hunting and pecking on the typewriter. You only have to write your letter once and it can be used over and over again with only minor changes in the copy.

There is a creative way to use computers to help you plan ahead in your prospecting efforts. Write a letter that sounds personal but can be sent to virtually any prospect. Generate a month's worth of prospects and have a computer operator print out the letters in advance. You do not, however, want to mail all the letters on the same day. Spread the mailings out over the month. For example, let's say you have eighty prospects to contact; that's four per day, five days a week for four weeks. Print out the letters with the dates they will be mailed. Four letters would say March 1; the next four would say March 2 and so on. On the envelopes, instead of a stamp, pencil in the date the letters will be mailed.

When you start the month's mailings, put the stamps over the penciled date and mail them. In your tickler file, enter the information on those prospects to be called after the letters arrive. Allow enough time for the delivery plus a day or two before you follow up.

This system is good for everyone, even if you don't have a secretary. Hire a professional word processor and the increase in sales will more than pay for the expense. For an additional fee you could have the word-processing company mail the letters daily and provide you with a weekly or monthly report so you'll know whom to call and when.

After you have introduced yourself with a letter, the next logical step is to call your prospects.

THE TELEPHONE

From a cost-benefit standpoint, the telephone is your number one communication tool. This is especially true for reaching established customers in the B and C categories. Letters take time, materials, and postage. It has been estimated that the cost of sending a single letter is $5.00 to $10.00. It is even more expensive to call on a prospect in person. Face-to-face calls have been estimated to cost well over $250.00. Obviously, telephone calls cost significantly less than either visits or letters. At the same time, they are less personal than face-to-face calls but more personal than letters.

Being such a time and money saver, the telephone is well suited for reaching customers and prospects for scheduling appointments and answering and asking questions. The telephone requires communication skills that differ from those used in face-to-face contact. The skills you learn for effective telephone calling, however, will also improve your face-to-face interactions.

The primary disadvantage of the telephone is that you are limited to the verbal and vocal aspects of that mode of communication. For this reason, some salespeople find it difficult to relate to people over the telephone. To overcome this problem, create a mental image of the other person as you talk. If you do not know the prospect, imagine a close friend and speak in the relaxed, friendly way you normally would. Many salespeople find visualization improves their attitude significantly.

Your attitude is conveyed through your voice. If you are in a bad mood, your voice will reveal it. Many telephone sales offices use mirrors on their employees' desks to allow the salespeople to see themselves as they talk. Research has proven that smiling while you are talking will affect the person on the other end of the line. The listener can actually hear the difference in your voice when you smile.

Test Your Vocal Quality

The way that you sound on the telephone is an important factor in determining the outcome of the call. One valuable tool for improving the vocal quality is to record your conversations with a cassette recorder, using, if possible, a telephone adapter so that you can hear both sides of the conversation. Call a friend, tell her what you are doing, and either have a normal conversation or pretend she's a prospect. Afterward, listen to your voice and see what kind of impression you get. Are you confident? Do you talk too quickly? Do you give the other person time to answer your questions?

Save the tapes so you can compare them to the ones you will make after you have worked on improving your vocal quality. Listening to the old tapes will constantly remind you of the speech habits that need to be improved. If you cannot judge your vocal quality, ask a co-worker or friend to listen to the tapes and evaluate your voice control. Often an objective listener will hear things that you miss.

You will find it useful to refer back to the chapter on listening and feedback. The principles that apply to your voice over the telephone also apply to conversations in person. Listen to your enunciation. Are you easy to understand or do you mumble? Are you repeating phrases such as "you know" or "like"? Do you say "uh" before every new thought? All of these conversational idiosyncrasies cause distractions that ultimately dilute the potency of your message.

Eliminate Background Noise

Have you ever called someone and tried to have a conversation while airplanes were taking off and landing in the background on the other end of the line? If so, you know how irritating background noises can be. The distraction becomes even greater when the other person interrupts the conversation to shout at the planes to be quiet. You can overlook these things when talking to friends, but a business call should be free of all background noises.

In addition to being a distraction, background noises also reflect on you. If you make business calls when there is a lot of background noise, you are telling your customer that you don't care enough to eliminate distractions. Naturally, there are extenuating circumstances in which you must call from a telephone booth outside an airport, but routine business calls should be made where it is quiet. If not, your customers will infer that you are inconsiderate and unprofessional.

Be Organized

If you have a large number of telephone calls to make every week, it is an absolute necessity to make them in an organized fashion. The first step in being organized is to establish a time each day that you will devote exclusively to telephoning. During that time, complete all your calls. Not only will this habit develop self-discipline, it will also make the calling sessions easier as time goes by. Calling prospects and customers is like most things that take practice: the more you do it, the better you become.

During your calling sessions, it is important to maintain your momentum. When you have completed a call, don't stop to fill out your log or order forms. Make rough notes so you can quickly wrap up the call and maintain your momentum. Later you can go back to fill in the details.

When preparing for your calls it is important to have all the information at your fingertips. If you were to set aside an hour each day for calls and spend twenty minutes looking for telephone numbers, you would only be cheating yourself.

A useful item to have on hand before starting your calls is a calendar. It sounds awfully foolish if you have to say, "Hold on, let me get my calendar," every time you set an appointment. Whether you prefer a large appointment calendar or a pocket calendar is unimportant as long as you have it in front of you.

When planning your calls, it is helpful to categorize them by the objective of the call. For example, you might call to gather information, offer promotional sales, follow up a complaint, collect money, or set up an appointment. Make all the calls in one category at the same time. This will establish a "mind set" in which to operate. Making similar calls will help you maintain your momentum.

Another reason to categorize your calls is to determine the best time to call. Group them by the types of people to be called; different people are available at different times. Here are some suggestions on when to call:

Type of People	Best Time to Call
Engineers, chemists	4:00-5:00 P.M.
Clergymen	Anytime after Tuesday
Contractors, builders	Before 9:00 A.M. or after 5:00 P.M.
Dentists	Before 9:30 A.M.
Druggists	1:00-3:00 P.M.
Executives/business owners	After 10:30 A.M.
Housewives	11:00-12:00 P.M.; 2:00-4:30 P.M.
Attorneys	11:00 A.M.-2:00 P.M.
Physicians	9:00-11:00 A.M.; 1:00-3:00 P.M.; 7:00-9:00 P.M.
Professors, teachers	At home 7:00-9:00 P.M.

CPAs	Anytime except between January 15 and April 15
Publishers, printers	After 3:00 P.M.
Butchers, grocers	Before 9:00 A.M.; and between 1:00-2:30 P.M.

Monitor Your Calls

To improve any skill, you need a baseline to which you can compare your progress. To increase your effectiveness on the telephone, keep track of your calls. A telephone log will structure the data you should keep on each calling session. This log is not concerned with the individual accounts. It is a day-by-day tally of what happened with each call you made.

The importance of keeping a log can be seen in the analysis of the results. Let's say, for example, you chose a different time to make your calls every day for two weeks. At the end of that time, your log would show you which times were productive and which were not. If you found you had to call a customer an average of three times before getting through, you may be calling at the wrong time. If you find, however, you are getting through to your prospects but not getting results, you should analyze your telephone habits. Without a telephone log, however, you would not be able to see the patterns and analyze your performance.

Sample Telephone Log

Date	Company	Industry	Person to contact	Outcome of call
1.				
2.				
3.				

Observe Telephone Etiquette

Brevity. Value your prospect's time as much as or more than your own; make your calls as short as possible. This does not mean you should talk in shorthand, but don't waste time either. Remember, your call is an interruption. It may not be an irritating interruption, but you are breaking the flow of your client's activities. For this reason, always ask if your prospect is free to talk. If not, find out when you should call back. The idea is to have the prospect's full attention rather than partial, resentful attention.

Correct Information. Part of your homework before approaching a prospect is to find out exactly whom to call. This can be done by calling the prospect's company and asking a switchboard operator, secretary, or receptionist. The advantage of finding out directly is that you will hear how the person's name is pronounced. All too often you have to call a prospect whose last name is a tongue twister. It's embarassing to ask someone how to pronounce his or her name. It is even worse if you assume you know how to pronounce it and say it wrong. So make sure you find out how to pronounce it correctly and if it is preceded by Ms., Mrs., or Mr. Remember, names such as Sandy McDougal can belong to a man or a woman.

Working with Secretaries. Most traditional salespeople view secretaries as obstacles and try to get past them to the boss. Non-manipulative salespeople don't try to get past them; they work with secretaries to reach decision makers. Part of building a business relationship with a prospect is also to build a relationship with her secretary. If you treat secretaries with respect and view them as allies rather than adversaries, they will become part of your team. Consider the following tips when you approach an inaccessible executive:

- Find out a secretary's first name, write it down, and use it when you talk to her. People respond when you treat them as individuals rather than robots. If you are personable, you are more likely to get help reaching the boss. Feel free to ask for advice. Most secretaries will be honest and help you if they can.

- When you call, ask for the executive by first name. The secretary may assume you are a friend and put your call through without delay.

- Call when the switchboard is busy; the operator will be in a hurry to route your call. If you use the boss's first name, you may be connected directly.

- Call early in the morning, late at night, or during lunch, when the secretary is not answering the telephone. If you call during lunch, a receptionist who is not trained to screen calls may answer and put you through. If things are busy enough, the boss may answer the phone.

- When a secretary asks you questions, answer one question at a time in a polite manner. If you don't volunteer more information than you're asked for, the secretary has to keep asking questions. She may want to get rid of the call, especially if she is busy. Answering one question succinctly could be construed as rude, so be sure you are polite, as in this example:

> **Secretary:** Ms. Pratt's Office.
>
> **Salesperson:** Hello. May I speak to Jennifer please.
>
> **Secretary:** May I ask who's calling?
>
> **Salesperson:** Of course. This is Tom Peterson.
>
> **Secretary:** And what company are you with?
>
> **Salesperson:** I'm with Tom Peterson and Associates.
>
> **Secretary:** And may I ask what this is regarding?
>
> **Salesperson:** Certainly. It's regarding a letter I sent her. She's expecting my call.

There is nothing dishonest about saying the boss is expecting your call. After all, you did send a letter and say you would be calling.

- If you are asked if the boss is expecting your call, say yes because this will always be true if you have written first.

- Often secretaries will say, "If you tell me the nature of your call, I'll ask Ms. Pratt if she wants to take it." Give a brief benefit statement, as for example, "I've been working with some of the hotels in the area such as the Sheraton, Westin, and Loews. We've been presenting a program that has been giving them a fifteenfold return on their investment within thirty days. Given our incredible returns, I wanted to talk to Ms. Pratt and see if she might be interested in exploring the option with me." If you have followed the guidelines above and treated the secretary courteously, she will go to bat for you.

- Ask for advice. If you've called several times, left your name, developed a telephone relationship with the secretary, and still have gotten nowhere, ask her, "When would be a good time to reach Ms. Pratt?" Usually you will be told the best time or told it is impossible to reach her.

- Be persistent without being a nuisance.

Use Creativity When Necessary

Unfortunately, there will be times when you just cannot get your foot in the door. This is the time to be creative. Find out what the prospect likes and capitalize on it. Perhaps she is a chocolate lover; do something creative with chocolate. Dip yourself in chocolate and show up at her door! Your prospect may be a golfer; use golf as a springboard.

One salesperson sent a prospect a box, in which was a helium balloon tied to a shoe. On the string was a note that said, "Now that I've got my foot in the door, I'd like to make an appointment to get the rest of me in." The prospect enjoyed the creative approach and granted the appointment.

Another creative approach is to send a letter to the prospect. In the envelope, put a check made out for $50 or $100 to the prospect's favorite charity. (You can ask her secretary about this.) The check is not signed. In your cover letter, say something to the effect of, ". . . enclosed is a check made out to your favorite charity. You'll notice it has not been signed. If you will give me fifteen minutes of your time to see if we have a basis for doing business, I will be happy to sign the check at the end of our meeting, regardless of the outcome."

Another tack is to go the prospect's office to set up an appointment. If you have developed a rapport with the secretary and show up in person, if the boss is in, she may let you talk to him briefly to set up an appointment. As a condition upon which she will let you in, promise to only take a minute of his time. If you make such a promise, no matter what happens, keep your word.

Announce Long-Distance Calls

When calling long distance, it is highly advisable to tell the secretary you are doing so. Most people give long-distance calls a higher priority. If someone says, "Do you mind if I put you on hold?" be careful. Some people are not in the habit of checking back with the caller every thirty seconds to make sure you still have vital signs. Your best bet is to tell the secretary you can remain on hold only for a short time; otherwise you will have to hang up.

The way you handle long-distance calls when you answer the telephone reflects on you and your company. If you have a hold button on your telephone and are in the habit of using it, be sensitive to your caller. Professionalism dictates that you check back with your caller every thirty seconds to give some feedback as to what is happening on your end of the line.

Be Aware of the Importance of Language

Over the telephone, a prospect only has your words from which to get your message; therefore, your choice of words by telephone is even more important than when you meet in person. Face to face, if there is any doubt as to your meaning, you can sense it from the person's nonverbal feedback. Over the telephone, however, you may confuse your prospect and never know it.

Be careful what you say and how you say it. For example, a common phrase is, "Let me ask you a question." It may be a subtle distinction, but this is a command, not a question. A command immediately puts someone on the defensive. A better way to say this is, "May I ask you a question?" or "Do you mind if I ask you a couple of questions so I may better understand your situation?" This shows you are respectful of the person's time and autonomy.

In addition to choosing your words carefully, you should also choose your attitude carefully. Be natural. Strike a balance between sounding overly friendly or too cautious. Talking on the telephone is just like making a personal sales call; you do your best when you are relaxed, courteous, and genuine.

Listen Effectively

Effective listening is required on the telephone as well as in person. To be an active listener on the telephone requires more effort than it does in person, so concentrate.

When talking to a prospect, ask as many open-ended questions as possible. Listen to what is being said, not just to the words being spoken. When pauses occur, try not to interrupt unless you sense the prospect is finished. Reinforce the prospect's participation by giving feedback. A simple "Yes" or "I see" will often suffice. Make sure you understand what the prospect is saying and avoid jumping to conclusions. Toward the end of the call, arrange for the next call, either in person or by telephone and express your gratitude for the person's time.

Let the Prospect Hang Up First

Have you ever concluded a conversation with someone and just as he was hanging up, you thought of one more thing to say? To avoid cutting off your prospect's thoughts, it is a good practice to let the prospect hang up first, even though the general rule is for the caller to hang up first. Stay on the telephone during the silence until you finally hear the click on the other end.

Identify Yourself When Answering the Telephone

When you answer the telephone in the office, immediately identify your company and department and give your name. If you are self-employed and have an office at home, answer by stating your name. Some people like to say, "Sylvia Jones" or "Sylvia Jones speaking."

Using the telephone wisely gives you control over your sales career. When you call for appointments and orders, you save time and money and increase the profitability of the account. You also increase your control of time and manage your day more effectively. The telephone is such an integral part of our lives it is hard to imagine how people conducted business before its invention.

IN-PERSON MEETINGS

The discussion so far has covered meeting a prospect by mail and over the telephone. The discussion on in-person meetings that follows is much briefer than the other two but not because it is less important. In fact, it is more important. However, the majority of this book addresses, either directly or indirectly, meeting the prospect in person. The key points that follow give a brief overview of procedure and are covered in more detail in appropriate chapters.

There is nothing like meeting someone in person. Telephone conversations and letters reveal only an inkling of someone's personality. Given that sales is such a personal business, it is no wonder the most highly valued form of contact is in person.

The easiest personal call is the one made possible by a referral or previous introduction. Traditional salespeople often experience "call reluctance" before calling on a prospect whom they have never met. This is not a problem for non-manipulative salespeople because they have done their homework, talked to the prospect, and secured an appointment. The non-manipulative approach decreases the tension for both the buyer and the seller.

In-person meetings can be made for any number of reasons: to introduce yourself to the prospect and gather information, to make a presentation, to confirm the sale, or to assure customer satisfaction. After the business relationship has been established, personal calls become easier. For this reason, the discussion will center on the introductory call.

The introductory call is designed to be an information-gathering meeting for you and your prospect. Before business can be transacted, both of you need to know and trust each other. Basically, the procedure is as follows:

Enter and introduce yourself. Be aware of your image, body language, and eye contact. Your prospect is sizing you up (on strictly superficial terms) to determine if you are the type of person he likes to do business with. By the same token, you should look for clues to his behavioral style. Observe the office, its decor, and his mannerisms and nonverbal behavior.

Establish the purpose of your call. Early in the meeting, make it clear why you are there, and when the time seems right, seek permission to ask some questions. Remember that time is money, so be careful how you spend your prospect's time. Imagine yourself as having a meter running during the meeting; the more time you spend with your prospect, the more it will cost both of you. Be sure you are quick and efficient with directors and thinkers. You can take more time with socializers, and relaters, unless they are in a hurry.

When setting up an apointment with a director or thinker, impress upon him the fact that you are aware that the person is busy. Say you will only need about twenty minutes of his time and honor that time limit. There is only one condition in which you can stay longer than promised—when you are asked. Otherwise, leave on time. If the meeting is supposed to last twenty minutes, start wrapping things up after seventeen minutes. Your credibility rests, in part, on your ability to keep your word. To be punctual in leaving, you should consider buying a watch with a timer. If you have to adjourn a meeting before you've asked all of your questions, ask your prospect when another meeting would be possible. It is better to come back than to overstay your welcome.

Uncover needs. After you have established the reason for the call and created some interest, you need a reason to continue. Explore your prospect's business situation by asking questions. This is best accomplished by first asking permission to inquire into his business and then using questions that require narrative answers. At the same time, listen actively and begin to develop trust. To review the art of questioning, reread chapter 4. The next chapter will cover the studying phase of the sale.

Propose a solution. Many times a sale will require a number of calls before a solution can be proposed and the sale confirmed. You may have to return for more information gathering or fact-finding, or your prospect may need time to think about your product. There are situations, however, in which a presentation can be given during the first meeting. Chapters 16 and 17 discuss the proposing and confirming phases of sale.

As stated time and again, it is the relationship that determines whether two people will want to do business together. The meeting phase, in turn, makes or breaks the relationship. It is at this point in the sales process that all your skills come together to create an impression.

The first few minutes with a prospect can forge the nature of a business relationship and literally determine your degree of success in this business.

8

Studying

EACH PROSPECT has a unique situation that requires study before you can make a judgment and recommend a solution. Studying a prospect's business may require research and repeated trips to his office, factory, or home.

PROBLEM SOLVING VS. OPPORTUNITY SEEKING

It is important to study a prospect's business with an open mind, that is, don't look solely for problems. Too many salespeople troubleshoot, as if they can only fix problems. There is another way to match the services or products of your company with the needs of the prospects. Look for opportunities; find niches that your prospect may not have been aware of. Perhaps your prospect would welcome a new system or an introduction to a new market. Whatever you have to offer, there is always more than the problem-solving approach to be taken.

A relationship with a prospect or client is not unlike a relationship with the family doctor. There are many reasons you might visit your doctor. One reason is your concern about a specific problem.

For example, you might have a simple rash. You would go and tell him about it, and after a quick look he would prescribe some ointment, and you'd be on your way again.

This also happens in sales. One day you get a telephone call from a prospect who knows exactly what she needs. She is out of printed carbonless forms and was not satisfied with her former printer. You meet with her and fill the order. It's a quick diagnosis and an easy treatment.

Another hypothetical reason to see your doctor is for general malaise. You go in and say you feel weak in the knees, unable to eat, and more absent-minded than usual. He asks you if you are in love. If your answer is no, he will have to spend time figuring out what your problem is.

Again, this happens in sales. You stop by a client's store and talk for a while. She complains about a lack of sales but doesn't know what to do about it. You listen, ask questions, and after some consideration, recommend an outdoor promotional device such as your company's multicolored hot-air balloon. She tries it, it works, and everyone is happy.

A third reason to see your doctor is for a yearly physical. You feel fine, but you want to make sure you are in good health. The doctor spends time asking questions, probing, taking blood, and so on. At the end of the exam, you are either given a clean bill of health or told to go on a diet. It is also possible for your doctor to find a major problem that you were unaware of. For example, your cholesterol level or blood pressure may be too high. He would warn you and thus head off a serious problem. From your point of view, the best medicine is preventive medicine.

One more possibility—after the physical your doctor may pronounce you to be in good health but may have suggestions as to how you could be healthier. He may commend you for exercising regularly and suggest a way for you to fine tune your workout. So even though nothing was wrong, you still derived some benefits from the visit.

The same principle applies to your clients. Give each one an annual physical. Make an appointment to stop by to chat and ask some questions. You may discover an opportunity that has arisen or a need gap that has reopened.

Looking for opportunities is one level above the problem-solving approach to selling. By looking for areas of positive overlap, the non-manipulative salesperson uses all her resources to find a match between what she does and what the client does. The match may be subtle, but that is one reason why studying is so important in non-manipulative selling.

Traditional salespeople are not, for the most part, opportunity seekers. They see themselves as problem solvers and problem creators. They *think* they can create needs because they have a solution that needs a problem in order to be saleable. This is prescription without diagnosis. *Needs exist, however; they are not created.*

By narrowing their focus and only looking for problems, traditional salespeople shortchange their customers. Non-manipulative salespeople, by contrast, look for both problems and opportunities by focusing on the prospect's present situation and future potential.

ASSESSING SITUATION AND GOALS

To determine if your product or service will be of any value to your prospect, you must know his current situation, all of its attendant problems, the potential of the business, and his goals and objectives. For example, if your prospect has a very unorganized payroll but no desire to be more organized, there is no sense in trying to sell efficiency in the beginning. Note the phrase, "in the beginning." At first you should accept your prospect's assessment of his situation as valid and objective. As you develop your relationship, you will be in the position to bring up new ideas that he might not have previously addressed. When you have a strong relationship, you can mention the unorganized payroll and show him a way to save time and money. Having confidence in your expertise at that point, the prospect will be open to your suggestions.

Since you need to know about the prospect's business situation and goals, which should you explore first? At first glance, it may appear the order is unimportant. That is not the case. Consider the fact that the current situation deals with something concrete, the present. Goals and objectives deal with something abstract, the future. Different behavioral styles prefer talking about different things. For example, a socializer is a dreamer, so your discussion would first revolve around his goals for the person and his business. After you have completely talked about the socializer's vision of the future, you can then move on to the present situation. Gentle, effective questioning will lead the way to discussing the socializer's reality-based, task-oriented goals. A more in-depth discussion of selling by behavioral style will appear in chapter 12.

One of the primary reasons for the study phase is to give you a picture of the *actual* conditions versus the *desired* conditions. Often prospects think their goals are being accomplished when, in reality, they are not. They are too close to the situation to see it objectively. After you have established a good working relationship, it is your job as a consultant to analyze the situation and point out opportunities your prospect may be missing.

After analyzing a prospect's business, if you find his need gap to be small (see figure 8.1), then your product or service may offer little or no improvement. In this situation, your advice would be not to buy. When this happens, wrap up the call so you will not waste either your time or the prospect's. You might conclude by saying something like, "Mr. Jones, based on what we've discussed, it looks as if I can't offer you a way to improve your sales. If in the next six months, however, you find your sales do not grow by more than 5 percent (or some other condition), we would have a basis for doing business. Do you mind if I keep in touch to see how your sales are progressing?"

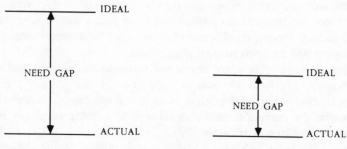

FIGURE 8.1

When you terminate a call in this manner, your prospect will remain open to future contacts because you did not try to sell him something he didn't need. You have created good will, which will not go unrewarded in one form or another in the future. Place that prospect's name on a follow-up list and call in six months. When you reach the prospect, ask how things are in general and then ask questions to see if those specific conditions have changed. If they have not, ask if you can call back again in six months. If they have, get together and look at the situation again. At this point, you will already have established a relationship, which will be an asset, and you will be able to pick up from where you left off.

In the majority of cases, after analyzing your prospect's need gap, you will find you *can* be of service.

TOPICS TO STUDY

Part of pre-call planning involves establishing a call objective. It can range from confirming the sale to simply introducing yourself and gathering some information. There will be times when it will be appropriate to simply establish the relationship without discussing business. Barry Woolf, the Northeast Sales Manager for Walsworth Publishing, learned this lesson a long time ago:

Barry: I was introduced to a prospect who immediately informed me that he had been happily working with one of my competitors for "more than six years" and was not prepared to look for a new supplier. I thought to myself, "Why not just try out what I learned in NMS and just make friends with this fellow." I began by easing the tension with a humorous remark about him not feeling threatened by me since I wasn't going to try to sell him. He relaxed immediately and we spent some time getting to know each other. In fact, he was a relater and before long we were confiding in one another. That first meeting lasted over two hours. He was "very loyal" to his old supplier, he told me during our first meeting, and I believe him even to this day; after all, he's now been a loyal customer of mine for more than twelve years!

The more information you seek from a prospect, the more you will need an outline of topics to be covered or a list of questions to be asked. Many salespeople think it looks amateurish to use a list of questions. On the contrary, it is very professional to have done your homework and have a list. It is also professional to take notes during the meeting. You can only be of service to your customer if you have the facts straight.

Every prospect will be different, but there are common areas to explore with all of them. Basically, you want to find out where the prospect stands in terms of the benefits your product or service can offer. You should also find out where he would like his business to be and what is keeping it from reaching that point. For example, if you sell advertising space in a publication, you would find out how much exposure your prospect is getting at present, how much he would ideally like to have, and what is preventing him from achieving that goal.

Uncovering a need gap requires you to delve into many aspects of the prospect's business: who the decision makers are, what the decision-making criteria are, how the prospect's thoughts and feelings enter into the decision-making equation, and so on.

Psychological Dynamics

In analyzing the current situation, consider the psychological dynamics of the sale. There are many reasons why people buy and most of them have nothing to do with business needs. This is something you should be aware of and look for in your clients' thinking. A psychological need can be just as strong as a concrete business need. There is nothing wrong with a customer wanting to buy for seemingly "superficial" reasons, but you must be certain your product or service will satisfy those reasons. Some of the emotional reasons people buy are as follows:

Prestige. People buy in order to gain distinction from others or the admiration of others. We see this every day in the form of conspicuous homes, automobiles, club memberships, clothes, and restaurants.

Love. People buy things to express their feelings, to protect or share with someone they love. Everything from diamond rings to smoke alarms can be bought from the motive of love.

Imitation. By nature, people are imitators. This is not entirely bad, especially if they are imitating positive qualities. In sales, this motive can work well when one company buys to imitate the success of a competitor.

Fear. Fear is a very strong, albeit subtle, emotion in sales. Physical fears would be those concerning loss of health, property, life, or freedom. For these reasons people buy health and life insurance, security systems, diet books, and so on. Psychological fears include old age, loss of self-esteem, poverty, criticism, loss of love, unemployment, or lack of fulfillment. These fears are often assuaged with how-to books, vitamins, investment plans, and psychotherapy, to name a few.

Variety. People like new things, even if the things are only slightly different from what they already have. Proof of this lies in the fashion industry. It thrives on the fact that people tire of their clothes after wearing them twice, especially if they have to be ironed!

Your Prospect's Feelings and Thoughts

How your prospect thinks and feels about her situation is something you should know. If she is ambivalent about spending money, take this into consideration. It is better to postpone a sale than to confirm it only to have it canceled later. You want your prospect to be happy with her purchase. This may require your creating some excitement in the prospect, which you can do by learning as much as you can about her situation, analyzing it, and then presenting solutions. Once the prospect sees the possibilities, she may become enthusiastic about your product or service.

You also want to learn what your prospect's feelings are toward you and your company. Her perceptions will undoubtedly color her feelings about doing business with you. If the prospect is part of a large corporation and sees you as a "Mom and Pop" business, she may not trust your company with her business. If the prospect is a small business and sees you as a conglomerate, she may feel a lack of personal service. There are all kinds of combinations and possibilities. Your knowledge of what the prospect thinks and feels will enable you to assure her that all will be well if she chooses to do business with you.

Key Decision Makers and the Buying Process

Simply ask, "Who, in addition to yourself, will be involved in the decision-making process?" Another way to ask is, "Could you describe the decision-making process for me?" Both of these questions allow the person to include himself in the process, whether he is officially part of it or not. In this way, you protect your prospect's self-respect. His answer will dictate the most efficient approach for penetrating the company.

In addition to the one seller-one buyer approach to selling, there are three other possibilities. A team approach would use several of your people to sell to one person in the prospect's company. For example, on your sales team you may have someone who is very strong on the technical details of the product, someone else who is an applications expert, and a third person who is the financial wizard. The prospect may want to meet with all of these people in order to get a different perspective from each.

There will be times when you will use a multifaceted team approach to sell a company. There may be three decision makers in three different departments: one in accounting, one in engineering, and the third the president of the firm. Each will be consulted by a different player on your team. You play the role of "quarterback."

The third type of sales situation is the multifaceted approach. You are the only salesperson who calls on the account, but you have to meet with several facets of the company such as the president, the purchasing agent, and the engineer. This requires you to be sharp in every aspect of your product, its application, and its design.

An important aspect of the multifaceted sale is positioning. Most salespeople try to go right to the top of a corporation to talk to the number one decision maker. This is often difficult. If you are trying to penetrate a company and you know you will have to meet with several people within the organization, don't go straight to the top. The president relies on other people for information. First, position yourself with the engineer, then with someone else, perhaps the purchasing agent, then again with someone in the accounting department (the people to contact will vary from situation to situation). After you have established relationships with these "lower" decision makers, you are in a strong position to go to the president. The people within the company whom you have already met will become a part of your sales team. They will be on your side.

When you penetrate a company in this way, it is essential to analyze the roles of the different people in the decision-making process. Some of these roles will overlap, but for the most part, they will be divided into six types:

The Initiator. This is the person who first suggests or thinks of buying a particular product or service.

The Gatekeeper. This is a person, usually a secretary or receptionist, who has control over the accessibility of someone you wish to speak to or see.

The Influencer. This person is a member of the decision-making process whose opinion or advice is heavily weighed in the final decision.

The Decision Maker. Obviously, this person is responsible for the ultimate decision of what to buy, how many, when, and from whom.

The Buyer. This is the person who actually makes the purchase.

The User. The user is the consumer or person who is employing the product or service regularly.

Knowing the people who play these roles will help you plan an effective strategy for penetrating the company. You can find out who they are by asking noncompetitive salespeople and secretaries and by using the means discussed in chapter 6.

Buying Urgency

In your information gathering and fact-finding, it may be important for you to know how quickly a prospect will want to act if the sale is confirmed. Knowledge of the time factor gives you a lot of insight. A prospect who recognizes a need but is in no hurry to change may be doing one of two things: either taking bids from competitors or gathering as much information as possible. It will be important for you to know which.

The urgency of the purchase will also affect your ability to deliver what you promise. If there is some doubt as to the speed with which you can deliver, you will have to be a liaison between your prospect and your company. Go back to your company and see if you can convince them to rush the order if it comes through. This difficult balancing act is part of being a consultant representing the desires and limitations of two parties. It is known as upstream and downstream selling. An example is seen in the insurance industry. An insurance salesperson has to sell you first and then go back to the company and sell them on your being a safe bet to insure.

Politics

Everyone knows that having connections is stronger than having knowledge, talent, and every other lofty virtue deserving of recognition. That's life. If you can't fight it, work with it. In the sales situation, ascertain what the politics are and how you will have to work with them. Part of this is finding out who the key decision makers are and what criteria they are using.

Another aspect of politics is loyalty and nepotism. You may run across a situation in which a prospect's nephew presently supplies a similar product to yours, immediately making you the underdog in the contest. If you hope to pick up the account, you will have to look for several good reasons why the prospect should buy from you instead of the nephew. You will have to take each area (pricing, quality, service, for example), analyze how you compare to your competitor, and uncover some strong selling points in your favor. It is possible that the prospect will be disillusioned with the nephew and willing to give the business to someone else. They may, however, lack the data needed to justify the switch. Your studying and uncovering the nephew's weak points could provide the ammunition the prospect needs to make the change.

When you discover a prospect who is loyal to one supplier, there is another tack to take. Talk to the prospect, giving all the information he needs to know about you and your product, as if he were going to give you an order. Say that the reason you want to go quickly through the motions of the sale is so he will know you are in the wings if something happens to the present vendor. You might also convince him that it is not a good idea to be dependent on one supplier. It would be in his best interest to give you 5 percent of the business as a way to become familiar with your company and to keep you ready to take up the slack if something should happen to the other source. By becoming his secondary source, you are getting your foot in the door and opening up the possibility of more business in the future.

Negative Past Experiences

There are few sales situations as difficult as confronting a prospect who has a chip on his shoulder from a past injustice. The best thing to do is listen to the client and assure him you will do everything in your power to see that the bad experience is rectified and never repeated.

If the customer's gripe is about your company, you have to be very diplomatic. Simply ask, "What happened?" and then take cover. Let the customer "dump his bucket." Listen and be empathic. You may feel as if you just started World War III, but when it's over your customer will feel much better. He may have been saving up anger for twenty years, just waiting to vent it on someone from your company. Whatever you do, *do not defend* your company against the specifics of his complaint. Instead, defend your company in general by saying things like, "I'm really surprised to hear this; my company is normally very good in this area."

After you have listened to the complaint, it is essential that you rectify the situation. Say something to the effect of, "Before we go any further, I want to make this right with you. What can I do to make you feel this injustice has been cleared up?" Remember: focus on *what* can be done to resolve the problem, not *why* it happened.

This exact scenario happened to a salesperson the authors know. When the customer finished his tirade the salesperson took out his checkbook and said, "My company owes you a $200 credit and I want to be the one to give it to you." He wrote out a personal check and gave it to the customer. The relationship was immediately patched up, and the salesperson went on to write an order for thousands of dollars. His commission on the sale more than covered the $200 reimbursement.

Product Specifications

If you are selling a technical product or service, you will have to be concerned with specifications. This is a fact of life for many businesses. Products or services that are custom-made for a client will require you to gather data on specifications.

These types of products sometimes need to be certified, approved, or endorsed by a third party. It is important for you to know this for two reasons. First, the approval may take a lot of time or red tape. Knowing this will help you fit this account's lag time into your overall plans. Second, this approval or certification may affect the chances of the sale being confirmed at all. For example, on the one hand, if you know your product could not be approved by a regulatory agency, you can stop pursuing an account that requires that. On the other hand, if the product has been approved or certified already, you can save time by providing proof of this and obviating the need to repeat the procedure.

Knowing the prospect's specification needs will also help you judge other things. For example, if a prospect needs a large quantity of a certain color or size of product, the manufacturer may have to make a special run to accommodate him. This will certainly affect the delivery time and possibly the price. These are things you have to know. The decision to buy may be based on these details.

Budgetary Constraints

In qualifying a prospect, you must establish their credit and buying power. As thorough as your studying may have been, it is entirely possible that the prospect's financial health has changed. This is an area in which you will have to question your prospect in a subtle, nonthreatening way. As mentioned earlier, it is not wise immediately to bring up the subject of money. Ease into it when it becomes relevant.

Every salesperson has had the experience of dealing with someone who said he was interested but claimed to have no money in the budget. This presents a situation in which you have to use your best judgment to determine your prospect's truthfulness. Granted, in some cases, the budget simply is not adequate. In the vast majority of cases, however, if a prospect likes your product or service, they are usually able to find the money to purchase it. If they do not like you or your product, there could be millions of dollars in the budget, but none of it would find its way to you.

"No money in the budget" at this stage of the sales process is often a defense mechanism. It is a sign that the *relationship* is not right. This is where you must determine if the monetary problem is real or a smoke screen. If it is a smoke screen, you need to work on developing the relationship. The bottom line is always: Does this person want to do business with me (money and other details aside)? In the sales process, it is important to get a commitment to your proposed solution before working out the monetary details. Too many salespeople try to work out the details before their prospect is committed to the solution. You must work the other way around.

Of course, there are situations in which a prospect is committed to your solution but has financial problems. In fact, he may mention the lack of funds at the beginning of the call. You should acknowledge that "money is tight for everyone, but alternatives do exist." One alternative is to see if the product can be presold for next year. Another option is to suggest breaking down the solution into smaller increments, thereby making the payments smaller and more manageable.

Another way to ease a prospect's budgetary concerns is to have him or her take money from one department's budget and put it in another. For example, imagine a company that has a huge advertising budget and a relatively small training budget. If you were trying to sell them a training program to improve their customer service, you could use the following perspective: "What is the point of advertising? Answer: To bring in customer inquiries. What happens if your customer-service personnel lose half of your prospects because of their poor attitude, lack of knowledge, and so on? Answer: You've wasted your advertising dollars. It makes sense, therefore, to take some of the money you are spending in advertising and spend it on customer service. That way you can capitalize on the success of your advertising campaign."

This principle applies to your company as well as to your customers'. It is essential to keep the back door closed while opening the front door as wide as possible. In other words, customer service prevents the loss of business (out the back door), while advertising brings more in (through the front door). In the same way that you are trying to become a secondary source for your prospects, your competitors are trying to become secondary sources for your clients. It is the objective of your customer-service department and your efforts in the assuring phase to keep customers from slipping out the back door. *Remember: It costs far less money, time, and effort to keep a good customer than to find a new customer.*

NEEDS SUMMARY

When you meet with your prospect to discuss various need gaps, present her with a well-organized and well-documented needs summary. The summary will give your view of her situation as it is now and as she would ideally like it to be. You are, in essence, defining the need gap for her.

When you have finished conveying your observations, ask if she agrees with your evaluation of her business. If you have been communicating well, there should be no discrepancy. You may want to state this as, "Do you agree with my observations of the problems you would like to solve?" On a more positive note, "Would you agree that these are the opportunities you are seeking?"

In your needs summary, delineate those problems you can help her with, which ones seem relatively unimportant, and which ones you cannot help her with. Keep in mind that it is always your option to seek other sources to help with those problems you cannot remedy directly.

There are times when you uncover many problems. If you over-sell your prospect, that is, try to solve all the problems with one gigantic solution, you run the risk of scaring him off and losing everything. The best tack is to prioritize the problems and address them one at a time. Obtain a commitment and implement the solution; then, after you have proven your ability as a consultant, go back and address the other problems.

ESTABLISH SUCCESS CRITERIA

After you and your prospect have agreed on his needs, ask him this question, "From your perspective, if you were to look back at the purchase six months from now, what are the criteria you would use to judge the success of our solution?"

The reason to ask this question is to give you a concrete basis on which to measure the efficacy of your product or service after the sale. To track performance accurately, you need to have success criteria that are realistic, specific, and measurable.

When you and your client have agreed on the success criteria, put them in writing and give your prospect a copy. If you and your prospect cannot agree on the success criteria, the study phase is not over yet. Continue to discuss the issues until there is clarification and agreement.

Occasionally you will run across a prospect who has unrealistic expectations. This is usually due to ignorance, so all you have to do is enlighten him. If his lack of realism is due to monetary constraints, work out a creative financing plan. If, after much discussion, the two of you still cannot agree, then split the goals in half; agree on some and hold off on the others. If you do this during the proposing phase, you will have to make two proposals: one that is an answer to the agreed-upon success criteria and one that solves the unrealistic expectations. Since the latter proposal will be way out of the prospect's price range, he may sober up to reality or dig deeper to find the money for the higher-priced solution.

ONE-CALL VS. MULTIPLE-CALL SALES

There will be some sales calls in which the entire sales process can be accomplished in one visit; others require extensive research and many sales calls. The one-call sale is possible for simple products and services that don't require long sales cycles. This way of selling should not be construed as contrary to the principles of non-manipulative selling. On the contrary, the steps of the sale and the integrity of the salesperson are the same; only the sales cycle is shortened.

During a one-call sale, it is absolutely necessary to do all the information gathering and fact-finding before giving a presentation. In addition, a bridge needs to be inserted between the studying phase and the proposal phase. That bridge is the needs summary and the establishment of success criteria.

Keep in mind that not all products lend themselves to one-call sales. It is all right to come back another time to give your proposal. Don't be impulsive; be patient. You might end a sales call by giving a needs summary and discussing the success criteria and then saying, "I'd like to go back to my company to discuss your situation with some people so we can determine whether we can help you. If we think we can, may I call you for another appointment to propose a solution to your problems?"

The study phase, perhaps more than any other step in the selling process, separates the pros from the amateurs. It is the trademark of the non-manipulative salesperson. The considerable time spent at this point of the sale will result in better customers, quicker confirmations of the sale, more vertical account penetration, and infinitely more repeat business. It is the groundwork on which you establish those long-term business relationships that will someday evolve into annuities for you . . . for life.

9

Proposing

IN THE STUDYING PHASE of the sale, you uncovered your prospect's need gap, and the two of you agreed upon the problems to be addressed. The proposing phase is the point at which you and your prospect mutually close his need gap. It is a process of taking your prospect's ideas and combining them with your ideas to arrive at a solution that makes sense to both of you. To a non-manipulative salesperson, the presentation is not a pitch; it is give-and-take exchange.

The give-and-take exchange can be thought of as an opportunity to "switch heads" with your prospect. Imagine saying this to your customer: "If you and I could switch heads, that is, if you could know what I know about my product and if I could know what you know about your business, assuming we both have the best products, where would you buy what I sell? The answer is, from me. And similarly, I would buy from you." The goal is an exchange of information that will allow you fully to understand your client's business and him to know as much as possible about your product or service.

The primary roadblock to such a thorough exchange of information is time. There simply is not enough of it. So keep in mind the three Ts of information exchange: Time, Trust, and Tension. If you decrease tension and build trust, the prospect will want to spend more time with you.

The goal of the proposing phase is to match a customized package of solutions to a specific package of your prospect's needs. The style with which you propose these solutions should be determined by the behavioral style of your prospect. The different ways of proposing to directors, socializers, relaters, and thinkers will be discussed in chapter 12, "Selling by Style." For now, it is safe to generalize and recommend that you don't offer several solutions at once, just the best one you have devised given the information you gathered during the study phase. Have other options available, but, in most cases, you will confuse the issue by offering them at the outset.

When you propose your solutions, relate them to the success criteria agreed upon in the study phase and explain how each one will work. In the beginning of your proposal, review the points agreed upon in the last meeting and get feedback to be sure your prospect is still in agreement.

The sales presentation in non-manipulative selling is not the slick, razzle-dazzle approach that traditional salespeople use. Instead it is a well-researched, customized presentation of realistic solutions to the prospect's need gap. Every presentation is different and there are several types commonly used.

THE CANNED PRESENTATION

A memorized or canned presentation is rarely, if ever, used by non-manipulative salespeople. By nature, canned presentations are generalizations that do not take into consideration the prospect's unique situation. Canned presentations are used by inexperienced, traditional salespeople for selling familiar products that everyone uses, such as newspapers, pens, light bulbs, and so on.

The only situation in which a non-manipulative salesperson would use a canned presentation would be for brief segments of the presentation in which precise data or technical information has to be accurately disseminated. If this is the situation, a written document with the technical specifications or data could be given to the prospect while you discuss it.

The non-manipulative approach is a flexible one in which the client's needs are always considered. A canned presentation does not lend itself to customized solutions and a give-and-take atmosphere during the proposal.

THE OUTLINED PRESENTATION

The outline that follows is the best approach to the presentation for non-manipulative salespeople. It makes the most sense to take all the success criteria and need gaps and address them one by one, presenting the solutions as you go along.

The advantage of the outlined presentation is that it allows flexibility and organization. With a written outline in front of you, there is no fear of forgetting major points if you digress or are interrupted. You can spend as much or as little time as appropriate in each area of the presentation, depending on the client's needs.

The outlined presentation allows the salesperson to bring up issues that may otherwise go unanswered. For example, during a computer sale, a tangential issue such as insurance, sufficient electrical wiring, or other logistical considerations can be brought up. Your thorough and thoughtful presentation will increase your credibility and your ability to fulfill your client's needs.

Beginning salespeople are often under the impression that they should give their presentations without notes. This is not so. There is absolutely nothing wrong with using notes as long as you do not read your presentation. To make your presentations interesting and effective, they should be characterized as follows:

Comprehensive. When you have finished with your presentation, ideally there should be no questions. If you have done your homework well, your presentation will cover every issue that could possibly come up. This does not mean that you discuss every feature with every prospect. On the contrary, cover only those that are relevant. Of course the ideal presentation is different from real ones, so be prepared to answer questions and repeat information as necessary. Giving a comprehensive presentation also means providing the entire solution to the prospect's problems. Do not propose a partial solution because they asked you to solve part of the problem or because you think the whole solution would be too expensive. Any discrepancy between your presentation and the previously discussed needs summary should be brought out into the open. You might say something as simple as, "I was home thinking about your situation and realize we overlooked something." Always present the optimum solution to the problems and opportunities you have uncovered.

Custom-tailored. Your presentation should deal with the problems that this prospect is experiencing, not the problems that similar businesses have experienced. Rather than generalize, make direct references to your prospect's business. Remember: you are a consultant dealing with the needs of one client at a time.

Well-positioned. You cannot eliminate the competition. You can, however, point out the features and benefits that make your product or service superior. Spend most of your time on features and benefits that are unique to your company. If you can, emphasize features of your product or service that the competition cannot touch. Keep in mind that there are secondary features and benefits that are also important. For example, your company's reputation and good customer service and your product's reliability are assets that you add to the primary features and benefits.

Well-organized. Your presentation should be clear and well organized. The order in which you present the features and benefits will depend on what you are selling and the priorities of your prospect. With some products, there is a natural or logical order in which to show or discuss the features. In addition, there may be an advantageous place to end. For example, when a realtor shows a house, she knows there is a natural order that most people follow to tour a home. They come in the front door, look at the living room and dining room, proceed to the bedrooms, and wind up in the kitchen, a part of the house that is a high priority for both men and women. Realtors let people follow their natural inclinations, but they also try to lead them to end up somewhere specific—the kitchen. They achieve this by using subtle direction.

If you are selling a product that does not dictate a natural order of presentation, use your prospect's priorities as a guide. Keep in mind the effects of primacy and latency. Primacy is firing your big guns first so they'll be remembered. Latency is firing them last. The best combination is the following: For your presentation, start big; give your most salient features and benefits first. When you give the benefit summary, however, leave the best for last.

Geared toward your prospect's style. When giving presentations to socializers and relaters, take most of the data out of your claims. Relaters like to hear personal guarantees. Socializers like to see charts and other visual aids. Directors want the data summarized on one page, and thinkers like a lot of data, especially on computer print-outs. Selling by Style will be discussed in more detail in chapter 12.

Flexible. In presenting the optimum solution to your prospect's problems, you may stretch one variable or another. For example, you may exceed the time or budget constraints in the interest of doing what is best. If your optimum proposal is not acceptable, have plans B and C ready in your back pocket.

THE IMPORTANCE OF BENEFITS AND FEEDBACK

The chapter on relationship strategies discussed the importance of being able to speak the prospect's language. During the proposal phase there is another language in which you have to be conversant. It's the language of benefits. A feature is some aspect of the whole product that exists regardless of a customer's needs. A benefit is the way that feature satisfies a need. *A benefit is a feature in action.*

Many customers think in terms of benefits. They don't care how something works; they want to know what it will do for them, how will it solve the problems they are having. Someone in the engineering department (a thinker) may care about features because quality and dependability are often related to features. The bottom-line benefit, however, is what the key decision maker will care about.

It follows, then, to talk about benefits with her. Most of the time, you cannot go wrong if you speak the language of benefits.

Imagine a real estate salesperson discussing homes with a client. The typical questions is, "What do you want in your new home?" The average person answers in terms of the number of bedrooms and baths, square footage, location, and so on. The realtor may ask things like, "Do you want a swimming pool, fireplace, balconies, two-car garage?" The responses to all these questions dictate which houses the realtor will show the prospect. This *feature* information-gathering approach creates limitations. The more features the prospect asks for, the more difficult it will be for the realtor to find a house that fits the bill.

A better way to approach the prospect is to ask not only about features but about benefits. For example, if a prospect is shopping for a condominium and says to the realtor, "I want a swimming pool," that preference may be flexible. Perhaps she wants a place to exercise and just automatically said, "pool." Upon further questioning, the realtor may discover that a gym or tennis court would be acceptable. The realtor could easily ask, "May I ask why it is important for your family to have a swimming pool?" This question asks for the specific benefits sought.

With further questioning, the realtor may discover that a pool in the backyard is not an absolute necessity. The client likes to swim, so a house near the beach or near the YMCA will suffice. In fact, there may be benefits of a house near a pool that outweigh the desire for a pool. Working with the benefits will give the realtor many more options than working solely with features.

One way to get the prospect involved in the proposal is to use the feature-feedback-benefit (FFB) method. Present a feature and ask for feedback. To go back to the realtor for a moment, when discussing the features of a house before going to see it, the realtor could say, "The house has a small, kidney-shaped pool with a jaccuzzi at one end, which is nice for parties and late-night dips before bed. How important is that to you and your family?" The client would then say yes, no, or otherwise. He may also say, "That sounds good. Instead of bathing the dog, I'll just throw him in the pool."

Encourage the client to come up with his own benefits. If he comes up with all the right ones, you don't have to add any. The prospect sells himself. If he leaves some out, however, you always have the option to fill in the blanks. You would then ask, "What other advantages do you see?"

The FFB method of consultation will keep you tuned to the benefits sought by your prospect. It will keep your customer involved throughout the sales process, and it makes the studying and proposing phases more efficient.

Keep these feedback questions in mind to involve prospects in your discussion of the solutions to their problems:

"How do you see this fitting into your situation?"

"What other advantages do you see in this?"

"This is how it fits into your business; how do you see it fitting into your family life?"

"How do you see this addressing the opportunity we discussed earlier?"

"Does this look as if it will meet your needs?"

When discussing features and benefits, consider your prospect's behavioral style. For example, thinkers will be more process oriented. Directors will be bottom-line oriented. Socializers look for novelty and originality, and relaters are more relationship oriented.

Remember that any feature can have more than one benefit, and any desired benefit can be accomplished with more than one feature. When pointing out each, be sure to cover all the possibilities. You can also ask your prospect if he sees any other benefits to a particular feature.

THE FIVE KEY ELEMENTS OF PRESENTATIONS

1. Never make a misrepresentation to a prospect.
2. Follow an order in presenting ideas.
3. Never plan to give a condensed version of your presentation. If a prospect unexpectedly finds herself short on time, you would be better off coming back another day than cutting your proposal short. This would be unfair to the prospect, who is trying to make an informed decision with your help as a consultant.

4. During the presentation, take notes of comments your prospect makes regarding additional benefits or the use of your product or service.

5. Keep customer-satisfaction units (CSUs) in mind throughout the presentation. CSUs are a hypothetical, psychological unit of measure of a customer's satisfaction. How much the customer is willing to pay is in direct proportion to the amount of CSUs they perceive they will receive from the purchase. The number of CSUs a client derives from a product or service depends on the benefits it will provide.

Your role as a salesperson is to raise the number of CSUs so that their perceived value is equal to or higher than the price you are asking. This is done by pointing out features and benefits and asking for feedback.

GAINING THE HOME FIELD ADVANTAGE

When you make a proposal in a prospect's office, you lose some control over the atmosphere of the presentation. Customers are not always sensitive to your needs, so you need gently to exert as much control as possible over the physical and environmental logistics of the presentation. Often this is simply a matter of making your needs and preferences clear to your prospect.

Find out in advance where you will have to work. Try to secure a private office in which there will be no interruptions. Arrange for necessary table space, lighting, electric outlets for your audiovisual equipment and so on. This is smart business. The more you can arrange in advance, the less will be left to chance. There is nothing worse than arriving at a client's office and being told you will be giving your presentation in a congested hallway or in the cafeteria at lunch time.

HOW TO HANDLE INTERRUPTIONS

It is not unusual for the prospect to be interrupted by an employee or a telephone call during your presentation. If this happens, busy yourself with paperwork, reading, or doodling. Whatever you do, do not sit there and stare impatiently at the client.

When the prospect hangs up the telephone or the employee has left, avoid the temptation to reiterate what you have covered so far. That would give the impression you are summing up for the end of the presentation. Instead, briefly review the last point you made and then continue the presentation. For example, you might say, "We were just talking about the benefits of a hard disk in the computer, and you said it would allow you to run more complex software. Some other benefits are . . ."

If you are interrupted by your prospect's customer, it is important to give the prospect the time and space needed to take care of business. This means you should physically rise and move away to give your prospect privacy. When the customer has left, pick up where you left off.

If there are too many interruptions, you can volunteer to reduce the noise by taking the client out of the office. Perhaps your presentation can be given across the street in a quiet restaurant or coffee shop. Another alternative is to ask if there is a conference room where the two of you can find some privacy. The last alternative, and perhaps the least desirable, is to offer to reschedule the appointment. Unfortunately, someone who is interrupted so often during the day will have a hard time finding seclusion on another day. Sometimes, however, there are extenuating circumstances, so coming back another day may do the trick.

If you point out the situation to your prospect, often he can change it. Remember to place the blame on the environment by saying, "It seems pretty hectic around here today. Is there someplace we can go for a cup of coffee to finish this?" That may be all the prospect needs either to take you up on your offer or to have the secretary hold all calls and interruptions for the next half hour or so. You can then enjoy the prospect's undivided attention.

After the proposal, regardless of the outcome, follow up with a letter that thanks your prospect for their time and the opportunity to work with them.

THE GROUP PRESENTATION

The outlined presentation, that is, the one-on-one proposal, is the most flexible presentation. There are times, however, when you will have to meet with more than one decision maker in a group presentation.

Many of the elements of a group presentation are similar to those of the outlined presentation discussed above. The primary difference is that either you or your team is presenting the proposal to a group of decision makers.

The group presentation, depending on its size, may be less flexible than a one-on-one meeting. The larger the group, the more structured your presentation will become. It would not work if everyone jumped in with feedback and ideas simultaneously, so a semblance of order has to be arranged. As the salesperson in charge, you can structure the presentation and provide a question-and-answer period at the end or during the presentation.

The ideal situation is to have most or all of the decision makers involved during the studying phase. That way they will have contributed to setting the success criteria and the points you discuss will hit on thoughts they have expressed regarding the problems at hand. There will be times when you will have to give a presentation to a body of people who were not involved in the previous phases of the sale but who need to hear your proposal in order to give their blessings to the sale.

This type of group presentation will be more formal than the one-on-one presentation. In the first three to five minutes, you should accomplish the following:

Give a proper introduction. Tell them your name and company and explain in one clear, concise sentence the premise of your proposal. For example, your statement might sound like this: "Good morning. I'm Jeff Baxter from International Hospitality Consultants. I'm here to share with you my findings, based on research of your company and my discussions with Mary Farley, that suggest that my company can help you increase your convention bookings by 15 to 30 percent."

Establish credibility. Give a brief history of your company that includes the reason the business was started, the company philosophy, its development, and its success rate. Mention a few companies that you have worked with in the past, especially if they are big names. This serves to "ground" the client and lets the group know who you are and the extent of your experience and credibility.

Provide an account list. Have copies of an account list available for everyone in attendance. It would be monotonous to tell each company you've worked with. Instead, hand out copies either in advance or while you are talking. This list will show the various sizes, locations, and types of companies you've helped in the past.

State your competitive advantages. Right up front you can succinctly tell the group where your company stands vis-à-vis the competition. Don't get into a detailed analysis of comparative strengths and weakness; just make it clear that you can do better than your competition.

Give quality assurances and qualifications. Get the group on your side by stating your guarantees in the beginning. This shows that you are proud of your product and are not skirting the issue of guarantees. You should also give your company's qualifications and credentials. For example, "We are certified by the United States government and licensed in forty-eight states to treat or move toxic waste" or "I have copies of the test reports from an independent lab . . ." If your company has an impressive money-back guarantee or an extended warranty, mention it. Chrysler used this tack successfully with their five-year/50,000-mile warranty.

Cater to the group's behavioral style. Every group is comprised of individuals with their own personal styles. However, a group also exhibits an overall or dominant style; that is, it takes on a mode of decision making that is characteristic of one of the four behavioral styles. If you can quickly determine the group style, you will be able to hold their attention and give them what they want more effectively. Some people are more impatient than others. If you don't address their needs, you will lose their attention, some before others, in this order: directors first, then socializers, thinkers, and relaters.

The four styles also differ in their priorities and concerns during the presentation. Directors want to know the bottom-line impact, the return on investment, and the relationship of your product or service to their goals. Socializers want to know how your product or service is new, unique, and exciting and who else uses it. Thinkers are concerned with how the product or service works and its safety and accuracy. Relaters want to know how it feels to use and whom it affects.

After you have established the credibility of your company, begin involving the group in the presentation. The first thing to do is go around the room asking for everyone's input into the success criteria and decision-making criteria. Preface this with, "I spoke to Fred, Sally, and Sue and found out their views on what your company would like to see changed in this area. In my research I discovered it would also be to your benefit to have X, Y, and Z improved. I'd like to hear all of your thoughts on this matter." Ask each person to add to the list of benefits sought and decision making criteria. Take notes, perhaps on a flip chart, on what everyone says to help shape your presentation.

After everyone has had a chance to speak, go through your presentation exactly as you would in a one-on-one presentation. The primary difference is that you want to be sure to answer all the questions, fears, and concerns that came up in the group. Meet each person's specific needs with a specific proposal.

When using this method, it is essential, during your preparation, to brainstorm all the possible concerns and questions the decision makers may come up with. This information will come from talking to people within the company, fellow salespeople, and other people in the industry. You should be so well prepared that there is nothing they could come up with as a decision-making criteria that you haven't already thought of and answered.

When you prepare for either a group or individual presentation, write a proposal document that will range from one page to an entire notebook with data, specifications, reports, and solutions to specific problems. The proposal document is a reference source that tells your customer what he bought if he said yes and what he didn't buy if the answer was no. This document will address everything you and your prospect discussed in the study phase: problems, success criteria, decision-making criteria, and how your product or service answers each. At the end of the document, include relevant documents and copies of testimonial letters from satisfied customers.

During your presentation, do not read from the document. It is not the presentation; it is strictly a resource of facts to give your prospect after a decision has been made. In addition, when making your presentation, do not expect to cover every point in the proposal, unless you are relatively brief. Your presentation will focus on the issues that relate to the customer's specific need gap; tangential information should be left in the document. Remember: proposal documents don't sell products; people sell products. The document in no way serves as a substitute for a first-rate presentation.

The best way to present a proposal document is without prices. There are several reasons for this. First, some people will go directly to the prices without reading through the document. Second, prices tend to prejudice nondecision makers, who should not be concerned with prices. If the decision maker asks you why the prices are missing, tell her, "I thought you would prefer the flexibility of showing the document to other people without their knowing prices. It's a matter of confidentiality." The third reason is politics. Imagine a board of directors who have not had a raise in two years looking at a document that proposes a $2 million computer for the company. This may stir up problems.

Make it clear that you are not trying to hide the prices and that you would be more than happy to talk about them with the appropriate people, that is, the decision makers. It is important to present prices in the proper perspective and context.

When you give your proposal, address each problem and give specific information about your solutions for each. Make sure you discuss features and benefits and get feedback from the group. Ask things like, "Can you see any other advantages to this?" or "How do you feel about that; do you think that would solve the problem?"

At the end, summarize your proposal by giving a benefits summary. "Here is what you will get if you accept my proposal . . ." Talk about how the benefits will address their specific problems.

Before your presentation, find out from your primary contact in the company if the group is going to make a decision while you are there or if they will discuss it and inform you later. You should also know if they are responsible for dealing with the financial aspects of the purchase. If so, you will have to talk about the costs and the benefits they will receive in relation to the costs. If they will not be concerned with prices, don't discuss them.

When you have completed the benefits summary, solicit the impressions of the group. Ask if they agree that the solution you proposed would solve their problem or meet their needs. Without asking for it, get a feeling for the disposition of the group. If you are working with one person, it is easier to ask for an impression.

At the end of your summary, ask if there are any questions. At this point you will be close to the end of your allotted time. When someone asks a question that is answered in your proposal document, refer her to the appropriate section of the document and assure her that a complete answer is provided.

Rick: In 1985 this method was successfully used by the Buffalo-Niagara Sales and Marketing Executives. Our convention committee went to the Sales and Marketing Executives International convention to bid on bringing the 1988 SMEI convention to Buffalo. Needless to say, there were a lot of other cities bidding, including some Southern resorts.

We used this method of presentation. The SMEI rules did not allow us to ask who the decision makers were, so we could not ask them for their decision-making criteria in advance. We brainstormed and came up with twenty-three different success criteria that we thought they would be looking for. Our proposal document was a thick notebook with twenty-three dividers. We were allowed a thirty-minute presentation and began by asking all the people on the committee what they considered to be the success criteria. As they told us, we wrote them on a flip chart. We addressed each success criteria in order and walked the committee through our proposal document, video tapes, and live presenters. All of these things answered their questions and met their needs. We were awarded the contract for the 1988 convention, which promises to bring millions of tourism dollars to the city of Buffalo. The committee later told us our thoroughness and the strength of our presentation were what won the contract.

THE IMPORTANCE OF USING ALL FIVE SENSES

During a presentation, appeal to as many of the prospect's senses as possible. A video demonstration would appeal to seeing and hearing. If there is something to be tasted or smelled, be sure to bring it and let everyone experience it. If your product is small enough, give it to them to feel and play with. If your product does not lend itself to more senses than one or two, add some elements of sense appeal to the situation. If you can, bring some good-quality food and coffee. The smells and the act of eating will relax your group. If your presentation takes place in mid-morning or late afternoon when people start to get hungry, taking away their hunger pangs will ensure you have their attention. Another way to hold your group's attention is to give a demonstration and encourage participation.

THE ART OF DEMONSTRATING

A demonstration, like a photograph, is worth at least a thousand words. Video tapes, slides, audio sound tracks, and live demonstrations are fun and effective and keep the pace of the presentation moving.

A demonstration aids in learning. By making your points vivid, you make them memorable. Associating new information with images that are already familiar will cement the connection and guarantee the impression. Analogies, especially humorous ones, are potent aids to memory.

It is important to make the demonstration relevant. Don't assume that the prospect will be able to visualize and appreciate the use of your product or service in her business unless you show her. This is especially true of technical, industrial, and office products.

Full-scale demonstrations can have a lot of impact. If the expense can be justified, it is effective to take a field trip to demonstrate a product operating in another facility. Before doing so, be sure to arrange for four contingencies:

1. Be certain all the key decision makers will be present.
2. Produce something of value for them to take home. This may be difficult with large industrial machinery in someone else's plant, but, if possible, provide a sample.
3. Give the prospect, especially the final user of the product, a chance at hands-on experience. Point out the benefits of its operation.

4. Provide a summary of the information gathered during the field trip. This can be either written or verbal, depending on the logistics of the trip and the structure of the presentation.

HOW TO DEAL WITH SEALED BIDS

Whenever possible, make a presentation in person. There are some situations, however, when you are given the specifications of the product or parameters of a service desired by a company and are asked, along with your competitors, for a sealed bid. When this happens, it is important to study that prospect as much or more than you would for a personal presentation. There are some things you can do to give your bid more impact.

• In writing, present an extensive comparison of your competitors. Be sure you are comparing apples to apples and not apples to oranges so your comparison is valid.

• If you can, sell your prospect on letting you write the specifications of the product or service. You could offer to do this free of charge.

Phil: When I was in the security business, I sold every museum in Georgia on Dictagraph security systems by selling myself into the position of writing the specifications. I wrote specifications that I was sure only we could deliver.

• Include testimonial letters with your bid. These add extra value to your product or service.

Rick: I knew a salesman who sold football equipment to high schools. His sales used to entail big contracts and were often based on sealed bids. He included three testimonial letters from schools who absolutely loved him. They loved him because he used to go to their Friday night football games and sit on the sidelines with a box full of helmet pads. He did this because everyone knew the pads became compressed when the helmets were hit a few times. When the kids came off the field, he would change the pads for them as part of the contract to supply the helmets. Coaches loved him because they didn't have to deal with injuries and lawsuits. He also eliminated the need for them to administer the helmet maintenance and keep parts on hand. The extra value he added and the letters attesting to it worked wonders for him.

- Meet the specifications and then add something extra. Describe what your company can do above and beyond the competition. All of you may have a similar product or service, so you have to offer extra benefits such as an extended warranty or specialized customer service.

- Include a list of references so your claims can be corroborated. The key to submitting a winning sealed bid is to take your product, which the customer perceives as a commodity, and make it a differentiated product. It must have more perceived value while being priced the same as or less than your competitors' product.

Traditional salespeople worry about the presentation because they see it as the only time to really "sell" the prospect. Non-manipulative salespeople don't worry. They know that if they have done their homework and maintained the relationship along the way, the presentation is simply another step in the sales process. The presentation is made infinitely easier because they have spent the time studying the prospect's situation and are confident that they can provide attractive solutions.

10

Confirming

AFTER THE PROPOSING STAGE, most traditional salespeople pray for success or prey on their client. Non-manipulative salespeople who have followed the methods described in this book, however, can be much more relaxed. You would not have reached this step in the sales process unless you had a strong relationship with your prospect and she had a clear need gap to close. If you have been conscientious along the way, working closely with your prospect, the two of you will naturally progress to the confirming phase together. Being a personal form of selling, non-manipulative selling takes the awkwardness out of confirming the sale. Non-manipulative salespeople never maneuver their prospects like cowboys lassoing steers.

CLOSING VS. CONFIRMING

One of the most distasteful aspects of traditional sales is the overemphasis placed on the "close." It is ascribed so much importance that it reeks of manipulation, trickery, and a disregard for the prospect's needs. This is the polar opposite of the way non-manipulative salespeople work; for them, the end does not justify the means.

Closing implies that your hard work is over and you are now free to reap the rewards. This is only half true. You will reap the rewards, but your work will continue. For the non-manipulative salesperson, the emphasis is not on the confirmation of the sale but on the relationship and the entire sales process. The confirmation is just the beginning of a commitment to an ongoing business relationship; in a sense, the sale begins when the customer says yes. The non-manipulative salesperson sees the customer as more than a source of orders and commissions. She sees the customer as an annuity and an important building block in the foundation of her sales career. The confirmation, therefore, is not a time to sigh in relief; it is a time to feel happy about having helped another customer.

You have already noticed there is no line drawn between "selling" and "closing" in non-manipulative selling. When the studying and proposing phases have been done well, the customer has expressed her needs and knows your product or service will meet them. You have used verbal and nonverbal feedback to see how the customer perceives the value of your product or service. In fact, before you enter the confirming phase of the sale, you and your customer should have agreed upon the solution to her problem. Therefore, the confirmation is not an *if* but a *when*. Complex or manipulative closing techniques are unnecessary. The non-manipulative salesperson and customer are doing business *together*.

In non-manipulative selling, an analogy can be drawn between the confirming process and asking someone to marry you. If you are worried about the answer, don't ask; you're premature. The decision to get married is a resolution of a mutually developed relationship. The question, just as in a non-manipulative sale, should be rhetorical; and the answer should be a date, not a yes or no. The question is simply the formal crystalization of already understood feelings.

Despite their differences, manipulative and non-manipulative selling have many things in common. In the confirming phase, regardless of your philosophy, you must be tuned into your prospect. She will determine *what* you do and *when* by her level of agreement. If she is ready to confirm the decision early in the presentation, then you need not finish it. If you do, you run the risk of overselling and boring the prospect. Most of the time, prospects will want all the information you have. Be cognizant of verbal and nonverbal signals that your prospect is projecting.

CONFIRMING OPPORTUNITIES

By the time that you reach the proposing stage you will know your prospect's personal style, typical body language, and ways of interacting with you. During the presentation, this knowledge will aid you in determining what your prospect is thinking or feeling. There will be times, however, when you do not know the prospect all that well. For example, your prospect may ask you to give a presentation to someone you've never met. Therefore, it is valuable to know the verbal and nonverbal indicators of buying decisions. Buying signals can be red (negative), yellow (neutral), or green (positive).

The prospect's questions will tell you a great deal about her thoughts. Some questions are more neutral than others and need to be evaluated in the context of the prospect's other signals. Some typical questions are the following:

1. Could I try this out one more time? (+)
2. This machine is supposed to be more reliable than mine? (0)
3. What sort of credit terms do you offer? (+)
4. How soon can you deliver? (+)
5. How can I even think of buying with interest rates so high? (−)

Questions that are concerned with terms, delivery, quantity, benefits, and service indicate a positive buying attitude. Questions that ask about product features, ease of use, and maintenance are neutral. Negative questions are usually obvious.

A prospect's comments about a product or service also indicates her buying tendency. You will hear statements like these:

1. That's very interesting. (0)
2. We could probably afford that. (+)

3. Hmm, I just don't know about this. ($-$)
4. Yes, I've seen these before. (0)
5. Things are tough these days. ($-$)

Body language was covered extensively in chapter 6. If necessary, review those concepts before the proposing and confirming phases. In addition, keep these clues in mind:

1. If the prospect is sitting, open arms indicate receptiveness; tightly crossed arms show defensiveness.
2. Leaning forward and listening carefully shows interest.
3. Supporting the head with one hand and gazing off into space shows you have lost the prospect's attention.
4. A tense posture is not a positive indicator. People tend to relax when they decide to buy.
5. Happy, animated facial expressions indicate the prospect is relating well to you.

Since you have developed a working relationship, you can do more than monitor your prospect's buying signals; you can ask how she feels or what she thinks. This is especially useful if the indicators are negative or neutral.

THE TENTATIVE CONFIRMATION

When a client shows some hesitation, frequently it pays to confirm the sale using the tentative confirmation. This can be a very effective technique because it gives the client the psychological ability to see "a way out" and ends the shopping process at the same time. For example, a travel agent calls up a hotel for a client. The agent asks the reservationist for a room on a specific date. The room is available, but the agent has to check with her client before confirming. The hotel reservationist can say, "Frequently the hotel sells out and I'd hate for you to call back and find your room unavailable. Why don't we go ahead and book the room for you and if your client says it's OK, you don't have to do any more work; the reservation is made. If your client doesn't want the room for some reason, all you have to do is call us back by six o'clock on the day of the reservation. There's absolutely no cancellation charge."

First, the beauty of the tentative confirmation is that it begins the commitment; and sometimes prospects need a little push to do what is truly in their best interest. Granted, it is not the strongest commitment, but at least it is *a* commitment. Second, people stop shopping once they've given a commitment. If they don't commit, they continue looking. Psychologically, once they've commited, even tentatively, they feel they have made a decision and don't bother to keep shopping. For example, imagine a woman shopping in a department store. She picks out a blouse that she likes and walks to the cashier. Along the way she sees another blouse she wants. She puts down the first one, picks up the second one, takes it to the cashier, and buys it. Now, if there had been a cash register closer to the first blouse, the woman would have bought it and probably not even noticed the second blouse because she would have been finished with her shopping. If she had noticed the second one, she would have had to evaluate whether it was worth the effort of returning the first and so on.

The tentative confirmation is not meant to be used as a trick. It is used when there is agreement on the solution to the prospect's problem and yet she is having difficulty making a commitment. There are some people who, despite their acknowledgment of their needs, still have a hard time making a decision. That's when you use this technique. It is for the customer who wants what you are selling, not for the customer who is not interested.

Some industries require long delivery dates because of manufacturing, production, or some other lag time. If you are in such an industry, consider using the tentative confirmation. An example of what you can say to an uncertain prospect is, "It's going to be six weeks before it leaves the warehouse anyway. Why don't we go ahead and order one? I'll give you a call at the end of the fifth week to confirm that you still want it. If you change your mind, fine. I'll use it for another client."

A good example is space reservations for print ads in local publications. A salesperson may say to a client, "Our deadline for the camera-ready ad is the tenth of the month. From time to time we run house ads. Why don't I reserve a space for you and you will have until the last minute to decide. If you don't want the ad, we'll put in a house ad."

This confirmation works well in situations in which a prospect has agreed to buy but has to wait for financing or some other contingency. In effect, the salesperson using a tentative confirmation is saying to the customer, "I don't mind if you tie up my inventory. I want to make this easy for you."

THE PILOT

A pilot is a technique that lets the customer sample your product or service. Most salespeople misuse the pilot. They use it as a confirming technique. Non-manipulative salespeople use it as an assuring technique. It is discussed here because it is so commonly misused during this phase of the sale.

The problem with using a pilot as a confirming tool is that it's not the way to get a commitment. The typical salesperson says, "Look, I see you're undecided, so why don't you take ten dozen and see how you like them. If you like them, we'll do business; if you don't, no problem." The customer takes the product and what does she do? She looks for all the things that are wrong with it and the reasons not to buy. Negative selective perception has replaced commitment. It's human nature.

The pilot should be a tool for assuring customer satisfaction. A pilot is offered after your customer has said to you, in essence, "If everything you have said is true, then I want to buy." The pilot is a way of proving everything you said is true. It's a way to help your client feel comfortable with what she has already decided to buy. If a client is already commited, selective perception dictates that she will look at what is right, not at what is wrong, with your product or service. *That* is why pilots are powerful assuring tools but terrible confirming tools. If you talk to a lot of salespeople who use it to confirm the sale, they will tell you that most of their pilots don't work.

You have probably experienced the difference between the two uses of a pilot in your own life as a consumer. Most of us have subscribed to magazines that allowed us to pay later or cancel when the invoice arrived. Most of the time we cancel. Have you ever bought a book that promised a money-back guarantee if you were not satisfied? Chances are good you didn't return it. Instead, you realized all the reasons you should keep it.

THE ALTERNATIVE-CHOICE CONFIRMATION

The alternative-choice confirmation, like the pilot, is, more often than not, misused. Most traditional salespeople give their customers manipulative choices as a way to obtain the commitment. In fact, they call it the "forced-choice close." Asking, "Would you like a half-page or full-page ad?" puts your prospect in a half nelson and applies pressure.

In non-manipulative sales, the only time an alternative choice is given is *after* a commitment has been formally made. Then it is a way to pin down the details.

The alternative confirmation is *not* to be used in the confirming phase because people insist on making their own decisions. The drive for autonomy is a very strong, unconscious need that people exercise either directly or indirectly. If you were to give an alternative choice to a director or socializer, she would react immediately. Your choice of two positives would leave her with only one autonomous choice—a negative! If you were to give the same choice to a thinker or relater, you would get a delayed reaction. They would let you manipulate them now and exercise autonomy in the future by canceling the order, finding something wrong with the product or service, not paying the bill, or giving your company a lot of bad PR.

WHEN TO SEEK CONFIRMATION

When should you try to confirm the sale? Most salespeople would say when the customer gives buying signals or indicates he's ready to make a commitment. That is only half the answer.

Phil: I have a client in the apartment management business. He routinely gives tours of an apartment complex to prospective tenants. Normally he confirms the rental in the office or clubhouse, but occasionally he has a prospect who is giving strong buying signals in the middle of the tour. My answer to him is that he should stash applications behind bushes and under towels near the pool. But seriously, if the customer is tugging at your sleeve to buy, accomodate them, but realize they may only appear ready to buy. The customer is ready based on his "guesstimate" of the price which, in turn, is based on what he knows at that point. What if the price is much higher? The customer may be shocked and become uninterested after all.

In a situation like this, it is important to give the customer all the information you have that will increase his perceived value of your product or service. If you were to stop your presentation midstream to give the price, you would be giving a lopsided picture of the value of your product. The customer would only have a partial picture of what the price is buying. If it is true that you get what you pay for, and if you know what you are paying but not what you're getting, you can't possibly judge if the price is fair.

It is essential to give prospects the whole picture before confirming the sale. In other words, the time to confirm the sale is after you have finished your proposal.

A logical question arises. If the anxious buyer doesn't want you to continue your presentation but wants you to tell her the price, what should you do? The first time she asks, you put the situation in perspective.

Let's use the example of someone shopping for a health-club membership. After a tour of the pool, gym, and locker room, the prospect is tugging on the salesperson's spandex leotard and asking, "How much?" The best answer is something to the effect of, "Lisa, I'd love to tell you how much it is, but there are a number of different plans. What I'd like to do is give you a feel for our different membership options and services and then together we can come up with the plan that best fits you. And then I'll tell you exactly what the price is for that plan." If you sense this is acceptable to your prospect, you would then ask some information-gathering or fact-finding questions.

If the prospect asks again, offer a range of prices; if you are asked a third time, give the price. It is better to give the price and risk a misunderstanding than alienate your prospect because you are ignoring her.

Giving price before value is a disservice to your customer. Alan Cimburg, one of America's leading sales trainers, uses an example of a woman shopping for a gold pen. She points to one in the display case of a store and asks the clerk the price. "Five hundred dollars," the clerk tells her. "Five hundred dollars! I don't want it!" the woman growls and storms out. The clerk turns to a co-worker and says, "Gee, I should have told her it comes packed with a Rolex watch." Again, *your customer must know exactly what she is getting*.

ASK FOR THE CONFIRMATION

There will be times when you ask the prospect what she would like to do. Use an open question with direction, such as, "Where do we go from here?" "How would you like to proceed?" or "What's our next step?" This is a straightforward, honest request that eliminates the tricky or manipulative characteristics of traditional sales. Since your prospect has participated fully in the entire sales transaction and has agreed on the solution, you will often be answered with a time, date, or other relevant reply. If there is some concern, your prospect should feel comfortable and trusting enough to speak up. You are, after all, problem solvers working together.

So far, this is all very simple if the sale is confirmed, but what if the prospect does not confirm the sale? Traditional salespeople are trained to overcome objections and ask for the order again. This method raises defenses, increases tension, and reduces trust. Instead, the non-manipulative salesperson manages the problem.

MANAGING CUSTOMER RESISTANCE

In traditional sales, you are taught to overcome objections. In non-manipulative sales, an "objection" is not a rejection; it is a correction. In NMS it is called resistance, not resistance in a negative sense but the type of resistance, like air pressure, that can be used to accomplish things.

When a customer offers resistance, indirectly, she is trying to guide you. By telling you what she won't buy, the customer is also leading you in the direction of what she would buy. Two analogies will clarify this. When you water ski, you make turns by putting pressure on the ski opposite the direction you wish to turn. If you want to go right, you apply pressure to the left. *Resistance changes direction*. The other example is a heat-seeking missile. It is never on the right course until the moment it makes contact with its target. It is constantly correcting its course based on the input of data from its sensors.

The same can be said of non-manipulative salespeople. They are never on target with their package of products or services until the confirming phase is complete. It is necessary to monitor your prospect's feedback and continually adjust your course. When a customer resists, it is simply a nudge in another direction. You are being told to take another tack until you either hit your target or are corrected again. The prospect's resistance is saying, "Don't go *that* way, let's go *this* way."

Ideally, you should meet little, if any, resistance. You would not have come this far through the sales process if your customer did not have a reasonable intention of doing business with you. In every phase you have sought agreement and kept the relationship strong. When you reach this point, the confirmation is just like a marriage proposal; it is the resolution of the mutually developed relationship.

Resistance should be viewed as an opportunity, not a roadblock. The prospect is letting you get to know her better and helping you uncover her needs even more. A customer who shows resistance to something is participating in the relationship instead of remaining aloof. This is what a non-manipulative salesperson wants, a *relationship*.

Resistance takes many forms, such as questions, statements, and body language, and it can mean many things. Occasionally it is difficult to ascertain the exact reason for the resistance because people use excuses to cover up their true feelings. You are actually lucky when someone is straightforward and tells you where you or your product has failed. This is one type of feedback from which you learn and improve yourself.

When this happens, gently question your prospect, keeping in mind that her resistance may be caused by one or more of the following reasons:

1. The prospect no longer has a need for your product or service owing to changes of which you have not been informed.
2. The prospect lacks the ability to buy. This could be due to lack of authority, budget cuts, high interest rates, or other logistical problems that are beyond your control.

3. The prospect's trust in you has diminished. Perhaps you have misjudged her personal style and have been treating her incorrectly. It is also not inconceivable that your prospect simply doesn't like you. It happens.

4. There is no urgency to buy. Time pressures usually motivate people; a lack of time pressure or the perception of no need can cause complacency. Perhaps the need gap is less wide that you thought.

5. The prospect has a lack of interest in your presentation. You have somehow failed to uncover needs or tailor solutions. You might have been working with incomplete data or wrong information.

Incorrect or Insufficient Information

If the reason for the resistance is incorrect or insufficient information, determine where you went wrong and why. Did you gather the wrong information or give erroneous or incomplete information, or was there simply a breakdown in communication? In any of these cases, you have to go back to the point of the communication breakdown, gather more information, and use the new information to design a plan that will work.

Resistance stemming from wrong or insufficient information can usually be corrected simply by providing new information. The four-step process to use in dealing with resistance based on lack of accurate information is as follows:

Listen and carefully observe both the verbal and the nonverbal message of the prospect. What is really being said?

Clarify the basis of the resistance so that there is no misunderstanding about what concern you are addressing.

React to the resistance, using the technique that seems to be most appropriate.

Confirm the prospect's acceptance of your answer to assure that your response was on target and additional resistance is no longer necessary to guide you further. Don't forget to check the trust and tension level at the end of this process.

For example, a prospect may say your service is desired only if you can implement it immediately. Clarify what "immediately" means before you go any further. Depending on the definition, you may be able to meet the requirements.

Personality Conflicts

The most difficult resistance to manage is the one caused by a lack of good chemistry in the relationship. The relationship is the foundation on which everything else is built. If the relationship collapses, so does everything it supports. This happens because somehow trust was broken. You might have mistakenly identified the prospect's behavioral style, or it may be something beyond your control that is unidentifiable. Maybe the prospect just does not like you.

Naturally, your prospect will not come right out and say, "I don't like you" or "Dummy, I'm a director and you're treating me like a socializer!" Instead they say things like, "It's too expensive" or "I don't want it in green." The traditional salesperson's reaction is to attack the stated objection rather than work on the relationship. The problem is that the prospect may not know why she doesn't want to buy, she just knows she's not interested.

If you discover this problem, see if there is time to salvage the relationship. Use your communication skills to reestablish the trust. Quickly reevaluate the person's style and start treating her appropriately. If none of these things work, come right out and ask if it is a personal problem. The way to ask such a direct question is to say, "My philosophy is that if two people want to do business together, the details never stand in the way. Let me ask you this; given where we are and what we've been through, do you feel comfortable enough with *me* to want to do business?" If the answer is yes, then say something like, "Let's quickly review the needs summary and make sure my analysis of your needs is correct and includes everything." After you have done that, review the success criteria the two of you established. Finally, review the CSU summary. If there is agreement on all of those elements and the relationship is not at fault, ask your prospect why she is not buying. Logic dictates that she should.

If the answer to your question is, "Yes, it's you. I'm not comfortable doing business with you," then you have to turn the account over to another salesperson. The *best* way to T.O. is to give the account to an expert. "Sheila Levine is the expert in graphic design. Perhaps she might be able to explain better how our system can meet your needs. May I have her call you?"

Stand By: Technical Difficulties

There are situations when trust is strong and resistance is due to technical problems beyond your control. For example, you may be expected to provide a color or style of an item that is no longer available. Unless the color or style can be changed, the sale may not be confirmed. These problems are difficult but not insurmountable. Help your client clearly see her priorities with this four-step process:

- Listen and observe.

- Clarify the concern.

- Answer via the "compensation" method.

- Confirm your answer.

In this approach, steps 1, 2, and 4 are similar to steps 1, 2, and 4 outlined for dealing with insufficient information on page 42. The difference between the two approaches lies in step 3. Using the compensation method, you acknowledge a deficiency in a particular area but try to compensate for it by pointing out other features and benefits that outweigh the shortcoming. For example, if you cannot meet a delivery date, suggest other times and stress the *advantages* of another date. This method is effective when the shortcoming is not of paramount importance. Suggested alternatives will often suffice.

Sometimes you can use the classic Ben Franklin Balance Sheet. Take a sheet of paper and divide it into two columns with "Reasons For" at the top of the left column and "Reasons Against" at the top of the right column. On this balance sheet, start with the "Reasons For" column and ask your client, "Of the ten criteria for success we discussed, which one would you rank as the most important?" Write it at the top. "Which is least important?" Write it at the bottom. Go through them all and rank them from high to low. When you are done, assign a weight to each. "Let's put a weight on them. If we could only do number one, how important would that be to you on a scale of one to a hundred?" Continue this process down the list.

Next, go on to the "Reasons Against" column and do the same thing. Keep in mind that traditional salespeople do this column wrong. They say, "Okay, what are some reasons not to buy?" The customer sits there dumbfounded and few reasons surface. Later, when the salesperson is gone, she thinks of lots of reasons. The non-manipulative way to use the Ben Franklin Balance Sheet is to take an active part in offering reasons not to buy. That honesty applies to the positive side as well; be willing to say, "No, I don't see that as a benefit for you."

The traditional way to conclude this approach is to say, "The thing I admire about Ben Franklin is that he acted on whichever side won." This is very manipulative.

Non-manipulative salespeople, by contrast, use the balance sheet as a study tool. Discuss the items on the "Reasons Against" side. Answer the questions they pose and offer a solution or explanation if one exists. For example, one reason could be, "It will decrease my cash flow." The answer to that concern could be, "Yes, for the first three months it will decrease your cash flow, but we both calculated it will increase your cash flow starting on month four." You can then ask your prospect if this item is still a negative or if it is now a neutral. It is *the prospect's choice* to delete it from the list or leave it, but at least you have shed some light on the issue. At the end of this process, ask your client how she would like to proceed.

Skills for Responding to Resistance
One of the most therapeutic processes is talking to someone. Non-manipulative salespeople use their listening skills and act as sounding boards for their prospects and clients. A lot can be learned by simply listening; sometimes it is appropriate to reflect back what has been said for reconsideration from a different angle. Your ability to clarify an issue will serve you and your client well.

Convert to a question. A statement is difficult to respond to. You can, however, convert the statement to a question and answer it. For example, to the statement, "I don't think I could use that product," you could respond, "What I hear you wondering is, 'What benefits are there for me in this product?'" You can then proceed to answer *the question*, not rebut the statement.

Reflect and listen. It is helpful to hold up a mirror to show people diplomatically what they feel; often they don't know. This is one of the many ways you call on your good communication skills. *Listen* to your prospect's voice inflections, *observe* her body language, and *hear* her words; then you will know how the prospect feels. You will be in a good position to reflect this back to encourage further discussion. This technique is especially helpful if the prospect's objection does not give you enough information. She might say, "The price is too high." Sensing the emotion behind the words, you could say, "You feel frustrated about the price?" The prospect might say, "Sure I feel frustrated. Have you tried to get a loan lately? How can I do business when money is so tight?" You will then save the day with, "That's not an insurmountable problem. We have several credit plans you might find attractive."

Break the resistance into small, meaningful increments. Traditional salespeople use a technique in which they reduce an objection to such small increments that the increments become ridiculous. For example, "That watch isn't expensive. Why, it will last twenty years. That's 7,300 days! It'll only cost you 1.4 cents a day."

This is not the way you want to do it. Instead, take a statement that seems to have enormous proportions to your prospect and reduce it to smaller, *more reasonable* increments. The classic example in advertising is the Mercedes-Benz. It is one of the least expensive cars to own, not because it is inexpensive, but because it holds its value so well. When you sell it, you will recover a higher percentage of your investment than with other cars. If you subtract the resale price from the original purchase price and divide that by the number of years you drove it, you will see how inexpensive it was to drive.

It may appear there is a fine line between the traditional and non-manipulative ways of using this technique. There is not. The premise of the traditional way is to deceive the prospect. The non-manipulative way is to put things in perspective for your client.

Use the boomerang method. Think of what a boomerang does. It is thrown out, makes a wide arc, and returns to the person who threw it. You can do the same thing when you react to resistance. Imagine a prospect saying, "We are too busy right now to put your product into service." The boomerang response might be, "The fact that you're so busy makes time saving all the more important to you. We have already agreed that my product will save you 50 percent of the time you are currently spending. If you invest a little time now to install it, you will find yourself with more time at the end of the month than you expected."

Change the premise. In this case, you take the premise on which the prospect is basing her response and change it so she can see it in a different light. For example, the prospect says, "This won't accomplish the XYZ process." Your response could be, "When we first spoke, you said you inquired about our product for its increased convenience. Then we discussed the fact that it might also accomplish the XYZ process as a secondary benefit. Is convenience still your number one priority? If not, how would you rate the relative importance of each priority now?"

SEEING THROUGH THE SMOKE

In traditional sales, a smoke screen is viewed as a ploy used by the prospect to avoid being honest. In non-manipulative sales, however, a smoke screen is merely something that obscures a clear view of the relationship or the decision-making process. Two very common smoke screens are, "Your price is too high" and "I want to think about it." Both are phrases that prospects use when they are uncomfortable communicating their uncertainty. When this happens, you will sense their uneasiness from a lack of eye contact, voice inflections, and other nonverbal clues. The solution is to work on the relationship. If your customer is not comfortable enough with you to tell the truth, something is drastically wrong.

"I want to think about it."
Let's assume your prospect is telling you the truth. How can you react to the statement, "I want to think about it"? First, ask if there

is any additional information you can provide that would facilitate the decision making, such as accounting-amortization schedules, tax-impact statements, maintenance costs or schedules, and so on. Perhaps she needs more data to help quantify her criteria for making a decision or to give her a larger base of information.

If supplying more data is insufficient, ask your prospect if there is a particular part of the proposal or some things about your product or service that she either feels uncomfortable with (for socializers and relaters) or thinks is unworkable (for thinkers and directors).

If your prospect gives you no additional information, simply say something to the effect of, "I don't want you to buy anything you don't want or need. By the same token, I don't want you to miss an opportunity to buy something that you should have. I understand that you want to think about it. When do you think you would be able to say yes or no on the proposal?" Let the prospect pick a date, but don't be like a traditional salesperson and try to force a date. Once you have a date, tell her, "If you make up your mind before then, give me a call. I'm going to leave you alone to think about it between now and then. Would you mind if I gave you a call the day after that date if I haven't heard from you by that time?"

"Your price is too high."

The other common statement, "Your price is too high," can mean one of three things:

1. Your price is higher than I can afford to pay.
2. Your product is not worth the price. I know where I can get something just as good for less.
3. Your product is worth the price, but not to me.

Let's examine these one at a time, using the same example for each. The situation is a realtor showing a house to a prospect. Imagine the prospect making one of these statements:

1. The house is worth $100,000, but I can only afford $75,000. (Your price is higher than I can afford to pay.)
2. The house is overpriced. If you look at comparable houses in the neighborhood, they are selling for less. I could buy

your neighbor's house for $75,000. (Your product is not worth the price.)

3. The house is worth $100,000, but I'm not interested in four bedrooms and a swimming pool. I'd be just as happy with two bedrooms and a large bathtub. And it doesn't have the view I want. So it's not worth $100,000 to me. (Your product is worth what you are asking, but not to me.)

This type of resistance can tell you many things and lead you in various new directions.

When a prospect claims that your product or service is higher than she can afford to pay, you have several options:

- Work out delayed payments, extended payments, or other creative financing alternatives.

- Propose a solution that is more affordable. This would be the time to take options B and C out of your back pocket. If the best solution is too expensive, propose the second best. For example, some services are often purchased in time increments that can be reduced and made less expensive. For example, a one-year contract for monthly consultations can be made less expensive by breaking payment down into monthly pay-as-you-go increments.

- Explore logical budget changes. As mentioned earlier, companies can, if they choose, take money from the advertising budget to use in another department. If your prospect really wants to do business, she will share the budgetary information with you so that you can consult her on the best way to implement the money shift. If you can present a logical argument for doing so, your prospect can go to the company decision makers and present a solid case.

Be sure your prospect appreciates the fact that your product is better than the competition, hence the higher price. You should also make sure the relationship is solid and she appreciates your willingness and ability to be of service. You can come right out and say, "If you sincerely want this, let's work together to figure out a way you can get it."

If your price is higher than the competition, there are a couple of things you can do:

- Increase the perceived value of your product or service. Do this by separating your company and its product or service from the competition by talking about the features, benefits, customer service, or reputation you can offer but the competition can't touch. Be sure you are comparing apples to apples. When your comparison reveals a discrepancy between your company and the competition, point it out to your client. Most of the time there is a good reason for your product to be more expensive. Your prospect gets what she pays for; make her aware of the added value you are providing.

- Concede that the competition has a better deal. For obvious reasons, this is the least desirable alternative. Before giving up the business, you *must* go back to your company and negotiate on your customer's behalf. Convince your company either to lower the price or increase the perceived value for your prospect. Remember, you are a liaison with the best interest of both parties in mind.

When a prospect says your product or service is worth the price, but not to her or him, there are two possible solutions:

- You can go back to the studying phase and uncover needs that will be filled by your product, if they exist.

- You can change the solution to reflect the prospect's needs more closely. In the example of the four-bedroom home being too costly, further discussion may reveal that the prospect's mother is thinking of moving in with the couple, so, in fact, they may need the extra bedrooms.

WIN-WIN SOLUTIONS

Integrity in business is essential and it dictates, among other things, that you work toward win-win solutions with everyone.

Tony: A company called me up after having read an article I wrote and wanted to hire me for their annual convention. I asked some information-gathering questions and then some fact-finding questions, and finally we got around to discussing their budget for a speaker. Their budget for an hour's speech was far below my usual fee. The woman on the other end of the line was silent; then she told me it was hopeless. Before we resolved the price issue, I said to the woman, "My philosophy is that if two people want to do business with each other, they're not going to let the details stand in the way. Let's make sure we want to do business with each other; then we'll work out the rest." I sent her some information that really sold her on me and a couple of weeks later she called and said, "Tony, we are sold on you. We want you!"

We still had the fee to resolve. I said to her, "You want me for an hour, but what do you have planned for the rest of the morning?" She said they were going to have another speaker. I told her my fee was the same whether I was there for an hour or for the morning and suggested I give more than one program. She liked that idea, but said they were still underbudgeted. I looked for ways of giving her more for her money. I included some books they would have bought anyway. In fact, they had a product budget but didn't think of combining it with the speaker's budget. By looking at all the options, we took what began as a hopeless situation and turned it into a win-win outcome.

Managing resistance is simply using different forms of logic to help you be a better consultant. There will be times when your prospect does not see clearly her problems or the solution to them. It is your job gently and diplomatically to return with her to a point of agreement and begin again from there.

NO NEED TO FEEL DISHONEST

Traditional salespeople often feel dishonest and coercive when they try to "overcome" resistance. This is not true for non-manipulative salespeople. As a consultant, you have been working with your prospect to solve her business problems. You would not have come this far if both of you did not think you were right for the job. When resistance arises, it could be because the prospect's needs, feelings, or financial situation has changed. Reacting to the resistance is your way of shedding light on the change for *both* of you. You never can tell what extenuating circumstances have come up. Your questioning could clarify your prospect's thinking, for which she may be grateful. After all, you *are* looking out for her best interest. If the situation has changed to the point that she is no longer interested in your product, you will at least find out the real reason why the sale is not being confirmed.

Just as spouses deal with resistance to each other, partners in a business relationship deal with resistance as a natural part of the sales process. It is a necessary ingredient in the building of a strong business relationship.

If, after discussing your prospect's objection, she is still opposed to the sale, you can put the ball in her court by asking, "Where do we go from here?" This conveys your continued desire to be of service, but gives the prospect the choice. She may make another appointment with you, ask you to explain an unclear point, provide you with more information, or simply terminate the sales process for this item at this time.

EVALUATING YOUR CALLS

Regardless of the outcome, make notes following each call so that you can evaluate your performance. Doing so after confirmed sales will point out your strengths. For those sales not confirmed, you will discover your weaknesses by evaluating what transpired and how it affected the outcome.

Use the final minutes of the call to pave the way for the next call, if there will be one. After you leave, write down all the new details you learned about your prospect and her needs. Summarize what transpired and include any mistakes you made and what you could have done differently. Note the resistance that arose, the reason for it, and how you responded. Also note any verbal commitments such as price quotes, delivery dates, or terms discussed. You should also enter the follow-up date in your tickler file.

The best way to learn by your mistakes is to record systematically the positive and negative aspects of the call. The Post-Call Checklist will guide you through a comprehensive examination of what took place during the call. Fill out this form while the events are still fresh in your mind. If you do not write down what happened during the meeting, there is a good chance you will not learn from the experience at all.

Post-Call Checklist

Account name: _____

Address: _____

Telephone: _____

Person contacted: _____

Product or service: _____

Date: _____

Directions: Circle how you rate yourself for each of the areas below:

	Rating				
	Excellent				Poor
Your image					
Appearance	5	4	3	2	1
Mood	5	4	3	2	1
Enthusiasm	5	4	3	2	1
Eye contact	5	4	3	2	1
Body language	5	4	3	2	1
Listening level	5	4	3	2	1

Comments: _____

_____

Planning/Studying

Knowledge of prospect's needs	5	4	3	2	1
Knowledge of personal style	5	4	3	2	1
Knowledge of buying criteria	5	4	3	2	1
Knowledge of key decision makers	5	4	3	2	1

Knowledge of competitors	5	4	3	2	1
Knowledge of product or service	5	4	3	2	1
Overall preparation	5	4	3	2	1

Comments: _____

_____ _____

Proposing

Presentation length	5	4	3	2	1
Organization	5	4	3	2	1
Demonstration	5	4	3	2	1
Relation of features to benefits	5	4	3	2	1
Prospect's reaction	5	4	3	2	1

Comments: _____

_____

Confirming

Managing resistance	5	4	3	2	1
CSU summary	5	4	3	2	1
Open question with direction	5	4	3	2	1

Comments: _____

_____

Product or service

Company image	5	4	3	2	1
Company reputation	5	4	3	2	1
Price	5	4	3	2	1
Delivery	5	4	3	2	1
Service	5	4	3	2	1

Comments: _____

_____

Prospect

Receptivity	5	4	3	2	1
Mood	5	4	3	2	1
Consistency with past	5	4	3	2	1
Freedom from distractions	5	4	3	2	1
Initial interest	5	4	3	2	1
Final interest	5	4	3	2	1
Reasons for resistance	5	4	3	2	1
Reasons for refusal	5	4	3	2	1

Comments: _____

As you can see on the checklist, everything from soup to nuts is covered, including the tip. To make it relevant to the calls you make, add whatever items you think will help evaluate your calls.

This worksheet will provide you with a wealth of information about yourself and your prospects.

The Checklist as a Visualization Tool

There is another invaluable use for the checklist. When you have time at the end of your day, you can sit down, relax, and reflect on the call. This is a prime opportunity to use visualization to improve your performance. Visualize the call and focus on the parts with which you had problems. Run the "tape" through your mind and envision what you did. Then imagine the scene again, but this time see yourself doing it right. Imagine the prospect's conversation and reaction to your new behavior. It is essential to visualize a successful outcome.

You should visualize your successes often. By doing so, you will reinforce the successful and effective things you do. The mental repetition of productive behaviors creates strong working habits.

Whether or not you will be returning to the prospect, the Post-Call Checklist will be especially useful to you and other salespeople who may call on the account or similar accounts in the future. It should, therefore, be kept in the account file.

After the call there are two more items to attend to: (1) always write a thank-you note, regardless of the outcome of the call, and (2) put this account on the appropriate mailing lists.

CONFIRMING THE SALE WITH A COMMITMENT LETTER

The other side of the confirming coin is the successful outcome. You've worked hard doing research, studying, and preparing your presentation, and it culminated in a sale. Now, what do you have to do before you go out to celebrate?

With your client, during the call, verbally clarify and confirm what each of you will do to make the solution work. Then put the facts in writing. The commitment letter includes delivery dates, installation details, criteria for judging success, service agreements, and so on. Keep these details independent of the contract associated with the sale itself. The commitment letter between you and your customer will serve to remind each of you of your responsibilities. It will also impress your customer with your professionalism.

Some examples of responsibilities and expectations commonly spelled out by the salesperson in the commitment letter are as follows:

- I promise to meet my delivery dates and that all merchandise will meet the specifications discussed in the sales contract.

- I agree to call you once a week to check and see that everything is running smoothly.

- I promise to handle all problems personally and to respond within one day of your call.

The customer makes these commitments:

- I agree to test all merchandise within one week of delivery and notify you if there are any problems.

- I agree to make myself available to you or answer your calls once a week to give you feedback on your system.

• I agree to call you immediately if I have a problem.

The commitment letter ensures that the lines of communication will stay open. Putting your expectations on paper creates a mutual commitment. In addition, each party knows he or she has some recourse if all is not perfect after the sale.

The drawing up of the contract of mutual responsibilities should be handled carefully with some personal styles. Relaters and socializers, who prefer relationships to tasks, may feel that personal, informal agreements are good enough. You should diplomatically insist, however, that everything be put in writing for the protection of both parties. You can blame it on yourself by saying that you have a terrible memory and prefer it in writing. Relaters and socializers tend to overlook structure and deadlines; therefore, it is up to you to provide the structure so that the tasks will be done.

When writing out tasks and responsibilities with directors and thinkers, be sure to give them the freedom to contribute to the list. Remember, directors like to call the shots and feel that they are always right. Thinkers will be less assertive but equally as interested in being methodical about the confirmation and implementation of the sale. They will also want guarantees that everything will go smoothly.

NON-MANIPULATIVE NEGOTIATING

Many salespeople are in the habit of negotiating during the confirming phase of the sale. Their products or services are big-ticket items that have many negotiable details. The negotiating process during the confirmation of the sale becomes a critical point that could affect the nature of the business relationship.

There are many negotiating styles that go by various names. For example, there are cooperative, competitive, attitudinal, organizational, and personal modes of negotiating. Most inexperienced negotiators operate in the competitive mode because they mistakenly think the shrewd business person is one who wins at the other's expense. With a win-lose attitude in mind, they "don't show all their cards" and use other strategies to gain the upper hand. This is often done at the expense of the business relationship.

If you see your prospects as adversaries rather than business partners, you will wind up with short-term, adversarial relationships. The tension, mistrust, and buyer's remorse you will create are not worth the small gains you may win by using this negotiating style. There is a better way.

Non-manipulative salespeople negotiate in a way that achieves satisfaction for both parties. They rely on trust, openness, credibility, integrity, and fairness. Their attitude is not, "How can I get what I want out of this person" but, "There are many options to explore that will make both of us happy." The philosophy of non-manipulative negotiating is the same as for non-manipulative selling: *If two people want to do business, the details will not stand in the way.* It is important *not* to negotiate the details before your customer has made a commitment to your solution.

Phases of Negotiation

If your product or service requires negotiating on a regular basis, you should get in the habit of setting the stage for the negotiation early in the sales process. There are things you can do to prepare for the negotiation from the very beginning.

Planning. Most books on negotiating tell you the number one asset of a strong negotiator is preparation. Although most of these books teach the manipulative brand of negotiating, preparation is an indispensible part of non-manipulative negotiating as well.

During the planning phase, after you have completed a competition analysis, you will know how your company compares to the competition in terms of price, service, quality, reputation, and so on. This knowledge will be important when it comes time to negotiate. You may be able to offer things your competition cannot. It will be to your advantage to point these advantages out to your prospect when the time is right.

Before you make a proposal to a client, go through your company's sales records to find any reports of previous sales to your prospect or similar businesses. If these records documented the successes and failures of the negotiating, you will be able to learn by other salespeople's experience. For this reason, your call reports should include details of what transpired during any negotiation. The knowledge you gain from these records is not a strategy per se but insight into the priorities of this market segment. For example, businesses in a certain industry segment may value service more than price, or they may care more about help in training and implementation than a discount. This is important for you to know.

During your preparation for the confirmation of the sale, go over the various bargaining chips you have. Some of the questions to answer are there: What extra services can you offer? How flexible is the price or the payment plan? Are deposits and cancellation fees negotiable? Is there optional equipment you can throw in for free? Can you provide training free of charge? What items in the negotiation will be inflexible for you? How can you compensate for these?

Meeting. When you meet a prospect, you start building the relationship by proving you are someone who is credible, trustworthy, and, it is to be hoped, the type of person your prospect likes to do business with. If you are all of these things, you will take the tension out of the relationship and thereby ease the negotiation process. As proof of this, imagine yourself selling a good car of yours to a friend. Now imagine selling it to a stranger. Who would be easier to negotiate with? The friend, of course. For both of you, the top priority is the relationship; the secondary priority is the car deal.

Studying. When you study a prospect's business, look at the big picture. As mentioned earlier in the book, don't focus on features; look for benefits you can provide. Look behind his demands for the reasons he wants them. You can come right out and ask, "What are you trying to accomplish by asking for this?" After you are told, you may be able to say, "We can accomplish that another way. Consider this alternative . . ." The more options you have for providing benefits, the more flexible the negotiation will be.

It is important, during this phase, to find out what other company's products or services your prospect is considering. This will give you insight into what they are looking for and willing to pay. If you are selling a half-million-dollar Cat Scan and your prospect is also considering a three-quarter-million-dollar Cat

Scan, you know your product is not priced too high. If, however, your prospect is looking at a lot of lower-priced units, it may be an uphill struggle to get him to spend as much as you're asking. Knowing who your competitors are will help you assess your bargaining strengths and weaknesses.

Every purchase is made with decision-making criteria in mind, either consciously or unconsciously. Find out what they are for your prospect and his company. Within those criteria, there are usually three levels of desire: "must have," "should have," and "would be nice to have." Be sure it is clear to you what these are and how they create limits to your negotiations. Obviously, "must haves" are much less flexible than "would be nice to haves."

Proposing. Proposing is another phase that indirectly affects subsequent negotiations. What you do in your presentation sets the stage for what may come up later. During your presentation, you will tie features to benefits and emphasize your *unique* features and their benefits. In this way, you will position your product or service and company above the rest. It is important to position yourself as well. Don't be afraid to let your prospect know he is getting you and everything you have promised to do after the sale.

Tips on Negotiating

When you give something up, try to gain something in return. When you give something for nothing, there is a tendency for people to want more. In all fairness to you and your prospect, therefore, you should balance what you give and receive. For example, "I'll lower the price if you pay in full within thirty days" or "I'll give you 10 percent off, but you will be charged for additional services such as training."

Look for things other than price to negotiate. For example, gain some flexibility by offering better terms, payment plans, return policies, and delivery schedules; lower deposits or cancellation fees; or implementation and training programs. Often these things can be provided for less than your company would lose if you were to lower the price.

Do not attack your prospect's demand; look for the motive behind it. Never tell a prospect his demand is ridiculous or unreasonable. Remain calm and ask for the reason behind the desire.

Do not defend your position; ask for feedback and advice from your prospect. If you meet resistance to an offer, don't be defensive. Say something like, "This is my thinking. What would you do if you were in my position?"

The successful resolution of a negotiation must first start with a commitment to do business together. It is then necessary for both parties cooperatively to maintain common interests and resolve any conflicts. The key to non-manipulative selling and negotiating is to always seek a win-win solution in which there is commitment and implementation.

COMMITMENT AND IMPLEMENTATION

In order for the sales process to work, you have to have both commitment and implementation from the customer. Commitment is the belief in the solution to the problem; implementation is the action that makes the solution work. Both are necessary for the achievement of success. On the one hand, if a prospect is committed to you and your product or service but is not interested in implementation, she might say, "I love you, your product, and your company, and I'll buy from you . . . some day." On the other hand, if there is implementation without commitment, the attitude is, "Well, if you say it's going to work, then why don't we go ahead and try it."

This is not enough. You want them to do more than try it; you want them to believe in it and make it work. Implementation without commitment leads to returns, underusage, nonusage, unfounded complaints, unreasonable expectations, and negative word-of-mouth advertising.

You customer's commitment and implementation combined with your systematic and continued follow-up will assure the customer of a long, satisfying relationship with you.

11

Assuring Customer Satisfaction The Follow-Through Process

THE GREATEST WEAKNESS of most salespeople, is the way they handle the assuring phase. Most traditional salespeople have the attitude that their job is to bring in contracts, not service the accounts. Nothing could be further from the truth, especially in non-manipulative sales.

If you play golf or tennis and have taken lessons, what is the instruction you hear most often from the pro? Follow through! Keep your eye on the ball and follow through; otherwise your motions will be choppy and inconsistent. If you are lazy and don't follow through, your golf swing or tennis serve will not work well.

The same can be said of sales. Professional sales requires a concerted follow-through. Like a good golfer, the non-manipulative salesperson does not chip or putt from the tee; he looks down the fairway and aims for long-term goals.

Traditional salespeople are afraid of the follow-through because it requires playing the game differently, that is, with a commitment. They are more concerned with short-term numbers than long-term success. They would rather take the time away from the assuring process and put it into prospecting or closing sales. In following such procedures, however, they miss the customer satisfaction and loyalty that comes with being a non-manipulative salesperson. They also miss becoming one of the top 5 percent in their profession and being a most valuable player.

The follow-through process in sales can also be called assuring customer satisfaction. It is an ongoing activity that solidifies your business base and establishes long-term, mutually beneficial relationships for you and your company. Assuring customer satisfaction requires servicing and maintaining current accounts and expanding the services you provide.

THE CUSTOMER IS YOUR BOSS

Non-manipulative sales people care about their customers, their customer's businesses, and their satisfaction with each order. Such care takes extra time, and from a strictly cost-benefit standpoint, it is time that you have calculated into the profitability of the account. From an attitudinal standpoint, you should be happy to devote the extra time to your customers.

After all, as Earl Nightingale (co-founder of Nightingale-Conant, the world's largest producer of audiocassette programs) is famous for saying, the customer is king. He, above anyone else, is your boss. "Every working person from the president of the corporation to the shoeshine boy has the same boss. He is—the customer. He is the one boss you must please. Everything you have ever owned he has paid for. He buys your home, your cars, your clothing; he pays for your vacation . . . he writes every paycheck you receive and gives you your promotions . . . and he will discharge you if you displease him."

The customer is king not only for people who deal with him directly but for everyone in the company. Marketing is a philosophy, not a department. It is the function of *every* employee to acquire and maintain customers. If this philosophy is reflected in your attitude and service, you will outdistance your competition with ease. They simply cannot compete with non-manipulative salespeople. There is no substitute for assuring your customers' continued satisfaction and maintaining an ongoing consultative relationship with them.

Although you may not have made a point of it, when your client bought your product or service, she received a significant bonus—you. Undoubtedly, she realized you were different from the very beginning, but she didn't know you were the type of salesperson who would continue the relationship and make future contributions to the client's business. By the way, there is nothing wrong with mentioning yourself as a benefit during your presentation.

The assuring phase of the sales process begins as soon as you confirm the sale. From this point on, your value to the customer takes on many roles:

You are a one-person customer-service department. By managing all future interactions with the customer, you add a personal dimension to doing business. Customers, for good reason, dislike dealing with large customer-service departments.

You are a friend. You are always willing to be a sounding board. You care about your customers and their businesses and are always available to listen to even their minor concerns.

You are a resource. Your depth of knowledge is an asset to each of your clients. Your breadth of knowledge allows you to help them with problems, questions, and opportunities, even if they are outside your industry. To them, you can be the center of a large network of helpful people.

You are a consultant and a liaison. Through you, your customers can reach people within your firm who otherwise might be inaccessible. After the confirmation of the sale, you represent the customer to the company as much as vice versa.

You are a business partner. Your customers know you have their best interest at heart for the long term. They will come to you for advice and will reciprocate by helping you when they can.

When most people think about the concept and practice of assuring customer satisfaction, they can easily conceptualize it for outside sales people. Assuring customer satisfaction can and should be an integral part of retail sales as well. Imagine buying something in a retail store and two days later receiving a telephone call from the salesperson or the store manager in which she asked you if you are satisfied with your purchase. You would be very impressed and quite pleased with her thoughtfulness. There is little doubt that you would continue doing business there.

The most successful retail stores use both simple and complex follow-up procedures to assure customer satisfaction. They make telephone calls and send direct-mail catalogs and promotional pieces announcing sales, extended warranties, and the arrival of new merchandise. Some stores send out discount-coupon books; others give "preferred customers" special hours to shop storewide sales. "Preferred customers" are people on their mailing list who have lines of credit or have made major purchases.

The more complex the product, the longer the sales cycle and the deeper the commitment will be in the relationship. The inverse is true for retail sales; however, the notion that retail sales are strictly a single-sale commitment is a thing of the past.

MONITOR SUCCESS CRITERIA

During the study phase, you and your customer determined the success criteria in terms that were measurable. You also set a date on which to take those measures or in some way monitor the results.

Before that date arrives, make an appointment to get together with your customer to compare the ideal with the real. If your test results are positive, you have done exactly what you promised; you closed your customer's need gap. A happy customer is an excellent source for testimonial letters; this would be the perfect time to ask for one. Another good time is when they compliment you on the excellent job you're doing.

Customers will frequently tell you they don't know how to write a testimonial letter. Tell them it would be helpful if they would answer these three questions:

1. Why did you buy from me? What factors were involved in your decision to buy from me rather than someone else?
2. How has my product or service helped you?
3. Would you recommend me to others?

Testimonial letters are evidence of good will and should be treated as an asset to you and your company. They should be photocopied and used in proposal documents. Another use would be in the sale of your own business. Having a lot of testimonial letters shows all the good will you have created and could help you increase the perceived value for the buyer.

If, however, the need gap is still open, you and your customer must arrive at a new solution. If technical adjustments are necessary, you will call in an engineer or technician from your company. If further training is indicated, you can arrange for it. In essence, when a need gap is still open, it puts you back in the study phase of the sale. The only way to solve the problem is to uncover its cause.

From time to time in your sales career you may find yourself investing so much time in solving a customer's problem that you are breaking even or operating at a loss with that account. Inasmuch as you agreed to meet the success criteria, your reputation and future are on the line. Don't hesitate to do whatever it takes to satisfy your customer. It will be far less of an investment than getting a new customer. In addition, your annuity and reputation for keeping your promises will remain intact.

In any type of business, things don't always go smoothly; that includes sales in general and assuring customer satisfaction. It is valuable, therefore, to have some insight into ways to manage a customer's complaints.

The more insight you have into human nature, the better your chances are of succeeding in any business. When assuring customer satisfaction, your understanding of the common emotional issues buyers experience will help you maintain the calm, compassionate attitude that is indispensible when dealing with complaints or questions.

DEAL WITH SELECTIVE PERCEPTION

Selective perception is the process in which a person sees only selected details of the whole picture. Sometimes inordinate importance is given to a small, annoying detail. For example, a customer may have a new copying machine that works like a charm, but she is irritated by the sound of the motor. She chooses to focus on what is wrong rather than on everything else that is right.

Selective perception occurs because buyers expect their purchases to be perfect. Regardless of the purchase price, they figure they deserve perfection. They do, within reason. When you run across someone who is practicing selective perception, resolve the problem by pointing out the compensating features and benefits. Paint a brighter picture. Put the negative detail in a different perspective so it becomes an insignificant part of the total picture.

Selective perception can apply to many things: performance characteristics, product operation, product idiosyncrasies, minor inconveniences, downtime, and the customer's idea of the solution to a problem. The latter is well illustrated with one of Bob Adamy's experiences.

Bob Adamy is the owner of two small hardware stores in upstate New York, including Blossom Hardware in Blossom, a tiny town in South Buffalo. Bob tells a revealing story about a customer who purchased a Toro tractor.

Bob: The customer called me up two years after he bought it. He was ranting and raving because his tractor broke down. I said to him, "Tell me what you want me to do and I'll do it for you." The customer demanded his money back. I tried to discuss some other options, but he was adamant. So I wrote a check for the entire amount of the original purchase and told the customer that one of my assistants would deliver the check and pick up the tractor.

My assistant came back an hour later and asked me to step outside. In the parking lot was my flatbed truck with the customer's tractor on top. Sitting on the Toro tractor was the customer, who had refused to budge. He had the check in his hand. I said, "I thought you told me you wanted your money back." He said, "No, what I really want is to get my tractor fixed. I love this tractor!" So I told him, "Well, if you just get down, we'll take it off the truck and put it in the shop." He said, "No, I'm not getting off this truck. I just want my tractor fixed."

So I got a mechanic, got the parts, fixed the tractor right on the truck, took him home, and got my check back.

Bob's approach to customer service has paid off well. He is now one of the top ten Toro dealers in the country, even though the floor space allocated to Toro is very small. Bob also has one of the most impressive records for market penetration; a full 5 to 10 percent higher than Toro's penetration in other areas of the country. He is so highly valued by Toro that they asked him to be in their training film with Arnold Palmer.

The moral of the story is, if you go out of your way to provide good service to your customers, they won't make outrageous demands. All they really want is a good return on their investment. In return, they will pay you back repeatedly with referrals and additional purchases. These customers are truly annuities.

COMBAT USER ERROR

User error is simply the inability of the client to utilize your product or service properly owing to lack of training. Many sales involve the installation of a new system or piece of equipment. Naturally, the buyer and/or his employees must be trained to use it. Given the fact that people tend to forget 75 percent of what they've heard after two days, it is not surprising that user error is a common cause of dissatisfaction after the sale.

Achieving the success criteria established during the study phase will hinge on the effectiveness of the training. It is imperative, therefore, that the salesperson follow through after the training period to make sure the customer is using the product properly.

The more complex a product or service is, the more training there must be. Computers are a perfect example. It often takes new computer users weeks or months before they can use their systems quickly, smoothly, and to full capacity. If a company were to install a new computer system in their office and not provide sufficient training, their commitment to the implementation of the solution would be less than 100 percent.

If user error is a common problem in your business, you should consider training your prospect before you confirm the sale. There are two advantages to this:

1. You reduce user error to practically zero. A well-trained customer will achieve his success criteria immediately or very soon after the sale.
2. It creates "golden handcuffs." Your prospect will be psychologically predisposed to doing business with you

based on the time and energy he or she has already invested in your product.

It is unlikely that someone would learn how to use your computer, for example, and then repeat that training to compare it to another. That's just too time-consuming. In addition, to learn the second system he must unlearn yours. That may make it seem that your system is easier to operate. Once a customer is comfortable with a new skill and the equipment he learned it on, he's going to buy that product.

User error is not limited to the world of high technology. For example, here's a story about a Vermont farmer who went into a hardware store to buy a new saw. He asked the owner for the best one in the house. The owner showed him a beauty and claimed it would cut five cords of wood a day. The farmer bought it, took it home, but returned a week later with it. "I'm sorry," he said to the owner, "but no matter what I do, I can't seem to get more than four cords a day out of this saw." The owner took it from him, saying, "Well, let me see if there's anything wrong with it." He reached down, pulled the starter cord and the motor roared to life. The farmer jumped back and said, "Wait a minute, what's that noise?"

You can't assume people know how to use your product. It never hurts to demonstrate and train them.

ASSUAGE BUYER'S REMORSE

Buyer's remorse is the regret someone feels after making a purchase. It can be caused by selective perception, user error, or just an uneasy feeling that he will not realize the full benefits of the product or service. Buyer's remorse could also be caused by the economic strain resulting from the purchase. Until the need gap is fully closed, the customer may question whether the benefits will prove to be cost-effective.

When a customer either directly or indirectly expresses some regrets for having made the purchase, assuage those fears by assuring him that his investment was wise. Repeat the success criteria and the time needed to achieve them. Remind him that employee training and other factors take time to affect the performance. If all else fails and you sense your business relationship will suffer, talk to your company about allowing the customer to return the product, if that is an appropriate solution. It is better to give up your commission and still have the good will.

MANAGE CUSTOMER COMPLAINTS

A customer's complaint is always important, even if it turns out to be unfounded. As soon as you can, follow up with a telephone call to see what the problem is. A telephone call may be all that is needed to provide some information or encouragement. It is often better to go to the customer's place of business to talk or rectify the situation. Use your judgment. If the problem is very technical, it's a good idea to take a technician or other "expert" along with you. He can solve the problem quickly, and you can prove you keep your promises.

If you are in the field when a customer calls in with a problem, have your company call you immediately. As soon as possible, call the customer to determine the severity of the problem. If you can, make an appointment to stop by later in the day. If that is not possible and sending a technician will do the trick, tell your customer you cannot make it but you are sending someone to fix the problem. Be sure to follow up with a telephone call after the technician has left to be sure everything is back to normal. You don't want to give the impression that you dumped the customer on a technician without any further thought.

If you are doing your job right, you should receive relatively few complaint calls because you will "head them off at the pass." In other words, you will have called or stopped by to see how things were going before your customer had a chance to call you. Their whole attitude is different when you call first. They are impressed that you called and are less emotional about the complaint. A simple telephone call creates an incredible amount of good will.

A sound system for following up sales is as follows:

- Immediately after the sale, send a letter or postcard thanking the customer for the order.

- Three to five days after the product has been put in use, call to see if everything is all right.

- A week or two later, send them something extra. It should be an item that they can use but don't expect. It can be a note pad with their name on it or a small option for the product they bought. For example, if your customer bought a computer, you could send some printer ribbons of different colors and enclose a note, "Thought you might have some fun with these colors." Often your company will have items that won't cost you anything. You might even suggest the procedure to your sales manager.

- One, two, or three months after the sale, review the success criteria with your customer to see if your goals have been accomplished. When you've accomplished your goals, ask for a testimonial letter and some referrals. A satisfied customer will bend over backwards to find more business for you.

There will be times when you have to manage a customer's complaint. It happens to the best salespeople. When it happens, keep these tips in mind:

Admit the problem and apologize. No one is perfect and the larger the company, the more people there are to make mistakes. As long as it's not a way of doing business, people will be forgiving if you are courteous.

Show compassion for your customer. Regardless of the extent of the complaint, keep the relationship strong by being sincerely concerned, looking into the problem, and solving it.

Be an active listener. Lending an ear will help your customer vent some steam and reduce his tension level. You may find his selective perception or buyer's remorse is caused by the stress of his business and not your product.

Don't pass the buck; there's no one to pass it to. You are the liaison between your customer and your company. It's your job to manage all complaints if you want to maintain trust with your client.

Assuring customer satisfaction requires a commitment to yourself: "My customers are as important to me as my career." Your customers are your career.

Use These Thirteen Ways to Assure Customer Satisfaction

Since your customers are your career, you should let them know how special they are. In addition to monitoring their implementation of and success with your product or service, they should be made to feel comfortable enough to call you at any time. There are many ways you can accomplish this.

Show your customers you think of them. Once a month or so look at your client list and think of a way to show your thoughtfulness. Cut out and send articles and cartoons. Send birthday or holiday cards and ideas to help them improve business. Start a monthly newsletter or send samples of new products.

Make appointments and go in to check up on things. Bring new brochures, products, or other little extras with you. While you're there, see if your customers are getting the optimal use of your product. If not, show them how to get the most out of it.

Offer a sample gift to enhance the use of your product. For example, a computer user would appreciate diskettes, printer ribbons, software, and so on.

Offer customers "preferred customer discounts" and encourage them to call you for all of their needs. Compile a coupon book full of discounts on things they will need, and you'll make it easy for them to place orders. After a while you will be the first person they will call when a need arises.

When customers hire new employees, offer to train them free of charge or at a reduced rate. The better trained their employees are, the more likely they are to use your product and the more sales you will realize.

Compensate customers for downtime. If your product or service has an unusually large amount of downtime, that inconveniences your customer; it creates a tremendous amount of good will to offset their loss somehow.

Accept returns without balking. They are much less expensive than finding new customers.

Respect your customers' confidentiality. Don't discuss their business with other clients, sales people, or friends.

Represent both your client and your company. If necessary, push your company to follow through on their commitments. Just as your behavior reflects on them, they can indirectly hurt your reputation if they are remiss.

Act on referrals immediately. Show your appreciation for your customer's referrals by contacting them as soon as possible and reporting back to your customer on the outcome. If the referral was successful, the positive feedback you give will encourage more referrals. You can show your appreciation with a modest but thoughtful gift. If the referral was unsuccessful, the customer may get more involved and try to make it work. For example, she may volunteer to telephone in your behalf.

Give your customers free publicity. If your company has a newsletter, ask permission from your successful customers to write about them. After publication, send them a copy.

Keep track of your customers' results. Meet with them once a year for an annual checkup. Discuss their business, the industry, market trends, emerging opportunities, competition, and so on.

Keep lines of communication fully open. Encourage customers to call you at any time with ideas, questions, grievances, jokes, feedback, and whatever else is on their minds. These are not interruptions of your work; they are the purpose of it.

The art of assuring customer satisfaction will take you a long way toward success. Aside from responding to problems and meeting for the evaluation of success criteria, there will be many other times when you will call on your customers.

Naturally, the classification of the account will dictate the frequency of calls. To determine when to follow up, be sensitive to the business environment and goings-on of all your accounts. Watch for changes in their businesses that suggest a call from you. Some of these are as follows:

1. Changes in sales volume. Increases or decreases should be investigated. They may be a reflection of the market, and

you should be aware of developing problems or opportunities.

2. An increase in the number of complaints about your product or service, customer service, pricing, or your company in general.

3. During telephone calls, repeated comments about the merits of the competition is a clear warning signal. Go talk in person.

4. Any time you feel a change in the relationship, go check it out. A decrease in your rapport, when unchecked, can mean problems if you don't take steps.

5. New management who are not familiar with or interested in your product or service can upset the apple cart. Make an appointment to meet them and establish relationships with them as well.

6. If your customer is absorbed by a larger firm, meet with the new decision makers. They may want to start over with a clean slate, which could mean the loss of the account. Therefore, you must try to establish relationships quickly and present a good case for not changing suppliers.

CONDUCT AN ANNUAL CHECKUP

Annual reviews are valuable tools for evaluating the activities of an account, the industry in general, competitors, and your company's strengths and weaknesses with your customers. Reanalyzing your market segments and accounts periodically will help you reclassify and prioritize accounts, if necessary, and give you insight into new markets and trends.

When you meet with your customers, encourage an open and honest discussion of where you have been and where you're going together. This special meeting will give you additional feedback about your customers' level of satisfaction, provide an opportunity to introduce new products or services, convey that you care, and strengthen trust between you. Give some thought to making the meeting effective:

1. Arrange a breakfast or lunch meeting, depending on the personal style of your customer.

2. Select a place that is well lit, quiet, and conducive to conversation. If your office or your client's office is not suitable, most hotels have boardroom-style meeting spaces that are fully equipped with audiovisual equipment, flip charts, and food service.

3. Invite everyone participating in the account from both companies.

4. You and your customer should bring all the records needed to discuss the previous year's business.

5. Allow an adequate amount of time for the meeting, but do set a limit. As much as you do not want to rush the discussion, you also should not let it continue beyond a reasonable amount of time.

6. Be organized. Know what you want to talk about and proceed in a logical, flexible manner. Take notes if necessary and afterwards send a clean, typed copy to the other participants.

7. Listen carefully for implied needs, concerns, and opportunities.

8. Reiterate your desire to be of service and maintain an open, trustworthy relationship.

9. After the review, offer a new idea, service, product, or special promotional deal when possible. This is an excellent opportunity to spark interest in something new.

10. During your conversation, look for opportunities above and beyond the customer's immediate horizon. Ask for referrals and letters of testimony, if appropriate.

EXPAND YOUR SERVICES

It is not sufficient to service your present accounts; you must also provide for the future. This means continually adding new qualified prospects and turning them into active accounts.

Opportunities are all around you every day, but you miss them by overlooking the obvious. The non-manipulative salesperson recognizes that her current customers are the best source of new business. It you have a strong relationship with your customers, you can feel comfortable asking them for referrals that may bring you additional accounts. There are several ways to expand your business through your customers.

Look for referrals within a customer's company. Whenever you talk to a customer, keep an ear open for clues that indicate needs and opportunities within his company. For example, a new office or branch might open and need your product or service. Ask your customer for a referral, either verbally or in writing. In these days of mergers, nearly every company owns a subsidiary or is a subsidiary of a larger firm. Be sure to ask for referrals to parents and subsidiaries.

Ask for referrals outside of a customer's company. It is important to ask your customers if they know anyone else who may have a need for your services. In doing so, it is helpful if they will write an introductory letter or make a telephone call on your behalf. Always ask your customers for permission to use them as references.

Sell more of the same. If, during your servicing of an account, you see the company has the capacity to buy larger volumes, suggest they buy more, especially if you can offer better prices. In this way, B accounts can sometimes be turned into A accounts. Of course, you would never try to sell them more if they didn't need it.

Sell additional products or services to your accounts. Offer new products or services to your present customers if appropriate. If they like your original product, they will listen to your ideas about expanding into other product lines.

Upgrade your customers. If a customer uses a medium-price product, you may be able to upgrade it to a higher-price, higher-quality product, especially if the company is growing and its needs are changing. For example, a company that uses a copying machine may find it needs one with more features such as photoreduction and collating. When you become aware of their increased needs, suggest the upgrade before your competitor does.

If you make assuring customer satisfaction a regular part of your sales routine and develop a vast and loyal business base, you will, in effect, be investing in your future the way people invest in life insurance. Think of a customer as an annuity. In the beginning, you establish the relationship. This is like taking out the policy. Over time you service and maintain that customer, always making sure he or she is satisfied. This is analogous to paying your insurance premiums. At some point in your sales career, you will have many customers who need litttle attention from you but give you lots of business nonetheless. You might consider this the annuity stage in which your previous investment is paying off quite nicely. The analogy of the customer as an annuity is meant to give you a long-term view of your sales career and the relationships you develop within it. There is no guarantee that each customer will become a low-maintenance annuity. Similarly, if one does become an annuity, there is no way to predict when. As you go along, you will see how much attention each customer needs to stay highly profitable. It's the philosophy that counts and the practice of it that makes it work. Your constant attention to customer satisfaction is one of the most important career-building blocks you have.

12

Selling by Style

THE BEGINNING of this book explained that the basic tenets of non-manipulative selling are embodied in building relationships and the six steps of non-manipulative selling. Integrating these approaches creates a winning combination; you learn to relate well to people and, in turn, use this ability to serve them better in your capacity as a non-manipulative salesperson. Practice will make these skills second nature and turn you into a top 5 percenter.

It is ideal if you can quickly identify someone's behavioral style on the telephone or in person. Listen and look for all the cues discussed in chapter 2. There will be times, however, when you haven't had the opportunity to determine exactly where someone falls on the two behavioral scales of openness vs. self-containment and directness vs. indirectness. If you can identify the person's placement on one scale, you're halfway there. For example, if you were to determine that your prospect is open, that would immediately eliminate the two self-contained behavioral styles, those who are thinkers and directors. Knowing that you are dealing with a relater or a socializer, you can start building the relationship.

How To Modify Your Behavioral Style

Before considering specific guidelines for being flexible with each of the four behavioral styles, it is helpful to look at what you can do to modify both your openness and directness in general.

To increase openness:

- Share your feelings; let your emotions show.

- Respond to the expression of others' feelings.

- Pay personal compliments.

- Take time to develop the *relationship*.

- Use friendly language.

- Communicate more; loosen up; stand closer.

- Use a few more "easy" gestures like leaning back, smiling, or gently patting the other person on the back or shoulder.

- Be willing to digress from the agenda; go with the flow.

To increase self-containment:

- Get right to the task, the bottom line, the business at hand.

- Maintain more of a logical, factual orientation.

- Keep to the agenda.

- Leave when the work is done; do not waste the other person's time.

- Do not initiate physical contact.

- Downplay your enthusiasm and body movement.

- Use businesslike language.

To increase directness:

- Speak and move at a faster pace.

- Initiate conversation.

- Initiate decisions.

- Give recommendations; don't ask for opinions.

- Use direct statements rather than round-about questions.

- Communicate with strong, confident vocal qualities.

- Challenge and tactfully disagree when appropriate.

- Face conflict openly, but don't fight with your prospects.

- Increase your eye contact.

To decrease directness:

- Talk, walk, and make decisions more slowly.

- Seek and acknowledge the opinions of others.

- Share the decision-making responsibilities with others.

- Allow others to assume some of the leadership.

- Show less energy; be more "mellow."

- Do not interrupt.

- Provide pauses when talking to give others a chance to speak.

- Refrain from criticizing or challenging.

- Choose words carefully when disagreeing and state opinions with finesse.

- Don't be pushy.

- Use less eye contact.

Selling by Style = Flexibility

When you have determined the behavioral style of your prospect, you will have the insight you need to know what will work best in every phase of the sales process. This insight will enable you to communicate more efficiently and effectively, that is, you will accomplish more in less time.

THE SOCIALIZER PROSPECT

Socializers like to interact with people on more than just a business level. A socializer wants to be your friend before doing business. When a client suggests you meet over lunch or dinner or asks you, "Any good parties happening this weekend?", you know you're probably dealing with a socializer.

Socializers like to wax poetic and exaggerate, so be nonjudgmental; after all, you don't have to agree with everything they say. Don't even bother trying to win an argument with a socializer. Socializers love a good debate as long as you don't dominate it; they don't like too much competition.

Be an active listener, as you would with anyone, and give reflective feedback. Let your prospect know you understand and emphathize with what he is feeling. When you talk about yourself, use the word *feel* instead of *think*. Share your vision of the world in terms of feelings, opinions, and intuitions. Tell stories about yourself, especially if they are unusual or humorous. The more entertaining you are, the easier it will be to win the heart of a socializer.

Planning

The planning phase of the sales process covers territory management, account analysis, and prospecting. Behavioral style bears on your handling of these phases in a subtle but significant way. When you plan to penetrate a company, determine as best you can what style the prospects will have. Generalizations can be made with some margin of safety. For example:

- Socializers love the people business; image, glamor, and show businesses; the persuasion business; the media; and any business that is fun and brings status.

- Directors generally gravitate to competitive, high-pressure businesses and become advertising executives, stock brokers, politicians, corporate presidents, and so on.

- Relaters are pulled toward the helping professions: psychologists, nurses, guidance counselors, social workers, elementary school teachers, and some doctors.

- Thinkers are comfortable in the exact sciences such as engineering, accounting, genetics, and biology, and library science.

These generalizations should be used for corroboration, not as a cut-and-dried rule for prejudging people. The occupations people gravitate towards are ones they feel comfortable in, but this does not mean that all engineers are thinkers, just as all salespeople are not socializers. There are all kinds of people in every occupation. The overall patterns, however, favor one behavioral style or another.

There will be times when you will have to team sell a company. In the planning phase, decide who in your company will meet with their people based on behavioral styles. A director from your company should meet their chief executive officer. A thinker should meet their engineering manager and so on.

Behavioral style also comes into play when analyzing your current accounts and prospects. In determining how much time to spend on each, take into consideration the style of the client or prospect. Plan to spend more time with relaters and socializers.

If you don't know a prospect's style, do your homework and try to find out. Ask people within the company; ask noncompetitive salespeople who know the person. Call his secretary and ask closed-ended questions based on the descriptions of openness and directness in chapter 2. Obtaining information from secretaries will be easier if you have built a relationship first. Even if you have not, however, it doesn't hurt to ask some innocent questions. Granted, you won't always receive answers, but, if *you don't ask, you don't get!* Here are some questions to start with:

> "Is Mr. Jenson easy to get to know, or does it take a while for him to open up?"

> "Does he only talk about business and the work being done or does he share his outside life, thoughts, and feelings with people?"

> "In a meeting, does Mr. Jenson readily voice his opinions, or does he prefer to listen?"

> "Does Mr. Jenson makes decisions relatively quickly, or does he like to take a lot of time to contemplate them?"

> "Is Ms. Hammond a bubbly person, or does she hold in her enthusiasm and act very businesslike?"

"Does she control her time rigidly, or is she flexible?"

"Does she prefer to work with others, or is she content working by herself?"

"Is Ms. Hammond a detail-oriented person, or does she look at the big picture?"

The more familiar you become with behavioral styles, the easier it will be to compose your own questions. If you spend five minutes on the telephone with a cooperative secretary, you will be amazed how much information you will collect. Soon you'll have every secretary in town knowing you on a first-name basis.

Meeting

When you write to or personally meet a socializer, give the letter or meeting an upbeat, friendly feeling and fast pace. Don't talk about features, specifications, or performance data. In your initial-benefits statement, stress those aspects of your product or service that will give them what they want: status, recognition, excitement, and being the first one on the block to have whatever you are selling. Be sure to back up your claims with testimonials from well-known people or corporations.

The first time you call a socializer, use an informal, friendly approach. Tell him who you are and say something like, "I'd like to come by and show you an exciting new product that will analyze and organize your accounts and help you become even more of a top performing salesperson."

When you call on a socializer at their place of business, make believe you are a politician running for reelection. Shake hands firmly, introduce yourself with confidence, and immediately show an interest in the person. Let them set the pace and direction of the conversation. Socializers like to talk about themselves a lot. You may say, "Tell me how you got into this business," and two hours later he is saying, ". . . and that was on my fifteenth birthday." For this reason, you must plan to have as many meetings with a socializer as necessary to build the relationship and gather information. After your first visit, you may want to meet for a meal. Keep in mind that your tight schedule may necessitate placing a time limit on the meeting. Breakfast and lunch are easier to limit than dinner.

Studying

Socializers become bored quickly if they are not talking about themselves. That is why so much of the information gathering has to revolve around them. You have to strike a balance, however, between listening to their life stories and gathering the information you need to be a sales consultant. When asking business-oriented questions, keep them brief. If possible, try to work the information-gathering questions in with the social questions. For example, you might say, "You mentioned people as being one of the keys to your success. How do you find (recruit) the people you work with? What kind of training do you give them?" The better your relationship with a socializer, the more willing they will be to cooperate and talk about the "boring stuff."

Proposing

The presentation should show a socializer how your product or service will increase his prestige, image, or recognition. Presentations should have impact, so involve as many senses as possible. Socializers want the presentation, and therefore the product, to feel great. They also want to be reminded of who else has it, but they don't care about the details of other people's success.

Confirming

Be open in the confirming stage and ask, "Where do we go from here?" or "What's our next step?" If your inventory is low, tell the prospect, "I see you really are excited about this. I have only three left; do you want to buy one right now?" Socializers are very spontaneous. If they like something, they buy it (all things being equal). You may have to hold them back because they also tend to overbuy, which both you and your customer will later regret.

Socializers don't like paperwork and details. They will try to resist spending the time to create a commitment letter. For this reason, you would be wise to write one out in advance and go over it with your prospect. Make any necessary changes and it will be done quickly and painlessly.

Assuring

In the assuring phase you have to be organized for a disorganized person. You have to be realistic in your expectation of how much time a socializer will take to monitor the success of your product or service. Socializers are the type of people who buy computers and never read the manuals. It is up to you, therefore, practically to hold the prospect's hand during the training, and implementation processes. Make appointments to stop by to be sure they are using your product or service correctly and getting the most out of it. If this requires extra training, so be it.

THE DIRECTOR PROSPECT

Directors are easy to deal with as long as you act like a director. They are impatient and intolerant of slow-paced people, especially if their competence is questionable. Be well organized, time-conscious, efficient, and businesslike. Directors don't want to be your friend; they want to get something out of you if you have something worthwhile to offer; and they are willing to pay a reasonable price for it.

Meeting

When you write to, call, or meet a director, do it in a formal, businesslike manner, which means getting right to the point. Be task oriented and fast paced. In your initial-benefits statement, talk about bottom-line results, increased efficiency, saving time, return on investment, profits, and so on. Over the telephone you can say something like, "The trend in your industry is toward computer-generated graphics. The research I've conducted with other typesetters in your area indicates increased profits of 20 to 30 percent over two years. I'd like to meet with you to show you the numbers and see if this concept interests you."

When gathering information, ask questions that show you have done your homework. Know the industry and the company. Be sure to ask questions that allow them to talk about their personal business goals.

Studying and Proposing

Although the two phases of studying and proposing are normally separate, with directors, they often have to be combined. Directors are busy people who do not like to grant several meetings. They like to hear the facts and make quick decisions. It is essential, when asking questions, to fine tune the questions as much as possible. Aim them precisely to the heart of the issue and ask them in a straightforward manner. You have to do your homework and ask only for information that is not available elsewhere.

In addition to being busy, directors are impatient. Keep your studying interesting by alternately asking questions and giving information. Do this in a logical manner; directors have to see the meeting as purposeful and they want to be able to see where you are going with your questioning.

Your presentation, whether it is combined with studying or given on its own, will have to be geared to the director's priorities. He is concerned with saving time, making money, making life more efficient and easier. He is also motivated to do those things that will bring more success. Present benefits briefly and quickly, focusing on the bottom line.

Owing to their lack of time, directors cannot contemplate and evaluate ideas. They want you to do the analysis and lay it out for them to approve or disapprove. Directors like quick, concise analyses of their needs and your solutions. You should offer options with supporting evidence and leave the final decision to them. "The way I see it, you can go with option A (tell pros and cons), option B (tell pros and cons) or option C (more pros and cons)." Directors are very big on autonomy, so *let them make the decision.*

Confirming

Directors are the type of people you can come right out and ask if they are interested. In the confirming stage, you might say, "Based on what we've just discussed, are you interested in starting our service or carrying our product?" A director will tell you yes or no in no uncertain terms.

At times, directors can appear to be poor decision makers. They will procrastinate and put you off as if they can't make a decision when, in fact, they aren't even thinking about it. They can be so busy they do not have the *time* to evaluate your ideas, especially when they don't have enough information. It is the salesperson's job to provide sufficient information and provide an initiative for the director to meet with you. For example, when you call, you could say, "Some of the ways I thought we might be able to work together are X, Y, and Z. Could we discuss those when I call you in a couple of weeks?" By planting a seed, you raise his interest level and the priority of your next call; unless, of course, he just isn't interested.

When you draw up the commitment letter, be conscious of the amount of time you are spending on something that the director may not care about. Explain your commitment to assuring her or him that the results are achieved and that the commitment letter is for both of you.

Assuring

Impress upon your prospect that you intend to stand behind your product or service. At the same time, ensure him that you will follow up without taking up a lot of his time. "You're buying this to give yourself more efficiency and save time. I want to make sure that it continues to work for you. What I'll do is periodically check back with you to make sure everything is running smoothly, but I don't want to waste your time with unnecessary calls. When I call, if everything is fine, just say so and that will be it. I'll call you next month. However, if everything is not letter perfect, I want you to call me immediately and I will rush out here with someone to fix the problem." You might also offer a money-back guarantee or a personal guarantee: "If you aren't happy, I will personally take back the merchandise and write you a check."

THE THINKER PROSPECT

Thinkers are precision people. They are efficiency experts who want to do their job the "correct" way and be recognized for being right. They go about things slowly and do not like to be rushed. To build credibility, use the word *think* instead of *feel*. Present data that are impressive and from reliable sources. Be intellectually oriented rather than emotionally oriented.

Meeting

When writing to, calling, or meeting a thinker, appeal to her logical side. Thinkers like systems, details, facts, and tangible evidence. Letters should include research findings and descriptions of features. When you call a thinker, be brief but slow paced. Carefully explain why you are calling and ask for an appointment. "Hello, Ms. Johnson, this is Salvatore Botticelli calling from the Italiano Pasta Company. Betty Bryant said she called you about me . . . good, I'm glad you remember. I'd like to come by your restaurant and talk to you about how you make pasta. You may be interested in our fully integrated, computerized pasta machine. It's a complete system that controls inventory while producing thirty-two types of pasta to within 1/100th of an inch of your specifications. Would you be interested in setting up an appointment to see more?"

Studying

Thinkers love to answer questions; they are the ideal interviewees. As long as your questions are logical and fact oriented, they will enjoy talking to you. Phrase your questions precisely and ask for precise answers. They typically give short, crisp answers even to open-ended questions. Ask for the *exact* number of things, not the approximate number. For example, "We are going to bid on the window washing service of the Empire State Building. How many windows will we be responsible for?" They'll tell you exactly how many windows. You could even ask, "And what is the total number of square feet of glass?" and you would find out.

Proposing

Show thinkers how your product will prove to their company that they are right in the way they do their jobs. They pride themselves on the accuracy of their analyses. Present your product or service in a way that shows them they will be correct in making the purchase. Base your claims on facts, specifications, and data that relate specifically to their need gaps. For example, point out cost-benefit analyses, maintenance costs, reliability data, tax advantages, statistics on increased efficiency, and so on. When you talk about prices, relate them to the specific benefits. Thinkers are very cost conscious; therefore, you have to increase their perceived value with hard facts.

Confirming

Thinkers are indecisive by nature, so make sure they have had enough time to analyze their options before you seek confirmation.

A problem that occasionally arises with thinkers is that they will say they need more information, but in fact, they are putting off the decision-making process. Provide them with the information they need until it reaches the point where additional information isn't moving them closer to a decision.

When you are asked for more information, be firm with them in a gentle way. Ask what specific information is needed to make the decision and if they will confirm the sale after you provide it for them. You might say it like this, "No problem, I can get that information for you. Will that information be enough for you then to make a decision?" If the answer is yes, then set up a hypothetical situation and see what he says. "Let's assume I get the information. If it turns out to be X, what will your decision be? If it turns out to be Y, what will your decision be?" What you have done is gained a commitment that is contingent upon something concrete that you are going to furnish.

If, however, he answered your question with, "No, It's not enough information," then ask, "What other information would you need?" Another approach is to use the weighted-average Ben Franklin Balance Sheet described in the chapter on confirming. When you discuss the commitment letter, spell out exactly how the success criteria will be measured. Thinkers are good at developing realistic, specific, and measurable means of monitoring results.

Assuring

For the assuring phase, set up a timetable that will indicate exactly when you will call or stop by to measure success criteria. Tell the prospect you will always call a day in advance to confirm your meetings. Keep in mind that monitoring results is *very* important to a thinker.

THE RELATER PROSPECT

Relaters love people. The relationship comes first; after all, if you haven't got a family and friends, what have you got? They are slow-moving, open people, who want to be cared about. You should use the word *feel* rather than *think* with them. They are most comfortable with familiar things; therefore, it is helpful if you explain new ideas in contexts or analogies that are familiar. When selling to a relater, you will have to become their friend first. Work on building trust and credibility.

Meeting

Letters to relaters should be soft and warm. They should talk about people, not things. Relate everything about your product or service to its impact on people and relationships. When you call a relater, sincerely ask how the person is. The best calls are those in which you can mention the name of someone who referred you. "Hello, Mr. Newhouse, I'm Sheldon Doolittle with the Pinpoint Acupuncture Clinic. Mary Walsh said you would appreciate knowing about me and my clinic. . . . Oh, she did call you, good. If you'd like, I could come by, we could get to know each other, and I can tell you about the ways other people have relieved their allergies with our treatments." Remember, you could have the best product or service in the world, but, if the relater doesn't like you, she will settle for second-best from a salesperson she likes.

When you meet, greet the relater with an easy handshake, a warm smile, and good eye contact. Be soft-spoken and work on creating trust first. Encourage them to open up, and take the time to talk about yourself as well. Give the meeting a slow, informal ambiance.

Studying

Relaters, along with thinkers, are excellent interviewees. You can ask them anything about the people side of the business, but get the hard facts from someone else. It is important to probe and ask sensitive questions gently. For example, if a relater does not have a good feeling about your product, company, or even you, they will not take the chance of hurting your feelings by telling you so. Relaters don't like to rock the boat. So a relater may tell you what he thinks you want to hear rather than what they really think.

The same reticence may apply in telling you about his dissatisfaction with your competitors. Even though this is exactly what you want to hear, the relater may think, "I know it hasn't been working well, but, gee, they're such nice people. I don't want to say anything negative about them."

Proposing

Relaters want to know how your product or service is going to bring people closer together or make life easier for them. Relate the benefits to these themes and spend very little time on features, unless the features make life easier. Involve the relater in your presentation by having him or her give you feedback and answer questions.

Confirming

Relaters are slow decision makers as well, but for other reasons than those of thinkers. One reason is that they are consultative decision makers; that is, they value the opinions of others and take the time to solicit those opinions before making up their minds.

The second reason is that they often lack the proper information. Unfortunately, relaters tend to tell people what they want to hear rather than what they need to know. In the study phase, if a relater tells you X, you act on X. When you propose a solution to X and the prospect keeps saying he wants to think about it, you become frustrated and confused. The problem started with the exchange of information in the study phase; you were given the wrong information.

In the confirming phase, relaters are too shy to tell you they need more information because that is not what they think you want to hear. So they skirt the misinformation issue by saying they want to think about it. The solution is to go back to the study phase, gather the right information, and start over again.

Another approach is to lead relaters. Once you have determined what would be in their best interest, lead them to the confirmation with your recommendation. Say something that shows you care, for example, "Jean, we've talked about a lot of things and I firmly believe this is the best solution for you. I would not recommend it if I weren't 100 percent convinced it will work for you." When you've won agreement, you can gently lead the relater to the next step. "If you agree with everything we've just discussed, I guess the next step is to fill out the agreement and get a deposit."

There is nothing manipulative or pushy about this. You have studied your prospect's needs and are now recommending a solution that you honestly believe is the best. It's a win-win situation.

Assuring

Follow the same procedure for assuring the relater's satisfaction as you would for anyone else, but go a step further. Impress upon your prospect that the two of you now have a relationship. "I want you to remember that you are primarily my customer and secondarily my company's customer. I will take care of you for them. If anything goes wrong, if you have a question or a problem, no matter how small it may seem, please call me first, any time of the day or night." Naturally you will give him your home telephone number. Rest assured, a relater wouldn't dare "disturb" you at home. Directors, on the other hand, you can expect to hear from . . . any time of the day or night.

ROOM FOR IMPROVEMENT

These insights into people and using the best strategies for working with them will smooth out the bumps that often accompany the sales process. One thing cannot be overemphasized: *If two people want to do business together, the details will not get in the way.* Selling by behavioral style will eliminate or reduce personality conflicts. With personal differences out of the way, you and your prospect will be able to focus clearly on the important aspects of the sale: the exchange of information, uncovering needs and opportunities, the design of solutions, and maintaining long-term, mutually beneficial relationships.

All your insight into behavioral style will not only help you relate to other people, but improve yourself as well. Knowing your behavioral style will suggest your strengths and weak areas where there is room for improvement. Table 12.1 summarizes the phases of the sale in which different types of people are comfortable.

Think about your personal style and determine if you are a director, socializer, thinker, or relater. Then look over table 12.1 to see if your strengths and weaknesses are the same as the majority of people in your category. If they are not, it only proves what has been said about the diversity and complexity of people's behaviors; generalizations reflect the overall picture; individuals may be exceptions to the rule.

Table 12.1

**The Strengths and Weakness of The Four Behavioral Styles
As Sales People**

Salesperson	Phase of sale most comfortable with	Phase least comfortable with	To improve:
Director	Planning Confirming	Studying Assuring	slow down, relax, participate more with client
Socializer	Meeting Proposing	Planning Assuring	organize for details; create checklists
Thinker	Planning Studying	Meeting Confirming	work on relationships; implement ideas
Relater	Studying Assuring	Proposing Confirming	focus on helping people solve problems

The third column of the table will give you much food for thought. A rule that salespeople have to learn is, *You have to be flexible with other people, especially if you have an insight into behavioral styles.* Some people may find it easier to be flexible than others, but ability should not determine practice.

Directors have to work on being more patient, tolerant, and slower-paced. They have to get involved with their clients, be less task-oriented, and work on their relationships.

Socializers need to become friends with thinkers. Seriously, they have to organize themselves so the details of their work do not fall through the cracks. Checklists and other paperwork will ensure that every step of the process is completed. This "safety net" will bring order to people who generally fly by the seat of their pants.

Thinkers need to work on relationships. This means being less businesslike and more people-oriented. They also have to realize that their great ideas are useless until they help their customers implement them.

Relaters need to realize they are helping people improve their businesses and personal lives by solving their problems. The only way a problem can be solved is if the customer makes a commitment to implement the solution.

When you sell *by* style, you also sell *with* style. Selling with style is knowing who you are, who your client is, and using all your communication skills to create good chemistry and not conflict. This is selling smart and it will, in the long run, give you a reputation as someone who does business with professionalism.

13

The Image of Excellence

IN BUSINESS and in private life, people keep score on other people. You can't help it. It is a way of determining whether to accept or reject another person. Every time you enter a new environment, you are evaluated and given a "score" on various characteristics that your evaluators consider important. You do the same thing. You use a system to evaluate and weed out people whom you don't consider worth your time or energy.

When the authors developed the concept of non-manipulative selling, they polled a large number of seminar participants with this question: "Of all the salespeople that you have met—from the door-to-door vacuum-cleaner peddler to the multimillion-dollar mainframe computer salesperson—what percent of those salespeople would you classify as 'professional'?" Or to put it another way: Imagine being in a restaurant with a friend. While you're eating, a salesperson with whom you spent an hour earlier in the day walks in and sits down. If that person were a truly exceptional salesperson, you would feel motivated to point her out and tell your friend how professional the person was. How many salespeople with whom you have done business would deserve such recognition?

When people are asked these questions, the most typical response is, "Less than 5 percent." Five percent of sales people stand out as exceptional. That 5 percent may be called *excellent;* the remaining 95 percent may be called *mediocre.*

What characteristics distinguish excellence from mediocrity? And which of those characteristics are learnable and practicable?

Assume that several business associates are talking about you. What words would they use to describe you when you are at your best? Ideally, what words would you want them to use when speaking of you? When the authors have used this exercise in the past, participants have responded with descriptive words such as these:

thorough	friendly	competent
professional	prepared	cool and calm
confident	self-assured	sincere
knowledgeable	polite	well-groomed
honest	creative	caring

Interestingly, their lists almost always described a *high-scoring,* non-manipulative salesperson.

In selling, a high score (seven to ten on an arbitrary scale of one to ten) based on the characteristics of excellence is called an *automatic* (a situation in which the customer tugs at your sleeve and says, "Can I buy now?"). An average score (five to six) means the customer is saying, "Sell me. Don't go away, I need more information." A low score (below 4) means the customer definitely won't buy from you. The final answer is no and both of you know it. End of conversation.

EVERYTHING counts in the scoring process. For example, how many points can a pen be worth? Maybe only a few, but an important few.

In his book *Dress for Success,* John Molloy writes that an excellent business person should carry a gold pen. Maybe a pen is worth only one or two points, but if you were winning by one point, the pen would become important. If a person has a very high or low score, it wouldn't matter, but with a borderline score it does. Imagine that the customer is ready to buy and the salesperson (who has a score of seven to ten) pushes the contract across the table with a chewed-up plastic pen bearing "Joe's Service Center" on the side. She may lose only two points, but that may be enough to drop her from an automatic sale to a "Gee, Susan, I like everything you've said to me, but . . ." The pen brought the score down to five or six. No sale.

Is it worth carrying a gold pen? Of course! *Every* impression counts. In fact, it is usually the *little* things that defeat our efforts.

There are things in life that we can control, and there are things that we cannot control.

Phil: I read a magazine article about a study that found that men over six feet tall tend to be more financially successful than men less than six feet tall. No matter how much I stretched, I stayed five feet seven inches. Knowing that height and success were correlated didn't help a bit. It's one of those things in life no one can control. So I stopped stretching and worked harder. Unfortunately, many people spend too much time, effort, and energy trying to deal with things they cannot control.

As a salesperson, you can't control the economy. You can't control your competitors' prices. You can't control your competitors' quality. But you *can* control the way you get dressed in the morning!

This chapter identifies twelve specific skills that excellence exhibits and mediocrity lacks. The twelve characteristics of excellence are personal attributes over which *you have complete control.* It is, therefore, very important for you to develop these skills so that you will win all the points possible in these areas. Every point you win in these areas is a point you don't need in the areas of price, product, and presentation. Being excellent gives you some leeway because you build stronger relationships based on your personal qualities.

Phil: Every time I hear a salesperson say he didn't get the sale because the price was too high, I wonder how he scored on all the characteristics of excellence. How was he dressed; was he punctual; was he sincere; how well was he prepared, and so on?

The following characteristics will help you achieve the "image of excellence" and join the elite 5 percent!

THE FIRST IMPRESSION

Upon meeting someone, you can't help but form a first impression. You note the person physically and pick up subtle verbal and nonverbal behavior cues. Unconsciously you gather information to determine what the person is like. The first few minutes can often make or break the sales call. Creating a favorable impression increases the possibility that your ideas will be accepted. The following elements help to create a good impression:

Dress

There are quantities of books on the market today that discuss dressing like a professional. If you are selling in a professional environment, there are some standard rules to keep in mind.

Men should wear conservatively cut, 100 percent wool suits (not sport coats) in blue, gray, or black. Dressing in shirt sleeves is taboo. Wear the appropriate fabric weight for the season. Patterns, if any, should be subtle pinstripes or very small plaids. The shirt should have long sleeves and be white or light blue. The tie is a major status symbol; satin or silk with a slight sheen is ideal. Lace-up wing-tip shoes or conservative loafers are best. You should wear little or no jewelry except a watch, which should be a thin gold one rather than a bulky sports model.

Image consultant Yvonne Kay recommends that women wear suits made of natural fabrics, preferably in gray or navy (black is too harsh). Cotton and linen are acceptable in the summer. Despite the women's movement, pants are still considered too casual for business. The skirt should have a kick pleat for mobility. Blouses should be cream, white, or pastel colored. A bow or scarf at the neck lends credibility, just as a tie does for a man. Leather, closed-toed pumps in a color that matches your suit are best; ankle straps and slingbacks are to be avoided. Hose should be a natural color and should be checked for runs before the appointment. Jewelry should be understated and elegant.

Depending on the product, there may be situations in which a man can wear short sleeves or a sport jacket. Some products even require the salesperson to wear coveralls. Bear in mind that your attire should be appropriate for the circumstances in which you will be conducting business. Regardless of what you wear, it should always be clean, well pressed, and neat. The big question to keep in mind is, Do your clothes reinforce or detract from the impression you want to make?

There will be times when you can use your clothes to help build the rapport with your client. For example, if your prospect is a relater who dresses very conservatively, you would make him feel better by dressing down and changing colors. A brown suit gives a friendly, down-to-earth impression. If you can, avoid the power colors of gray, dark blue, or black when meeting relaters. Of course, the opposite is true for meeting directors or socializers.

Eye Contact

Good eye contact is culturally rather than universally defined. Americans prefer the "glance-away" technique. Notice what happens when a crowd of people enter an elevator. Rather than make eye contact, everyone stares up at the floor numbers. If you were to turn around and look at people or be friendly, everyone would think you were behaving inappropriately. People don't like to be stared at. If a salesperson were to lock eyes with a prospect and never blink or look away, the prospect would feel very uncomfortable. It is best to let your eyes drift away occasionally to relieve any tension.

Carriage and Posture

How do you walk? Do you stride or saunter? Do you stand and sit tall with your shoulders back and stomach in, or do you lean against your presentation material, slouch, or stand with one hand on your hip? Good posture communicates confidence.

Handshake

Your handshake should be strong and firm but not overwhelmingly so. The question is often asked, "When should a man shake hands with a woman?" The traditional rule was to shake hands with a woman when she extended her hand. In contemporary business and personal introductions, you should shake hands with a woman in any circumstance in which it would be appropriate to shake hands with a man.

Imagine being introduced to a group of people. You shake hands and introduce yourself to the men, but for the women you put your hands behind you, smile, lean forward, and say hello. They would be offended.

Smile

A smile is contagious and can be a powerful tool. Imagine walking into a room with a big smile on your face and encountering four poker-faced individuals. A smile is far more powerful than a frown; it even requires fewer muscles. If you were to insist on smiling, you would see four faces smiling with you in seconds!

Hygiene

There should be no need to explain to adults the importance of taking baths or showers, brushing the teeth, and shampooing regularly. There, however, are two related issues worth mentioning: smoking and drinking on the job.

Traditionally, smoking has been considered acceptable if the customer is smoking or if the customer gives permission. In truth, it is *never* acceptable to smoke with a customer. Besides the fact that the smoke may bother the customer, there is no such thing as a neat smoker. As Phil put it, "I can remember my smoking days when I had a closet full of suits with burn holes in them." Cigarettes can ruin clothes and fall out of ashtrays onto desks or carpets. In addition, smoking is an unnecessary distraction that may lower your score by several points.

There was a time when drinking on the job was a requirement in some businesses, for example public relations and advertising. Today, virtually no companies or industries encourage drinking; very few find it acceptable; and many regard it as unacceptable behavior. Drinking is a bad idea for two reasons. First, alcohol stays on your breath for at least three hours. Your lunch date knows you had only a glass of wine, but what will your 3:00 P.M. customer think? Second, even one ounce of alcohol can impair your performance. Why would you want to perform at anything less than 100 percent?

Often there are situations in sales when you are entertaining a prospect over lunch or dinner. That person might order a drink and put a little friendly pressure on you to do the same. In a case like this, it is absolutely acceptable to order Perrier with a twist of lime. You could also order an alcoholic drink and not drink it. Play with it, but don't drink it. Today, we have expanded our thinking to include sobriety in the definition of being sociable and having a good time.

Voice Quality

A person's vocal quality conveys a message that is independent of the words spoken. Every sentence you speak is uttered with sounds that say as much or more than the words themselves. The best example is the word, "Oh." It has absolutely no meaning without the voice inflection accompanying it. Think about it. Depending on how you say it, "Oh" can convey surprise, understanding, cynicism, doubt, anticipation, or fear.

Being aware of the emotion behind your voice will allow you to communicate precisely what you intend to say. It is easy for doubt, fear, boredom, and fatigue to color what you are saying to the customer. If you are aware of your vocal quality, you can convey the enthusiasm, confidence, and sincerity that characterize a non-manipulative salesperson. Be aware of your voice and keep in mind the following points:

1. A strong, full voice projects confidence.
2. Speaking clearly and distinctly indicates intelligence.
3. A higher pitch and volume and faster rate of speaking convey enthusiasm.
4. Vocal changes can add emphasis by drawing attention to the important parts of your message. If you slow down and lower your volume when you say something important, your message will sink in.
5. Avoiding monotonous speech by varying your vocal qualities will keep the listener interested and make you more interesting.
6. Let your voice ebb and flow naturally. Be relaxed. This helps establish trust and reduce tension because you are being yourself. Using these vocal skills should be natural and spontaneous; otherwise you will appear artificial and uncomfortable.
7. Stay tuned to your customer's vocal qualities. Just as your voice conveys information, so too, you can infer the hidden

messages in their speech. Use your listening and questioning skills to discover the root of the change you hear.

Courtesy and Punctuality

Be polite! All the common courtesies that have been taught to us all of our lives, such as saying "please" and "thank you," apply in business. Courtesy also includes using the customer's name correctly and frequently. Don't use a customer's first name unless permission has been given. If a customer is introduced as John Jones, use John. If he is introduced as Mr. Jones, use Mr. Jones.

A part of being courteous is being punctual. Whether or not the customer is punctual, you be on time. When a prospect gives you an appointment, you have an obligation to respect and use his time well.

All of these facets blend together to create a strong, positive first impression. As the familiar saying goes, you only get one chance to make a first impression. Professionalism dictates you make it a good one every time.

DEPTH OF KNOWLEDGE

The second characteristic of excellence, depth of knowledge, refers to how well you understand your area of expertise. The more you know about your subject, the more professional you are. It is, therefore, essential to learn as much as possible about your industry, your company, and the relative strengths and weaknesses of your competitors.

Learn the policies and the procedures of your company and your competitors. Be familiar with all of your company's products, not just the products with which you are involved. Learn about the other departments in your company.

Phil: When I started in the burglar-alarm business, my sales manager used to insist that I didn't have to know anything but how to sell our products. He used to say, "You don't have to know how it works; you don't need to know technical specs; just learn application." Most of the other salespeople listened to him. Not me. I used to hang around with the installers and the service men and spend time in the parts department. In short, I learned as much as I could. Eventually I became vice-president of marketing for the company while my former boss remained sales manager.

Learn everything you can. Study industry trends. Read trade journals and determine how your company rates within the industry. Take advantage of any training programs your company offers. Whatever your field, become an expert.

BREADTH OF KNOWLEDGE

Breadth of knowledge refers to the extent to which you can be conversant on a broad spectrum of subjects. If you are a limited conversationalist, the number of people to whom you can relate will be limited. For a salesperson, this is a serious handicap.

Research has proven that customers buy from people they like and feel comfortable with. One of the major factors in determining how much you like someone is *perceived* common interest.

Imagine you have just met someone and you bring up a subject that interests you. He knows a little bit about it and the two of you talk for a while. A few minutes later, you introduce another topic that he is familiar with, and again you have a conversation. If enough common interests are discovered, you will feel comfortable and have a relationship with that person.

The salespeople that customers always make time to see have mastered the art of conversation. No matter what topic is brought up, they can talk about it. This ability helps the other person relax. At the other end of the continuum, uninformed people tend to be repetitious and boring. A preoccupation with one topic shows how shallow a speaker is.

Unlike *depth* of knowledge, for which your company shares the responsibility to educate you, *breadth* of knowledge is your responsibility. Reading is absolutely essential to expanding your breadth of knowledge. You should read a reasonable number of books each year. As the noted speaker Jim Rohn says, "When you start falling behind [in your reading], you are in trouble. If someone is reading two books per week, after ten years he is 1,000 books ahead of you if you haven't read any." How would you like to enter the marketplace 1,000 books behind your competitors? More importantly, how would you like to enter the marketplace 1,000 books *ahead* of your competitors?

If you are not a regular reader, become one. If no one instilled the love of reading in you, heed the advice of Maxwell Maltz from his book, *Psychocybernetics*. It takes twenty-one days of discipline to establish or break a habit. If you have poor reading habits, every major school system in the country has an adult remedial-reading program. Attend one. This could be the best present you ever gave yourself.

Establish the habit of reading for your growth. Every night, for one hour, sit down and read for reading's sake, not to find out the day's baseball scores, but for pure enjoyment. Before long, you will look forward to it because you will have discovered that reading is fun. Those of you who are regular readers, diversify your reading to develop a breadth of topics you are interested in and can talk about.

Expanding your knowledge requires a faithful *daily* reading of a major city newspaper. Skim it from front to back. Even the classifieds and the obituaries can be relevant. Should one of your customers experience a death in the family, being aware of it will affect what you say and the way you act on your next visit. You may even want to send a condolence card.

Pick up a local business weekly as well. It is essential that you keep your finger on the pulse of business in your geographical area.

Find out what is happening throughout the world. Read *USA Today, Time, Newsweek,* or *U.S. News and World Report* on a regular basis. They summarize events in every facet of life from entertainment to politics and provide an interesting menu for a week's worth of informed, casual conversation.

This emphasis on reading may imply that television serves no useful purpose. No so. As a source of knowledge there has been nothing as powerful as television since the Gutenburg press, which made the printed word available to everyone. The opportunity to see an outstanding play such as *King Lear* with Lawrence Olivier and Diana Rigg was not possible for everyone until television was invented. Today, history can be seen by millions as it occurs and is recorded for future generations, thanks to film and television. Quality programming *is* available if you look for it. With the advent of cable TV, there is a quality program on virtually every hour of every day. Television is not meant to replace reading as a source of knowledge but to be an adjunct to it. TV is like any other tool; if you use it well, it rewards you.

Another way to expand your knowledge is to use unstructured time productively. Salespeople are always looking for a way to stretch a day into twenty-five hours. There *are* ways to expand your use of time. Many activities, such as driving, riding an exercise bike, and running, do not require the part of your brain that listens to and absorbs information. During such activities you can listen to self-help tapes that are available on a variety of subjects. This "passive" form of learning has been proven to be very effective and is highly recommended by the authors. Participate in cultural and athletic events. If you have never heard a live performance of a symphony orchestra or been to a baseball game, experience these things. Besides expanding your horizons, you may discover a new source of enjoyment while coming into contact with a whole new circle of people.

All of these things—reading, doing, watching, listening—will increase your ability to establish a common interest with others, making you someone people will want to be around. All of the 5 percenters, that is, those with excellence, have great scores in breadth of knowledge.

FLEXIBILITY

Flexibility is the willingness and ability to adapt your behavioral style to the style of the person with whom you are meeting.

David Merrill conducted a study on the effect of flexibility on a person's success. He hypothesized that people with low flexibility would perform poorly in professions that require good communication skills, such as sales and management. The assumption was, the higher a person's flexibility, the more successful in "people jobs" she would be.

As expected, inflexible people made poor managers. Surprisingly, however, people with very high flexibility were also poor managers and salespeople. Two well-known characters illustrate this pattern: Archie and Edith Bunker of the television show "All in the Family."

Archie Bunker is the personification of low flexibility. He is bullheaded, single-minded, dogmatic, and nonnegotiable. Many people would find working with or for that kind of individual very difficult. Edith Bunker is the opposite extreme. She is too flexible, unpredictable, and wishy-washy. Few people would want to work for her or deal with a salesperson who is like her.

The flexibility discussed here is vital to the relationship strategies concept presented in chapter 2.

SENSITIVITY

Sensitivity, the ability to be affected emotionally and intellectually, is another characteristic for which excellents receive high scores. Unfortunately, sensitivity is not taught in school along with the other basics of survival such as reading and writing. Instead, we learn sensitivity from our parents and from society.

All of us are desensitized to a certain extent by the news media. Watching the news every night causes you to turn off the feelings you would normally extend to people experiencing hardships. You do this to protect yourself from emotional burnout. Another pattern in American society is to raise men to be "tough." Granted, this quality has its use in the business world, but it becomes self-defeating in personal relationships. So it comes as no surprise that many of us have a hard time getting in touch with our feelings. Knowing what you feel, however, is a prerequisite to having compassion for others.

Non-manipulative salespeople need to be sensitive. The give and take of a working relationship requires recognition of the other person's needs and feelings. To cultivate this ability, practice! When communicating with people, put yourself in their place and try to imagine what they are feeling. Tune in to what people feel as well as what they say.

ENTHUSIASM

Phil: Sammy Davis, Jr., is a consummate entertainer. My wife and I went to see him in Los Angeles many years ago. I don't remember how much we paid, but, to make my point, let's say it was very expensive, like $100 cover charge and $10 per cocktail for a total investment of $140. What do you think we expected as a return on this sizable investment? A great performance!

How do you think we would have felt if Sammy had come out on stage, walked up to the microphone, put his hands behind his back, sung fourteen songs, said "thank you" to the audience, and walked off the stage? We would have been outraged because we had been cheated! What would have been missing from his act? Enthusiasm!

It would have made no difference to us or anyone else in the audience if Sammy had been sick or had had an argument with his wife that day. Excuses would have been worth nothing to those of us who came to spend an evening with Sammy Davis. It just so happened that that evening he had pneumonia. Earlier in the day he had left the hospital against his doctor's orders so he could make his performance commitment. That night he projected more enthusiasm than a lot of entertainers have when they're healthy. What was his secret that night? He is a professional. He knows how to give the level of energy and enthusiasm that makes his audience feel good about their investment of time and money.

Excuses are often heard in sales offices. For the salespeople offering the excuses, what do you think their chances are of making a sale? Quite negligible.

If your level of enthusiasm is really low, stay home! More opportunities can be lost as a result of lack of enthusiasm than you could ever lose by staying home for a day.

Everyone has an occasional bad day. You should, however, be able to bring your enthusiasm up enough to get through the day. Exceptions should come only once or twice a year. If you experience a chronic lack of enthusiasm, it is a sign that it's time to review your job, personal life, or health and make some changes.

The non-manipulative salesperson knows how to rise above his problems. When he walks into the office or interacts with customers, he puts personal problems aside. Zig Ziglar, the famous motivational speaker and author, says that every day is either terrific or semiterrific! If the day doesn't start out great, make it great—*you* are the one in charge.

The preacher Norman Vincent Peale used to tell the story of his walking every day from home to his church. Each day he would greet the corner newsboy with a friendly "hello", but the newsboy never responded. When Peale was asked why he continued to be friendly, he replied, "Why should I let him determine my attitude? If he chooses to be unhappy, that's his choice. I'd like to see his attitude change, but it's not a requirement. What *is* a requirement is that I not let him change *my* attitude. My day should never be determined by someone else's rudeness." For the professional salesperson, this concept holds a lot of truth.

Ralph Waldo Emerson said, "People seem not to see that their opinion of the world is also a confession of character." In other words, if you think this is a miserable world in which to live, you are probably a miserable person. Your attitude will be reflected in everything you do. The same holds true of your attitude toward your customers. If you see them as people whom you can manipulate, then you will never be a truly non-manipulative salesperson. One way or another, they will sense this and will not do business with you.

A healthier attitude is to see your customers as fellow business people with whom you probably have a lot in common. Think of them as people who are worthy of respect, if for no other reason than that they are human beings. Your customers are the people who will make it possible for you to be successful. Think of them as gates through which you must flow rather than as dams (obstacles), who will impede your progress. Only your positive attitude toward them as people will ensure the mutual trust that is so vital to doing business.

Most managers like enthusiastic employees; they seem to work harder, longer, and more efficiently. An enthusiastic person can share and spread the good feeling to the other members of the sales team.

Closely related enthusiasm is the ability to be self-motivated. When you enjoy your work and find it meaningful, it is easy to motivate yourself. Being self-motivated is indispensible in sales and can make or break a salesperson's success. Work at what you love, set goals, focus on achievement, and take action to accomplish all that you can; that, in a nutshell, is the formula for self-motivation and success.

SELF-ESTEEM

Self-esteem is an internal measure of how you judge yourself in relation to the world, rather than a measure of what others think of you. It is so easy for a salesperson to define her worth by whether or not a sale is made. Too often she feels that if a sale was made she is a good person, and if the sale was lost, she is a failure. This is definitely not true.

Every salesperson has had the experience of making an excellent presentation but not making the sale. Similarly, there are times when the presentation is poor but the person makes the sale. The bottom line is, if you give an excellent presentation and don't make the sale, you still gave an excellent presentation. If you gave a bad presentation and still made the sale, *you still gave a poor presentation*. The question when leaving a presentation should not be, "Did I make the sale?" but, "Did I do a good job?" If the answer is consistently yes, then success is virtually assured. If the answer is consistently yes and sales are *not* being made, then your standards for judging the presentations are not high enough or you are not giving enough presentations.

You should never judge your value as a person by the result of a sales call. The excellent salesperson understands this concept. Your self-esteem must always be based on a higher set of standards—those of knowledge, justice, goodness, and equality. Thus, the top 5 percenter is able to maintain a positive self-esteem regardless of the outcome of a presentation. People admire and respond to this kind of consistent confidence.

GESTALT FOCUS

Focus is the next characteristic of excellence for which non-manipulative salespeople receive high scores. Excellent salespeople have a clear sense of where they are going. Their goals are specific, written, measurable, and divided into easily attainable segments. They focus their energy on these goals; they are not easily distracted; and they reach resolution. In addition to focusing on the specific, the excellents also look at the big picture. Their ability to focus simultaneously on the details as well as the big picture is called a "gestalt focus."

Many talented people float from one great project to another and yet never achieve closure on any of them. They lack *focus*. At the other extreme are people who focus so narrowly that they lose sight of the big picture. A good example of this is the railroad industry when people decided they were in the railroad business rather than the transportation business and refused to change and diversify with the times. The ability to focus on both the forest and the trees separates excellents from mediocres.

SENSE OF HUMOR

"Conversation never sits easier than when we now and then discharge ourselves in a symphony of laughter, which may not improperly be called the chorus of conversation," according to the eighteenth-century essayist Sir Richard Steele.

Humor is a social lubricant. It gives us something to share and creates bonds of appreciation. We are automatically endeared to people who make us laugh.

Although the excellents take their commitments seriously, they never take themselves or life too seriously. Above all, they have the ability to laugh at themselves. People appreciate those who can see the humorous side of any situation.

A non-manipulative salesperson should incorporate humor into her or his personal style. This humor should be appropriate, however, if it is going to be effective. Keep the following suggestions in mind:

Keep it in good taste. Know your audience and the type of material that they will appreciate. Some people are more inhibited than others. Use discretion and respect their standards of good taste.

Don't go overboard. If you are making someone laugh, do not assume that being "on a roll" justifies going on indefinitely. If your customer's body language indicates that it is time to get back to work, then get back to work! People appreciate digressions as long as they are short and sweet. You do not want to be known as "that clown who doesn't know when to stop."

Humor is not just telling old jokes. If you rehash jokes that have been circulating for years, you will be regarded as a jerk rather than a person with a great sense of humor. The best humor consists of original, spontaneous comments that flow with the conversation or the ideas being discussed.

Look for humor in everyday life. This is the best way to improve your sense of humor. Some people believe that a sense of the comic is a God-given talent, but it can be cultivated. There are numerous opportunities for you to increase your repertoire of humorous anecdotes and comments. If you make an awkward mistake, remember: Don't take yourself too seriously.

The television star Lucille Ball is a perfect example of someone who has learned to take her tasks seriously but not herself seriously. Ball was given the opportunity to audition for the part of Scarlett O'Hara in *Gone With the Wind.* In the middle of this serious dramatic reading, she dropped the entire script on the floor. As she kneeled down to pick it up, she tried to continue reading. She was so nervous that she continued to read right from the floor, picking up the papers as she went. The director was shrewd enough to realize that although she was wrong for the role, she was a talented comedienne who had the ability to laugh at herself but take her tasks seriously. He ended up giving her her first big break.

The advantages of humor in sales are numerous. Customers will relax more readily with you, they will appreciate and respect you and most importantly, they will remember you.

CREATIVITY AND WILLINGNESS TO TAKE RISKS

Two characteristics of excellence, creativity and the willingness to take risks are closely related.

Creativity is the ability to take several ideas or individual bits of information and combine them in new ways to develop a new idea. Breadth of knowledge plays an important role here. The more information you have at your disposal, the more idea options you will have. Creativity, therefore, also requires curiosity. As a Yiddish proverb suggests, "A man should live if only to satisfy his curiosity." There is so much to know and do that it is a wonder that we accomplish any work.

We are not born with creativity; it is a learned, acquired, practiced skill. The excellents are not locked into doing things the way everyone else does. They are not even locked into the way that they were doing things yesterday. They are always exploring new marketplaces, new applications, new ways to benefit their customers.

To paraphrase Albert Einstein, it is not the quality of ideas that makes genius. It is the frequency of ideas that you put into action. Einstein believed that everyone at some point in his or her life has ideas that could change the world. Unfortunately, minutes after a brainstorm, most people turn to their spouse and say, "What's for dinner?" and never think of the idea again. A true genius thinks the idea through and is willing to take the risk involved in bringing it to fruition.

Excellents do not just have ideas. They have the courage to put those ideas into action. There are hundreds of salespeople with great marketing ideas for their products, but few with the guts to implement them. The marketplace rewards successful risk takers with extraordinary payoffs.

Walt Disney's businesses failed many times before he turned twenty-seven. If he had not continued to take multimillion-dollar risks, he never would have become the patriarch of the vast empire that bears his name today.

A SENSE OF HONESTY AND ETHICS

Having a sense of honesty and ethics is essential for excellence. We all know what honesty means: being truthful, frank and sincere. Ethics can be thought of as honesty in action.

In our daily lives, we often tread a fine line between honesty and dishonesty. In many situations there are no clear ethical choices. But being honest and ethical will open up far more opportunities than you would gain by taking advantage of others. Being honest and ethical will earn you respect, an important aspect of being a non-manipulative salesperson, as well as the long-term reward of a positive reputation in the marketplace.

Ultimately your conscience will have to live with whatever action you take. Being honest and ethical means answering to a higher law. Living honestly and ethically is its own reward.

No one is born a brilliant salesperson. The 5 percenters who are excellent are successful because they are willing to develop themselves and constantly improve their professional and human qualities. It takes work, but the rewards are bountiful. The twelve characteristics just outlined are qualities over which you have *complete control,* and they are learnable and practicable. Improving yourself will not only help you achieve the image of excellence that non-manipulative salespeople possess; it will also make you a more likable person.

14

Developing Self-Management Skills

ONE KEY to a successful career in sales or in any field of endeavor is the effective management of yourself as a business. To do so, you must develop the fundamental skills of self-management. These skills include defining specific goals, establishing plans of action for their accomplishment, and effectively managing one of the most important assets of any business—time.

GOAL SETTING: SHOOTING FOR THE STARS

"Most people aim at nothing in life . . . and hit it with amazing accuracy." This anonymous statement is a sad commentary on people, but it is true. It is the striving for and the attainment of goals that make life meaningful for most people. As you travel through life, if you don't know where you are going, you'll never know if you have arrived. Taking any road will leave your fulfillment to chance, and that's not good enough. Setting goals not only tells you *where* you are going but helps you see *how* you are going to get there. As Charles Kettering once said, "We should all be concerned about the future, because we have to spend the rest of our lives there."

240

Think Positive

Before you can define your goals and establish a plan of action, you need to do some serious self-assessment. Feeling good about yourself is a necessary step in reaching your goals; otherwise, you may give up before you've gone very far.

As a preliminary, you must stop being a negative thinker. Negative thinking is self-defeating. Too many people focus on their limitations rather than their potential. The fact is, there are millions of people in the world who are succeeding every day. So the odds can't be that bad. If so many others can do it, *so can you*!

In order to succeed, you need to understand what success means. Success in America is often defined as the sudden achievement of a goal such as attaining money or power. Success, however, is deeper than this. Earl Nightingale defines success as "the *progressive realization* of a worthwhile goal or ideal." In other words, by choosing a goal and beginning to move toward it, you are, in fact, achieving success.

Negative thinking leads to negative assumptions. You set up internal roadblocks that limit your perceived options. One of the most common negative assumptions in sales is, "I'll never get the account, so why should I waste my time?" This becomes a self-fulfilling prophecy. You should never determine the outcome of a sales call before you make it. For that matter, sometimes you cannot foresee the outcome while you are in the midst of it. Tony has a story he affectionately calls "The Three Sisters," which he may someday develop into a three-act play.

Tony: When I was young and selling cookware door-to-door, I had a period of two weeks without a sale. Finally, one night I broke my slump and made a sale for $600. It was nine o'clock and I had one more lead to pursue. I knocked on the prospect's door and an eight-year-old girl answered. I asked for Mary and, before I could stop her, she said, "I'll go get her" and ran down the street to Mary's friend's house. A few minutes later Mary and her little sister returned. I introduced myself and said I was selling cookware. Mary was furious that she was pulled away from her friend's house at this hour for this reason. She vented her anger, saying how ridiculous this whole thing was. Inside, I agreed with her and thought my chances of making a sale were close to zero. In spite of it, I said,

"As long as I'm here, would you please just give me a couple of minutes and listen to what I have to offer?" She agreed.

We went inside and I asked if her mother was home because I had to have someone over twenty-one at the presentation. The mother wasn't home, but Mary's twenty-five-year-old sister was. Mary convinced her to join us. A few minutes after I began my presentation, the older sister took her baby into the kitchen and started giving him a bath in the sink! Every time I tried to get her involved she would poke her head around the corner of the door and say, "I'm with you." I had my doubts, but I continued to go through the motions. Suddenly the oldest sister came home. She was about thirty-two. She took one look at me and when she realized I was a cookware salesman, she started ranting and raving. It turned out that her husband used to be a cookware salesman and he ran away! She asked me if the cookware was expensive, knowing it was, and I told her, "Yes, it is expensive." She got the second sister, the one with the baby, and they all sat in front of me while I gave the rest of the presentation. They were glaring at me; I felt I was in the hot seat. Everything went wrong. I demonstrated how strong a cup was by stepping on it, and it broke! The only thing that kept me there was sheer persistence. At the end of the presentation, the twenty-five-year-old bought a $600 set of cookware, and the thirty-two-year-old, the one who was yelling at me, bought a $300 set. I couldn't believe it; I walked out with almost a $1000 sale!

If Tony had said to the sister, "You're not interested in this, are you?" she would have said, "No, get out." Instead he persisted and did not let his doubts dictate the outcome.

Assumptions are a form of mental rehearsal. If you assume that you cannot do something, you will act in ways that guarantee your failure. If you rehearse failure, you get failure. This vicious cycle could continue until you either force yourself to quit sales altogether or stop your negative thinking. Practice positive thinking instead!

Many famous success stories have involved people who were failures early in their careers. Frank Betcher, author of *How I Raised Myself from Failure to Success in Selling*, almost flunked out of school before he turned around and made a fortune selling life insurance. Abe Lincoln lost many races for public office and failed in business three times before becoming one of the most famous presidents in history. Henry Ford didn't make his first car until he was close to forty. All of these people attributed positive thinking to helping them achieve their goals. As Ford used to say, "Whether you think you can or you think you can't, you're right."

Even though in recent years the concept of positive thinking has been overcommercialized, the fact remains—positive thinking works. If you are serious about succeeding, it is to your advantage to embrace and practice positive thinking. As Henry David Thoreau put it, "If one advances confidently in the direction of his dreams and endeavors to live the life he has imagined, he will meet with a success unexpected in common hours." The key phrase is "advance confidently." Don't give up before you've started!

An important correlate to positive thinking is self-confidence. Self-confidence is absolutely indispensible to achievement. Self-confidence means nurturing and believing in your intrinsic worth as an individual. It stems from knowledge of and respect for yourself, as opposed to a comparison of yourself to others. A wise person once said, "Don't compare yourself to other people because you will either feel pompous or bitter . . . and neither one is desirable."

Take time out to evaluate critically your strengths and weaknesses in light of your current situation. If you can expand your thinking to accept more possible options for yourself, you can set higher goals. Each new goal achieved will make you feel capable of accomplishing more. Your belief in yourself thus increases, which opens up more options. The effect gains momentum and in this way, you achieve greatness through continual little steps.

The best way to increase your self-confidence is to increase your *competence*. When you know you can handle yourself in every area of your life, you feel confident. Don't leave the house in the morning until you feel good about yourself in every respect, from looking your best to being ready for your presentation. Confidence comes from knowing you are capable and prepared. Now you are ready to set goals.

Define Your Goals and the Steps to Achieve Them

When most people are asked, "What are your goals in life?" they respond with something like, "To be happy and healthy and have plenty of money." On the surface these may seem fine, but as goals that inspire actions they are useless. Try this exercise. First, take five minutes to brainstorm. Write down a complete list of every possible goal you would like to achieve in your lifetime. Consider spiritual goals, social goals, personal goals, community goals, family goals, career goals, and financial goals. You'll be amazed: you'll probably run out of goals before the five minutes run out.

Second, break these goals down into five-year goals and one-year goals. If you're married, have your spouse do the same exercise and then compare notes. What are the differences? You don't have to have identical goals to be compatible, but you should have some areas of positive overlap to work on together.

Third, to reduce the list to a more realistic series of goals. Pick one to three at a time to work on seriously, along with one or two secondary goals, so that you can stay focused in a particular direction. Fourth, once you've narrowed down your goals, check each goal to see that it meets the following criteria:

Your goal must be personal. It must be something that *you* sincerely *want* to do based on your personal convictions, rather than something that you think you *should* do.

Your goal must be positive. A positive goal motivates you through positive statements. "I will feel comfortable around new customers" is more effective than "I will try not to feel uncomfortable around new customers."

Your goal must be written. When goals are put into writing, they are transformed from vague thoughts to tangible entities. Writing them down imprints them on the brain and strengthens your commitment to accomplish them. If you have faith in your ability to achieve them, you won't have any problem putting them in writing. If you're having trouble, perhaps it's your fear of failure that's holding you back. Face the fear and commit yourself. Once you're committed, you'll have the strength to carry those goals through.

Keep those written goals in front of you: on the refrigerator, the bathroom mirror, your cigarette pack if you're trying to stop smoking, under the glass of your desk, or on your car visor. Better yet, record them on tape and listen to them during your nonproductive time. Listen to them *often*. After all, out of sight, out of mind.

Your goal must be specific and measurable. A goal needs to be specific and measurable in order to avoid the lack of commitment that comes with being vague. Don't set a goal of, "I will increase my sales next year." "I will increase my sales next year by 10 percent" is a more workable and motivating goal, because it defines specifically the desired increase. "I'll be running three miles instead of two in four to six months" is more effective than saying, "I will be running more in four to six months." If you reach that goal sooner than expected, you can set an even higher goal.

Your goal must challenge you. A goal must motivate you to work harder than you have in the past. It must move you forward. Set your goals just beyond your reach so that you have to stretch a bit. The more you stretch, the more limber your goal-achieving abilities will become. As Zig Ziglar says, you should enjoy the price that you pay to reach your goals. You have to decide what kind of effort you're willing to put forth to achieve those goals and then stick to it. Remember, if you don't challenge yourself, you won't reap higher rewards.

Your goal must be realistic. Where you set your goal is your decision. You should aim high, but if you aim too high, you may become frustrated. You should have an 80 percent chance of achieving your goal. Anything lower than that becomes demotivating and unrealistic. If you have a 100 percent chance of achieving it, you're not stretching enough. It is necessary, therefore, to set goals that are attainable and yet challenging.

Now that you've determined whether your goals meet all of the requirements of the above rules, it is time for another exercise. Take a separate sheet of paper for each primary and secondary goal that you want to achieve. For each goal, do the following:

Define your goal. If your goal meets all of the criteria listed above, state it as clearly as possible at the top of your worksheet.

Examine obstacles that stand in your way. This is a time to guard against negative assumptions and other self-defeating thoughts. An obstacle blocks you only if you let it. You should also write down innovative ways of overcoming any obstacles.

W.I.I.F.M.—What's in it for me? Write down *why* you want to achieve the goal. What kind of reward is motivating you? When you've answered that, ask yourself why again. And keep asking yourself why until you get to the psychological essence of why you really want to achieve that goal. When you reach that bottom line, you can focus on those feelings and needs when the going gets tough.

Plan your action. As the poet James Russell Lowell said, "All the beautiful sentiments in the world weigh less than one single, lovely action." Your goals are worthless unless you put them into motion. The best way to get started is to write out an "idiot sheet" outlining in complete detail what needs to be done, how, and by whom. If anyone could pick up this game plan, execute it, and achieve the goal, then you've used enough detail. Carefully list every step you will take to bring you closer to your goal. The smaller the increments, the easier they will be to accomplish. As the German proverb says, "He who begins too much accomplishes little."

Project a target date for your goal. Set specific starting and ending dates for your mind to focus on. Work from the deadline backwards to see if it's a realistic time frame, given time constraints, tasks, and other responsibilities. Allowing too little time will create unnecessary pressure and frustrate you. Too much time may reduce your drive. Allow some leeway for the unexpected.

Plan time to review at the end of each week, month, and year. Nothing ever goes exactly according to plan, so you may have to make adjustments to your idiot sheet in order to stay on track. Change the game plan so you can still reach your goal, but *don't change the goal*! In a football game, if it's the third down and your team hasn't scored, you don't move the goalpost. You figure out a way to score from where you are, given your strengths and time limitations.

Stay on track. Don't go to bed until you've accomplished your daily goals. Remember, winners do the tasks that losers don't like to do. Do what you hate to do the most first.

Rick: The one thing I hated most when I started in sales was asking for money. I wanted people to have my product, but I was afraid to ask for the money. I felt that I was unworthy of asking or that I was doing something dirty or mean. When I learned to do the thing I hated forthrightly and with confidence, realizing that the customer would gain as much or more than I would, that's when my career really took off.

Reward yourself. When using these worksheets, check off items as you complete them. This way, you can chart your progress and take pride in your accomplishments. It's important to promise yourself a reward each time you reach a step toward your goal, regardless of the cost in time or money. If you break promises to yourself, you'll keep yourself from achieving your own goals.

TIME MANAGEMENT

Time is like money. Unless you have more than you know what to do with, you need to control your assets. For a non-manipulative salesperson, the management of your time is one of the keys to success. Efficient and effective time management requires practice and self-discipline, but it is well worth the effort.

Know Your Circadian Rhythm

Circadian rhythm refers to the ebb and flow of your energy during the day. Some of us are morning people; others are night owls. Most of us have a sense of our up times and down times. It is important for you to determine when you're at your best so that you can organize your sales calls to coincide with your peak time and take advantage of that energy. Do you sell more in the mornings? Or are you in a fog until noon?

Besides daily peaks, there are times in your sales cycle when you are more effective than others. When you've just made a sale, turn around and try to make another right away. Often what happens is that you build up momentum, you're enthusiastic, you're confident, you think you can't miss, and in fact, you don't. When you're *not* effective, when your circadian rhythm is on a downswing, use that downtime to plan, take care of paperwork, service clients, relax, write letters, or set up appointments. Sell during your peak time.

Rick: I know a salesman who sold eighty-eight insurance policies in one day. When I asked him how he kept up the momentum after thirty or forty instead of quiting, he said, "Hey babe, when you're hot you're hot. You don't stop selling until you hit a cold streak." Your prime time is always immediately after a sale.

Make a Time Log

In order to learn to manage your time, you need a clear sense of how you currently use it. Try this exercise for two weeks. Make a time log that breaks your day down into fifteen-minute intervals. Record your activities throughout each day. The insight that you gain from this record will help you recognize and eliminate time wasters and set time-management goals.

Eliminate Time Wasters

You aren't the only one responsible for creating time wasters; other things waste your time as well. Below is a list of time wasters compiled in a study by Leo Moore of M.I.T. These time wasters are at the top of most people's lists:

the telephone	delegation	delays
meetings	procrastination	reading
reports	"fire-fighting"	emergencies
visitors	the boss	special requests

Use a To-Do List

A list of things to do for each day and week is a valuable aide to managing your time. A to-do list organizes your thinking and planning and prioritizes your activities so that you can be more efficient. A list helps you handle more work without an increase in stress.

Because people are creatures of habit, it is a good idea to establish a routine of writing up your to-do list at the same time every day when you feel the least pressured: perhaps the evening before your day begins or the first thing in the morning. Routine helps keep you *committed*.

List your activities in order of priority with high-priority items first. Spell out the desired result as well as the process. For example, you might list, "Go to manufacturers' rep luncheon *and get at least three business cards from prospects.*" This increases your chances of doing such activities successfully.

After you've completed your list, determine the amount of time each activity requires. Then total up the times and you'll know whether or not it's realistic to achieve those goals in one day.

As you check off completed activities, tally sales and contacts made so that you can keep track of your daily batting average. Tomorrow's to-do list should include any activities you could not complete today. Always save your to-do lists for future reference and as documentation of your activities for tax purposes.

Prioritize by the Four "Ds"

John Lee, a professional speaker and colleague of the authors, suggests using the four "Ds" to help prioritize your schedule. Take a look at a task and ask yourself, can I *delete* it? If it isn't essential, get rid of it. If you must complete the task, ask yourself, can I *delay* it? If there are consequences to a delay, weigh them against the consequences of delaying other tasks and make a choice. If you can't delay it, try to *delegate* it. Can you get somebody else to do it? If not, then *do* it yourself. Put it on your list and check it off as quickly as possible.

Delegation of work to subordinates is essential to the efficient management of your time. Delegation extends your abilities from what you can *do* to what you can *control*. It develops a subordinate's skill, knowledge, and competence. Most important, it frees your time for more important activities.

Since delegation saves so much time, the value of a secretary can't be emphasized enough. In almost any kind of white-collar work, you can easily justify paying a secretary out of your own income to increase your productivity. It may be a part-time secretary, a secretarial service, a college student, or an intern. They can handle paperwork, set up prospects, conduct research, and take care of countless other duties so that you can use your energy for higher-priority tasks.

If you don't have a secretary, speak to your sales manager about hiring one. Once you have one, you'll wonder how you survived without one. If you have a department secretary, learn how to work with him and depend on him.

Secretaries are not the only people to whom you can delegate work. A salesperson in San Diego, Sam Kephart of Westec, hired an assistant to make appointments for him over the telephone. He paid her $5.00 an hour plus 10 percent of all the sales made from the appointments she booked. This gave Sam enough time to fit at least one more appointment a day into his schedule. The extra five or so appointments a week yielded two or three more sales a week, and the commissions more than paid for the help he hired.

Handle Paperwork Efficiently

The first step in handling paperwork is to delegate as much as you can to your secretary or other subordinates. Establish a time for opening your mail each day during a low-productivity time. Screen your mail with your secretary: rapidly throw away junk mail and show him step by step what needs to happen with each piece so he can handle any follow-up. Prioritize your mail so that you can act on the most important pieces first.

Try to answer correspondence immediately. After you have read a letter, write your reply on the back or dictate it and leave the rest to your secretary.

Naturally, there will be more than mail accumulating on your desk. You should adopt a policy of picking up paperwork only once. Don't look at something and put it back down where you found it. Decide what to do with it and move it along to the next step toward completion.

Avoid Procrastination

Procrastination is like a virus. It creeps up on you slowly, drains you of energy, and is difficult to get rid of if your resistance is low. There are ways to overcome procrastination, but first you have to recognize and take responsibility for it. Don't plead laziness. Laziness is simply not caring enough to act. The suggestions below will help you defeat "delaying tactics":

Pick one area in which procrastination plagues you and conquer it. For example, if you are avoiding calling prospects, set a goal of calling X number every day. If you send out prospecting letters, force yourself to follow up with a telephone call. This is known as a *leading task*; it gets you moving on a task that you find difficult or unpleasant.

Give yourself deadlines. If there is no tension, there is no action; without action, there will be no productivity. Pressure in moderation increases motivation. Set appointments, make commitments, and write out your goals. Don't push yourself too hard; find your comfort zone.

Do not avoid difficult tasks. Every day we are faced with both difficult and easy tasks. Tackle the difficult ones first so that you can look forward to the easy ones. If you work on the easy ones first, you might expand the time that they take in order to avoid the difficult ones waiting for you. Tackle the difficult tasks during the peak period of your circadian rhythm. If you can't muster the motivation to tackle the tough stuff first, do some warm-ups with easier tasks, but *limit the amount of time* you spend on them.

Do not let perfectionism paralyze you. Don't allow yourself to get so caught up in one task that you successfully avoid other responsibilities. Be prolific in your efforts. You can always go back later and polish them up. Better yet, you can delegate the polishing to someone else.

Everyone is susceptible to procrastination. Effective action is the best prevention for procrastination. Reward yourself as you learn to kick the habit. Tell yourself over and over, "I'm a do-it-now person."

Control the Telephone

There are only two ways to control the intrusion of telephone calls: a skilled secretary or an answering machine. Your secretary should have a list of callers who always get through, who never get through, and who sometimes get through depending on your approval. The secretary shouldn't have to guess. An answering machine only postpones the time you receive the call. A skilled secretary is more efficient, for this person can assist you in creating a standard procedure for handling telephone calls.

Don't feel guilty about not taking all calls. No one expects a judge to answer while in court. Professors do not leave their classes to take calls. Why, then, should a busy executive or salesperson be available to answer the telephone anytime during the working hours?

Returning calls can also be accomplished more efficiently. Determine the best time of day to return calls. If you establish a set time, your secretary can let callers know when you will call them back.

If you plan to return calls in the late morning or late afternoon, chances are greater that you will catch the other person facing a lunch engagement or leaving for the day and, therefore, less likely to tie up your time and more likely to stick to the business at hand. This is not to say that you should be curt or unsociable. It is important to build relationships with customers, whether it takes two minutes or two hours.

The point is, you don't want a reputation of being lengthy, because then people won't take your calls. This may seem obvious, but how can you avoid being long-winded? One effective way is to stand up while you talk, because you will be less comfortable and less likely to chat overtime.

Another effective way is through your opening. Instead of saying, "Hi, Tom, how are you?" be specific about your agenda. Try this: "Hi, Tom. I need to ask you three quick questions. Is this a convenient time for you to spend ten minutes?" Be organized with a list of questions or topics in front of you. Then launch into the questions as soon as you get the word. There is nothing worse than saying, "Oh, I forgot the other question I was going to ask you . . ." It is also important to be able to terminate your calls promptly. Be decisive and say, "I guess that covers it, Tom. Thanks for your time. Speak with you soon. Good-bye." If you carry on business conversations succinctly, people will respect your ability to get things done and will not waste your time when they call. With relaters and socializers you can be a little more flexible if *they* are not in a hurry.

Try to return your calls in a group by type, such as sales, service, and introductory or appointment calls, because this gets you into a specific thinking mode. You will not have to "change gears" for every other call, so your momentum stays high.

Try to make all of your outgoing calls in one day and then wait for them to be returned. Salespeople often create their own games of telephone tag by placing a call and then leaving their desk. If you can set aside time each week for telephone calls, you'll save time. Think about it. If you make fifty calls, forty of those people may not be available. You can then say, "Well, I'll be in all day," and you continue to make outgoing calls while waiting for calls to be returned.

Control Visitors

Visitors can have the same time-wasting effect as telephone calls. Again, the ideal solution is to have a secretary run interference for you in a non-manipulative, diplomatic way. Let your secretary handle appointments and screen visitors.

During appointments, have your secretary block all interruptions, including telephone calls. Your secretary can monitor the length of the visit, and if it goes on for too long, she can call or come in to tell you about a previous obligation. Then you have an easy way to terminate the meeting if necessary.

Terminate your visits by standing up. This is an obvious sign that it is time to go. Walk your visitor to the door and say good-bye without standing by the door or elevator chatting unless *you* want to.

A non-manipulative salesperson takes pride in what he does. Pride comes from knowing that you are important, worthwhile, and capable of realizing your potential. This self-knowledge can be gained through such self-management skills as setting goals and taking decisive actions to achieve them. Setting goals allows you to stay focused on what it is you choose to accomplish in life. Time management will help you to reach those goals on schedule. Ultimately, only you can effectively control your career. Self-management is essential to your success in sales.

But besides achieving your goals, there are other more important reasons to set goals. First of all, we feel better about ourselves the minute we set a goal. Second, as explained earlier, we become a success just by the act of setting a goal. Third, we grow and evolve as human beings in the process of achieving our goals. What we become in the process is more important than achieving the goal itself, because we become the kind of person who can accomplish that goal. Hence, we can set loftier and loftier goals, challenging ourselves to become better human beings and better salespeople.

Thoreau once said, "If you have built castles in the air, your work need not be lost. That is where they should be. Now put foundations under them." Don't be afraid to make your dreams come true. That's what time management and goal setting is really all about.

15

Three Keys to Success

A professional is defined not by the business he is in, but by the way he is in business. Professionalism takes many forms, and it can and should exist in every business.

Rick: I was in Atlanta and I hailed a cab to take me to the airport. I noticed immediately this was not an ordinary cab; it was brand new, had velour seats, and was immaculately clean. The driver greeted me with, "Good morning, Sir. Where would you like to go?" I told him I was going to the airport. He continued with an initial-benefits statement, "I'm going to get you there today comfortably and efficiently. What time do you need to be there?" I told him when. "That won't be a problem, sir. In fact, you should have time to spare."

As we got underway, the driver pointed out some magazines and newspapers in the back seat; the current *Wall Street Journal, USA Today, Forbes, Fortune,* and *Newsweek.* I was very impressed and asked the driver if this was a regular cab or more posh than usual. He said, "This is a regular cab. I've noticed most of my customers are executives who travel back and forth to the airport, and they like a more comfortable seat than the plastic seat in most cabs. I know they're busy and don't have a lot of free time to read, so the cab is a good place for them to catch up on what's happening."

254

About that time the telephone rang. When he hung up, I asked him if it was a cellular phone. He said, "Absolutely. I always give my customers my phone number so they can reach me directly. If they call the dispatcher, sometimes it takes a few minutes before he can relay the message to me. Besides, if they have some complicated instructions for me, it's much easier to take them myself over the phone. And if I give someone my word that I'll be there at a certain time, I'm there. Sometimes my customers will call to ask me to pick up theatre tickets for them so when I pick them up later, they can just go to dinner and I already have their tickets for the theatre. The phone allows me to do that."

His attitude was one of total customer service. I was very much impressed. He asked me if I wanted to listen to some music and said he had some classical tapes that he found business people seem to like. He explained to me that they were relaxing tapes that allowed you to bring your stress level down on the way to the airport. Sure enough, I found myself more relaxed after he put on the tape I had chosen.

I told him I thought it was unusual for a company to allow a driver to have such an expensive car and asked how he managed to do it. "Oh, I own the company now." he said. "I started out as a driver and took care of my customers the best I could. Soon I was getting more calls than I could handle myself. So with my savings I bought a used cab and started driving on my own. After a while I got some other drivers to work with me and now I have my own company and a fleet of cabs."

When I got to the airport he gave me his card with his telephone number on it and told me, when I came back to Atlanta, if there was anything I needed, to call him. He gave me a receipt and pointed out, on the back of the receipt, there was a telephone number to call in Atlanta if I ever had a complaint about his cabs or any cab in the city. He encouraged me to use the number because the cab companies of Atlanta wanted to know what they could do to improve their service.

The message is clear. Any business can profit from an increase in its level of professionalism. And what is professionalism when you come right down to it? It's customer service. From beginning to end, you must treat your customers as if your world revolved around them; it does.

Three things will guarantee your success in any business endeavor: *knowledge*, *courage*, and *practice*. The first will give you what you need to know in order to do what you want to do. The second will enable you to take the risks necessary to do what you want to do. The third will turn fear into familiarity, hone your skills, and increase your knowledge and courage.

This book gives you the knowledge to change your life. It is, in effect, a blueprint for success. The best way to tackle the information in this book is to break it down into bite-size pieces and digest them one at a time.

The learning process you go through to implement the principles in this book must be a conscious effort sustained over a period of months. You have already achieved the first step in the process; you have gone from the "ignorance" stage to the "awareness" stage. Ignorance is simply being unaware of something. The term does not imply stupidity, just a lack of knowledge. We are all ignorant about a lot of things.

Having read this book, you have the knowledge of the techniques and benefits of non-manipulative selling. You can now develop an action plan to take you where you want to be. Develop a vision of your goal and you will significantly increase your chances of achieving it. Imagine trying to put together a jigsaw puzzle without first seeing a picture of the finished product. It would take forever to accomplish. Having a picture of your goal does the same thing; it allows you to make sense out of the myriad pieces of the puzzle.

During the learning phase, when you put into practice the steps you learned in this book, you will be aware of every move you make. The self-consciousness that comes with a new activity is inevitable. Use this self-consciousness to develop yourself, catch mistakes, and get feedback on your progress. Don't fight it if it feels awkward; just keep practicing and know that it is for a very worthwhile cause—YOU. Rest assured that everything improves with practice.

To improve yourself, find a partner to practice with. Perhaps your sales manager or a fellow salesperson will learn non-manipulative selling with you. This would be ideal. There is nothing so valuable as a support group when you embark on a new challenge. Learning non-manipulative selling with your co-workers will also help you with role playing, team selling, sharing research duties, and setting up systems and checklists and so on.

While you are changing your behavior and attitudes from the traditional approach to non-manipulative selling, you may find your sales productivity decreasing for a while. This is a common occurrence owing to a shift in your emphasis from the "close" to the beginning phases of NMS—planning, meeting, building the relationship, studying, and proposing. Rest assured that this decline is strictly temporary. In the long run you will build a solid foundation of relationships, good will, and more profitable, long-term prospects.

Once you are past the self-conscious stage you will enter the level of "habitual performance." This is the point at which everything becomes second nature. It will be like riding a bicycle with no hands. You will be on automatic pilot, navigating a career that is so much more rewarding than before you put NMS to work.

Roy: If I were to give a salesperson advice on how to succeed, I would say it is important to analyze all the people you really admire in the world and determine if they are manipulators or not. I'm convinced you will find the people in the highest positions in business are non-manipulative, although they aren't always aware of it. It's the way they are naturally.

Non-manipulative selling is not only something you practice when you are dealing with clients; it's a way to treat employees, employers, potential employees, and potential employers. To use a cliché, it's almost a way of life.

It is the authors' sincere hope that you will use this book as a catalyst for self-improvement—and we're sure your customers will benefit too.

INDEX

Account analysis, 76, 80-84: account classification, 83-84; account profitability, determining, 82; potential sales, estimating, 81; time, calculating worth, 81-82
Adamy, Bob, 193
Ali, Mohammad, 21
Alternative-choice confirmation, 164
Are You Listening? (Nichols and Stevens), 59
Arthur, Bea, 24
Asner, Ed, 24
Assumptions, testing, 75

Balance Sheet, Ben Franklin, 170-71
Ball, Lucille, 21, 237
Behavioral flexibility, 32-33
Behavioral styles: direct vs. indirect behaviors, 17-19, 30; directors, 22-24, 207, 211-13, 215; and discussing features and benefits, 147; and interpersonal problems, 27-29; modifying, 205-8; open vs. self-contained behaviors, 15-17, 30; reading, 14-27; recognizing styles, 29-32; relaters, 26-27, 207, 215-18; selling by, 204-20; socializers, 20-21, 207-11, 215; thinkers, 24-25, 208, 213-15
Benefits, language of, 145-47
Betcher, Frank, 242
Bids, sealed, how to deal with, 156-57
Body language, 63, 66, 70-75, 99, 161; tension and, 71
Budgetary constraints, and qualifying a prospect, 136-37
Burnett, Carol, 21
Buyer's remorse, assuaging, 195-96
Buying decisions, signals of, 160
Buying urgency, 133-34

Call objective, establishing, 129
Call preparation, 76; pre-call planning, 92-98, 129; call objectives, setting, 94; decision makers, uncovering, 93; in-person contact, 97-98; pre-call grid, 95; telephone contact, 94, 96, 97
"Call reluctance," 123
Calls: evaluating, 178-82; checklist, post-call, 178

Cammarano, Roy, 11
Cimburg, Allen, 165
Circadian rhythm, 247
Civic groups, as source for prospects, 87
Close-ended questions, 43, 44, 47
Close of a sale, 4, 6, 9, 99; vs. confirming, 158-60
Cold calls, 35, 36
"Comfort zone," and tension, 36-37
Commitment letter, confirming sale with, 182-83
Company knowledge, importance of, 77, 228
Compensation method, and overcoming customer resistance, 170
Competition analysis, 77-78, 80, 184; importance of, 228
Computer-generated letters, 107, 113
Confidence, body language of, 73
Confirming the sale, 158-87; alternative-choice, 164; asking for the confirmation, 166; calls, evaluating, 178-82; closing vs. confirming, 158-60; commitment letter, 182-83; customer resistance, managing, 166-73, 177-78; implementation, 187; negotiating, non-manipulative, 183-87; opportunities, 160-61; pilot, 163; smoke screen, seeing through, 173-76; tentative confirmation, 161-63; when to seek confirmation, 164-66; win-win situations, 176-77
Contacts: making, 7, 99-101; calculating contact yield, 103; maintaining supply of, 101-2; quality of, 99; *See also* Prospecting
Conversation, expanding art of, 229-30
Courtesy, importance of, 228
Creativity, 237-38
Credibility, establishing, 150, 151-52
Customer complaints, managing, 196-97
Customer resistance, managing, 166-73; incorrect or insufficient information, 168-69; personality conflicts, 169-70; skills for responding to, 171-73; technical difficulties, 170-71
Customer satisfaction, 10; and pilots, 163; and prospect referrals, 86; units (CSUs), 148; *See also* Follow-through process

258

Davis, Jr., Sammy, 232-33
Decision makers: uncovering, 93, 132-33; roles of in decision-making process, 133
Delegation of work to subordinates, 249-50
Deluise, Dom, 21
Demonstrating, art of, 155-56
Deshmukh, Ash, 56
Dictation, 111
Direct vs. indirect behaviors, 17-19, 30, 204, 205-6
Direct mail campaign: computer-generated letters, 107-8; form letters and, 106, 112; as least effective way of making contacts, 100; as source for prospects, 89
Directories, as source for prospects, 89
Directors, 22-24, 53, 63, 69, 108, 123, 147, 183, 207, 211-13
Discounts, perferred customer, 198
Disney, Walt, 238
Dress for Success (Molloy), 222
Dress, appropriate, 224-25

Eastwood, Clint, 24
Ego, need to control, 59
Einstein, Albert, 238
Emerson, Ralph Waldo, 234
Emotional information, listening for, 63
Enthusiasm: body language of, 72; as characteristic of excellence, 232-34
Environmental indicators of behavioral style, 29
Ethics, as essential to excellence, 238-39
Evaluative listening, 61-62, 71
Excellence: characteristics of, 222-39; creativity, 237-38; enthusiasm, 232-34; first impression, 224-28; flexibility, 231-32; focus, gestalt, 235-36; honesty, sense of, and ethics, 238-39; knowledge: breadth of, 229-31, 237; depth of, 228-29; risk taking, 237-38; sensitivity, 232; sense of humor, 236-37
Eye contact, proper, 225

Fact finding, 47: See also Information-gathering
Failure, fear of, 244
Fear, as motivation for buying a product, 131

Features: product, vs. benefits, 145-47; feature-feedback-benefit method, 146-47
Feedback, 62, 66-75, 99, 167; assumptions, testing, 75; clarifying questions as, 44; and defining words, 74; nonverbal, 70-72; transitions between phases of sale process, 75; verbal, 67-68; voice inflections, 68-70
Flexibility, effect of on success, 231-32
Focus, as characteristic of excellence, 235-36
Follow-through process: and customer satisfaction, 10, 129, 187, 188-203; annual reviews, 200-201; buyer's remorse, assuaging, 195-96; customer complaints, managing, 196-97; selective perception, dealing with, 192-94; services, expanding, 201-3; success criteria, monitoring, 191-92; thirteen ways to assure, 198-200; user error, combatting, 194-95
Ford, Henry, 243
Form letters, 106

Gestalt focus, 236
Goals and objectives: actual vs. desired conditions, 128; assessing, 127-29; defining and achieving, 243-47; setting, 240-47
Group presentations, 149-54: catering to group's behavioral style, 151; competitive advantages, stating, 151; credibility, establishing, 150, 151-52; group involvement in, 152; prices, 153; proposal document, 152-53

Handshakes, 225-26
Hartman, David, 26
Honesty, sense of, and excellence, 238-39
How I Raised Myself from Failure to Success in Selling (Betcher), 242
Humor, importance of sense of, 236-37

Imitation, as motivation for buying, 131
Indifference, body language of, 73
Indirect vs. direct behaviors, 17-19, 30
Information-gathering phase, 12, 58, 133, 139; vs. fact finding, 47; feature vs. benefits, 146; information exchange, 141-42; and questioning, 41

Initial-benefit statement, 103-4
Interpersonal problems, and behavioral styles, 27-29

Jargon, avoidance of, 50

Kay, Yvonne, 224
Kettering, Charles, 240
Knowledge, breadth and depth of, 228-31, 237

Lee, John, 249
Letters, 104-13; of commitment, confirming sale with, 182-83; computer-generated, 107, 113; dictation, 111; form, 106, 111-12; personal, 105-10; purposes for, 105; testimonials, 191-92; tips for writing, 110-11
Lincoln, Abe, 243
Listening, 54, 55; active, 30, 59, 60, 62, 65, 68; bad habits, 65-66; evaluative, 61-62; guidelines for listening, 62-64; marginal, 60-61; and memory, 60; noise, reducing, 64; note-taking, 64; on telephone, 121-22
Lowell, James Russell, 246
Loyalty, overcoming politics of, 134-35

Maltz, Maxwell, 230
Marginal listening, 60-61
Market analysis, 76, 78, 79-84; account analysis, 80-84; competition analysis, 80; and market segmentation, 78
Marketing effort, vs. sales effort, 100
Market segmentation, 78-79, 80
Mediocrity, vs. excellence, 222
Meeting, introductory with prospect, 99-124, 185; contacts, maintaining supply of, 101-2; first impression, 224-28; initial-benefit statement, 103-4; in-person, 122-24: planning for, 97-98; letters, 104-13; payments, 102-3; telephone, 99-100, 104, 113-22
Memory, vs. listening, 60
Merrill, David, 231
Molloy, John, 222
Moore, Mary Tyler, 26
Multifaceted approach to selling, 132-33
Multiple-call sales, vs. one-call, 139-40

National Society of Sales Training Executives, 66
Needs, 42, 124, 143; gaps, 126, 128, 129, 130, 141, 158, 168, 192, 195; opportunity seeking and, 125-27; psychological, 130; summary of, 138, 139; tension, 38-40
Negotiating: non-manipulative, 183-87; phases of, 184-86; meeting, 185; planning, 184-85; proposing, 186; study, 185-86; tips on, 186-87
Nepotism, 134
Nervousness, body language of, 74
Nightingale, Earl, 189, 241
Nimoy, Leonard, 25
Noise, reducing, 64
Non-verbal behaviors, 29; feedback, 70-72

Objections, overcoming, 4, 9-10
One-call vs. multiple-call sales, 139-40
One-seller-one-buyer approach to selling, 132
Open questions, 43-44, 47
Open vs. self-contained behaviors, 15-17, 30, 204, 205
Opportunities, 42; vs. problem solving, 125-27
Orphan accounts, 88

Pauley, Jane, 26
Peale, Norman Vincent, 234
Perfectionism, 251
Performance, product, tracking, 138-39
Personality conflict, 13, 169-70
Personality theories, 14; *See also* Behavioral styles
Philosophy of non-manipulative selling, 1-12; guiding principles, 10-11; negative sales images, sources, 1-6; and personal tension, 35-36; traditional vs. non-manipulative selling, 6-12
Pilot, use of as a confirming tool, 163
Pitch of a sale, 4
Planning, 76-98; company and product knowledge, 77-78; market analysis, 79-84; market segments, 78-79; pre-call, 92-98, 129; prospecting, 85-92; territory management, 78; territory objectives, 84-85
Politics of the sales situation, 134-35

Posture, 225

"Preferred" customers, establishing list of, 81

Presentations: canned, 142-43; comprehensive, 143-44; custom-tailored, 144; demonstrating art of, 155-56; geared toward prospect's style, 145; group, 149-54; key elements of, 147-48; outlined, 143-45, 149; sealed bids, dealing with, 156-57; senses, appealing to, 154-55; traditional vs. non-manipulative, 8; well-organized, 144-45; well-positioned, 144

Price, high, getting around, 175-76

Problem solving vs. opportunity seeking, 125-27

Procrastination, avoidance of, 250-51

Productivity, and tension, 36-37

Product knowledge, 33, 77-78, 228; and training, 3-4

Product specifications, 135-36

Professionalism, 221-22, 254; *See also* Excellence, characteristics of

Proposals, 8, 141-57; benefits and feedbacks, importance of, 145-47; canned presentation, 142-43; goal of proposing phase, 142; home field advantage, gaining, 148; interruptions, how to handle, 148-49; outlined presentation, 143-45; *See also* Presentations

Prospecting, 76, 85-92; feelings and thoughts of prospect, knowledge of, 131-32; introductory meeting with prospect, 99-124; potential sales estimation, 81; and product knowledge, 77-78; and sales slumps, 86; sources of prospects, 86-90; system for, 91-92; and territory management, 78-79; timing in, 90; top-quality prospects, identifying, 90-91; in traditional selling, 7

Psychocybernetics (Maltz), 230

Psychological dynamics of the sale, 130-31

Punctuality, importance of, 228

Questioning: art of, 41-57; answers and insights to, 54-55; behavioral style and, 53-54; composing, 48-53, 68; fact finding vs. information gathering, 47;

flexibility in, 48; list of, 129-30; open vs. closed, 42-44; use of questions, 44-47

Readiness, body language of, 72

Reading, importance of to breadth of knowledge, 229-30

Reagan, Ronald, 21

Relaters, 26-27, 54, 63, 69, 109-10, 147, 152, 183, 207, 215-218, 220

Relationships: business, 7, 11, 12, 66, 125-26, 159; "Golden Rule" and, 13-14; meetings and, 124; personality conflicts, 169-70; and resistance, 167, 177-78; strategies, 13-33; *See also* Behavioral styles

Relationship tension, 36-38

Reselling, in traditional sales, 10

Resistance, customer, managing, 166-73

Return on time invested (ROTI), calculating, 82

Reynolds, Burt, 21

Risk, willingness to take, and excellence, 237-38

Rogers, Fred, 26

Role playing, 97

Sales: confirming, 158-87; cycle, 86, 102; effort vs. marketing, 100; employee turnover, 1; expenses, minimizing, 76; feedback, use of in sales process, 75; planning, 76-98; politics, 134-35; process, 101-2; psychological dynamics, 130-31; slumps, avoiding, 86, 102; stereotype of salesperson, 1; training, 1-6, 59, 77

Sales records, as documentation of negotiations, 184-85

Savalas, Telly, 24

Sealed bids, *see* Bids

Secretaries, working with, 118-20

Selective perception, 192-94

Self-confidence, and achievement, 243

Self-contained vs. open behaviors, 15-17, 30

Self-esteem, basis for, and excellence, 235

Self-management skills: developing, 240-53; goal setting, 240-47, 253; time management, 17, 247-53

Self-motivation, importance of, 234

Selleck, Tom, 21

Sensitivity, and excellence, 232
Shatner, William, 24
Smoke screens, seeing through, 173-76
Socializer, 20-22, 54, 63, 69, 109, 127, 147, 151, 183, 207-11, 219
Solutions, proposing, 124, 142
Sources for data on sales, trends, and projected sales, 79-80
Source of prospects, 86-90
Speaking voice, *see* Voice quality
Specifications, product, 135-36
Stapleton, Jean, 26
Steele, Sir Richard, 236
Stereotypes, of salespeople, 1-6
Strategies, relationship, 13-33
Studying a prospect's business, 125-40, 185-86; needs summary, 38; one-call vs. multiple call sales, 139-40; problem solving vs. opportunity seeking, 125-27; situation and goals, assessing, 127-29; success criteria, establishing, 138-39; topics, 129-37
Style: personal, determining, 19; flexibility in, 32-33
Success criteria: establishing, 138-39; monitoring, 191-92
Success: keys to, 254-57; meaning of, 241; visualizing, 97, 181

Team-sell approach, 93, 132
Telephone: as means of making contacts, 99-100, 104, 113-22; creativity in, 120; etiquette, 117-20; long distance, 120-21; monitoring calls, 117; noise, eliminating, 115; organization for, 115-16; vocal quality, testing, 114-15; when to make calls, 116-17
Telephone contact, 94, 97; controlling, 251-52; planning sheet, 96; returning calls, 252
Television, as source of knowledge, 230-31
Tension management, 34-40; and active listening, 60; need tension, 38-40;

personal tension, and traditional vs. non-motivational selling, 34-36; relationship tension, 36-38, 71
Territory management: effective, 76, 78; and market segments, 78-79
Territory objectives, 84-85
Testimonial letters, 191-92, 197
Thatcher, Margaret, 24
Thinkers, 24-25, 53-54, 63, 69, 107, 108-9, 123, 147, 208
Thoreau, Henry David, 243
Thought, positive vs. negative, 241
Tickler files, 91-92
Time management, 17, 247-53; circadian rhythm, 247; paperwork, 250; prioritizing by four "Ds", 249-50; procrastination, avoiding, 250-51; telephone, controlling, 251-53; time log, 248; time wasters, eliminating, 248
Trade shows, as source for prospects, 88-89
Traditional selling: and follow-through, 188; and personal tension, 34-35; problem solving and, 127; training, 4-6; vs. non-manipulative, 6-12
Training, sales, 1-6, 59, 77, 229
Troubleshooting, vs. studying a prospect's business, 125
Type A and B personalities, 18, 23

Upstream and downstream selling, 134
User error, combatting, 194-95

Verbal behaviors, 29
Vocal inflections, and feedback, 68-70
Voice quality, 227-28

Walters, Barbara, 24
Webb, Jack, 25
Woolf, Barry, 129

Ziglar, Zig, 233, 245